Advance Praise for *BrandED*

"Eric Sheninger and Trish Rubin provide a great read for all concerned with taking education to the next level in a competitive, digitized social media world. The time is now to learn how to brand yourself and your organization to unleash the power of your story. If not someone else will, and your school or district may suffer because of it! Thank you Eric and Trish for paving the way through the power of branding!"

—*Dr. Darryl Adams, superintendent, Coachella Valley Unified School District*

"If you think about how students discover, communicate and learn outside of school, it's remarkable that we still insist on compromising their scholastic experience with yesterday's approaches. Eric and Trish help us not only re-imagine how to make learning intuitive but also how to build an engaged community where we co-create the future together."

—*Brian Solis, digital analyst, anthropologist, futurist, and author of* X: The Experience When Business Meets Design

"Eric Sheninger and Trish Rubin pave the way for educators across the globe to dive into the world of social media transparency in their new book *BrandED*. The authors take you on a journey as they walk through step by step on how to strategically enhance your school's branding power by engaging in '8 Conversations' to support you in moving beyond the status quo, providing a rich and meaningful professional development experience that will leave you wanting to continue the conversation."

—*Jimmy Casas, leadership coach, author, speaker, 2012 Iowa Principal of the Year, and 2013 National Principal of the Year Finalist*

"In our work as journalists and as the founders of 'Stand up for Heroes,' the power of storytelling is a foundational part of our brand and allows us to share the truth of our mission. School leaders can learn the lessons of building a unique brand that serves, honors and grows a community in the pages of Eric and Trish's book, *BrandED*, and can understand the need for communicating brand value that develops our next generation."

—*Bob Woodruff, ABC correspondent, and Lee Woodruff, author and journalist*

"*BrandED* provides an innovative platform for educators to engage in meaningful discussions about the purpose of their work, program delivery, and expected outcomes. As the leader of a College of Education, I believe that *BrandED* serves as a powerful mechanism in assisting me to develop our niche in the preparation of education professionals and national discourse on public education. Eric and Trish have created a space for business and education to coexist and energize each other."

—*Monika Williams, PhD, dean and professor, College of Education, Rowan University*

"*BrandED* opens the door to a creative, collaborative, brand-building process that results in connected school culture, performance and resource gains. As a former teacher, entrepreneur, marketing author, and most important, parent, I give this book two huge likeable thumbs up!"

—*Dave Kerpen, NY Times bestselling author of* The Art of People

"Every school has a brand, but it may not be what you hoped! Turn staff, students, parents, and your community into co-creators and co-owners of a trustworthy, relevant educational brand using Trish and Eric's 'why,' 'what,' and 'how' of brand relevance. The future of education is a connected and transparent, changing place of robotics and algorithms where a relevant, relational school brand can drive learning through intelligent listening, skillful adjusting and bold experimentation."

—*Annalie Killian, curator of Creative Intelligence Networks at sparks & honey, and founder, Amplify Festival*

"As a Head of School for an international school in India, *BrandED* has been essential in helping me understand how to lead my school. The simple idea that transparency drives improvement has had a large impact. Being in a city with many international schools, the question of how I can help my school stand out was one I grappled with. This book has become a guide for helping my school do things well, but more importantly, ensuring that all stakeholders know what is happening."

—*Bruce W. Ferguson, head of school, Sreenidhi International School, Hyderabad, India*

"Communication has experienced a revolution. Expectations, methods and opportunities have all grown and changed dramatically in recent years. *BrandED* lays out the why and the how to develop and use your own and your organization's brand through storytelling, relationship-building, and the use of cutting-edge technology and tools. The primary audience for *BrandED*—principals—will find it a groundbreaking, invaluable tool, and other educators—like superintendents—will find it extremely valuable as well."

—*Deborah A. Gist, superintendent, Tulsa Public Schools*

"*BrandED* is a valuable practical guide for educational leaders. They will learn to enhance their impact through innovative communication strategies."

—*Dr. Nelson Lim, executive director, Fels Institute of Government at the University of Pennsylvania*

BrandED

BrandED

Tell Your Story, Build Relationships, and Empower Learning

Eric Sheninger and Trish Rubin

JB JOSSEY-BASS™
A Wiley Brand

Published by Jossey-Bass
A Wiley Brand
One Montgomery Street, Suite 1000, San Francisco, CA 94104-4594—www.josseybass.com

Jossey-Bass books and products are available through most bookstores. To contact Jossey-Bass directly call our Customer Care Department within the U.S. at 800-956-7739, outside the U.S. at 317-572-3986, or fax 317-572-4002.

Wiley publishes in a variety of print and electronic formats and by print-on-demand. Some material included with standard print versions of this book may not be included in e-books or in print-on-demand. If this book refers to media such as a CD or DVD that is not included in the version you purchased, you may download this material at http://booksupport.wiley.com. For more information about Wiley products, visit www.wiley.com.

Library of Congress Cataloging-in-Publication Data

Names: Sheninger, Eric C., author. | Rubin, Trish, 1952- author.
Title: Branded : tell your story, build relationships, and empower learning /
   Eric Sheninger and Trish Rubin.
Description: San Francisco, CA : Jossey-Bass, 2017. | Includes
   bibliographical references and index.
Identifiers: LCCN 2016053479 (print) | LCCN 2017003564 (ebook) | ISBN
   9781119244561 (cloth) | ISBN 9781119244585 (pdf) | ISBN 9781119244578
   (epub)
Subjects: LCSH: Educational leadership—Marketing. | Branding (Marketing)
Classification: LCC LB2806 .S3544 2017 (print) | LCC LB2806 (ebook) | DDC
   371.2—dc23
LC record available at https://lccn.loc.gov/2016053479

Cover design: Wiley

Printed in the United States of America

FIRST EDITION

HB Printing   10 9 8 7 6 5 4 3 2 1

To my wife, Melissa, and children, Nicholas and Isabella. You motivate me each and every day to be my best. Your love and support are the ultimate currency. —Eric

For my kids, Alexandra and Zachary Rubin, and Jordan and Ryan Hughes, with thanks for allowing me to savor my brand, "MOM," in my memories, in today's moments, and into the days to come. —Trish

Contents

About the Authors

 **Eric Sheninger** is a senior fellow and thought leader on Digital Leadership with the International Center for Leadership in Education (ICLE). Prior to this role, he was an award-winning principal at New Milford High School, which became a globally recognized model for innovative practices under his leadership. Eric oversaw the successful implementation of several sustainable change initiatives that radically transformed the learning culture at New Milford while increasing achievement. He is the creator of the Pillars of Digital Leadership, a framework for transforming school cultures through sustainable change.

His work focuses on leading and learning in the digital age as a model for moving schools and districts forward. Eric has emerged as an innovative leader, best-selling author, and sought-after speaker. His main focus is purposeful integration of technology to facilitate student learning, improve communications with stakeholders, enhance public relations, create a positive brand presence, discover opportunity, transform learning spaces, and help educators grow professionally.

Eric has received numerous awards and acknowledgements for his work. He is a recipient of Center for Digital Education's (CDE) Top 30 award and PDK Emerging Leader Award and winner of the Bammy Award, National Association of Secondary School Principals' (NASSP) Digital Principal Award, and Learning Forward's Excellence in Professional Practice Award. He is also a Google Certified Innovator, an Adobe Education Leader, and an ASCD 2011 Conference Scholar. He has authored and coauthored five other books on leadership and technology.

Eric has also contributed to the *Huffington Post* and was named to the NSBA "20 to Watch" list in 2010 for technology leadership. *Time Magazine* also identified Eric as having one of the 140 best Twitter feeds in 2014. He now presents and speaks nationally to assist other school leaders in embracing and effectively utilizing technology. His blog, "A Principal's Reflections," was selected by Edublogs as the Best School Administrator Blog in 2011 and 2013 and was also recognized by Smartbrief Education with an Editor's Choice Content Award in 2014. Connect with Eric on Twitter (@E_Sheninger) and at ericsheninger.com.

Trish Rubin is the founder of Trish Rubin Ltd., a communications consultancy based in New York City since 2005. From her first entrepreneurial business, The EDventures Group, a professional development training company, Trish has developed her unique consulting brand. In her journey from a classroom educator to a business consultant, she draws from over 25 years of communication success in local, state, national, and international educational settings. Change process and innovation of teaching and learning for children and adults power her work and thought leadership.

Trish's career began as a middle school language arts teacher at Mt. Pleasant Junior High School. She currently teaches Marketing and Brand Management to international business students at CUNY's Baruch College in the CAPS Division.

A self-described "educationalist" with a natural ability and a passion for strategically developing powerful networks and authentic relationships, she has worked as a K-16 teacher, reading specialist, literacy coach, program developer, and administrator and now as an advocate for schools. She combines her love of teaching with a passion for business development, opening the collaborative leadership conversation between business and education that can create engaged 21st century school communities. Connect with Trish through her energetic tagline "All Roads Lead to Trish" on Twitter (@trishrubin) and at trishrubin.com.

BrandED

Introduction: Our BrandED Short Story

Someone give me a seatbelt, because the ride in public education is getting pretty interesting.

—*Trish Rubin (2009)*

ERIC'S PATH

Prior to 2009, I detested all social media, as I perceived it as a huge waste of time, let alone that it had no connection to my professional practice. As a result, I developed quite the fixed mindset and made the conscious decision not to let this fad enter into either my professional or my personal life. Unlike all my friends at the time, I wasn't on Friendster or MySpace, two social media sites that would eventually meet their demise. When Facebook became all the rage in 2005, I resisted all the requests from my friends and family to join. Not only did I see it as a huge time sap, but I was certain it would meet the same fate as the social media sites that came before. It would be a few more years before my opinion of social media would be changed forever by a little-known tool called Twitter.

When I first dipped my toe into the social media waters in March 2009, I did not know what to expect. My sole purpose for embarking into this uncharted territory was to improve my professional practice by becoming a better communicator. This was a natural connection to my work as a high school principal, as you will not find an effective leader who is not an effective communicator. Successful principals have always built highly functioning learning communities by clearly and consistently articulating a school's vision of—and commitment to—student success (Ferriter, Ramsden, & Sheninger, 2011). Twitter represented a great tool to accomplish this leadership goal. Sending short messages in no more than 140 characters was not only efficient but also an effective means of disseminating important information to my stakeholders. I finally saw value in social media as a means to improve professional practice, and thus my outlook on social media and technology in general changed.

So there I was churning out tweets about everything going on at New Milford High School. Little did I know that my tweeting would lead to a feature story on CBS Channel 2 NYC during November 2009 and in the process catch the eye of business maven Trish Rubin. It was at this time that I was exposed to the concept of branding in education (Rubin, 2009).

When Trish contacted me out of the blue, I was really caught off guard. She passionately explained that what I was doing was creating a brand presence for my school as well as for myself professionally. At first I wasn't buying it, but after I spent some more time speaking with Trish, her conversation began to make sense. I began to see brand more clearly and understand what it was about. Brand is about creating a unique identity that relates to a specific audience or stakeholder group. The value of a brand can be defined in many ways. For example, some brands promise durability, health, style, safety, taste, convenience, or savings. Brands are designed to stand out and ultimately influence the consumer in a fashion that builds trust in the product. Sustaining a sense of trust is an integral component of a brand's ability to promise value. The definition of brand I've given here provided clarity, but it was still missing some integral components in order to make the concepts of branding more applicable to the education world. Here is a synopsis that Trish and I developed back in 2009:

> BrandED tenets are about trust, loyalty, promise, and creating better offerings and innovations that distinguish the education brand experience for every user, including kids, parents, teachers, and community. A brand isn't a short-term fix or a fad, but a way to strategically build a school's assets in a transparent digital world. No more ivory tower. BrandED is about a genuine personality that can impact school culture, achievement, and resources.

Schools are considered a brand. They promise value to residents of the district in terms of academic preparation to succeed in society. Many families will choose to reside in a specific district if the schools have a track record of academic success. By establishing a school's identity or brand, leaders and other stakeholders can develop a strategic awareness of how to continually improve pedagogical and management practices that promise, as well as deliver, a quality education to all students.

As a high school principal, I felt that it was my responsibility to continually develop and enhance my school's brand through innovation, risk-taking, building of relationships (with students, teachers, parents, community stakeholders, institutions of higher education, businesses and corporations, etc.), and a commitment to the community. In my opinion, this vision can assist all educators in establishing a brand for their respective schools that not only promises but also delivers value to residents of the district.

By developing and enhancing your professional and school brand, you move toward a credible perception of your work for stakeholders to embrace. Thus a brand in education has nothing to do with selling, but instead is all about showcasing the work of students, staff, and leaders in an effort to become more transparent. Educational leaders understand the importance of branding in their work, and by leaders I mean any and all educators who take action to improve learning opportunities for their students and themselves.

TRISH'S PATH

I didn't meet Eric Sheninger on a social media site, a Google Hangout, through a hashtag, using a PLN, or on a Twitter chat. I met Eric on an "old school" channel: TV. The man came right into my NYC apartment and stopped me in my professional tracks. I saw the connected future in a segment highlighting his encouragement of his teachers' use of Twitter in their high school lessons. Who was this innovative guy?

Since 2005, after a long career in education where I tested out my ability to deliver value in unique ways on a national education stage, I became entrepreneurial in the world of business. It was an easy transformation. I was *educating* my clients to communicate an image, create value, and sustain brands. I used my education heart. I also had a unique idea resulting from my work at the intersection of education and business. I'd been thinking about something I called *brandED*—something that could improve leadership by bringing innovation to schools through marketing and brand. As a former school administrator, I saw brandED as a professional development tool for school leadership. But I didn't have a leader in mind who would get it, until I serendipitously stumbled on Eric Sheninger's CBS TV segment. A few quick Twitter posts later, I presented my theory of brand to this educator. In Eric's New Milford High School office, I tested my pitch: Brand thinking is a necessary part of 21st-century professional leadership. An informed leader can adapt marketing and brand as I had been doing to improve schools in three areas: culture, performance, and resourcing.

After that meeting, Eric's brand quickly developed to include worldwide digital leadership, which is best defined as establishing direction, influencing others, initiating sustainable change through the access to information, and establishing relationships in order to anticipate changes pivotal to school success in the future (Sheninger, 2014). I watched his path and knew that my theory had moved into action. My own career path further deepened my ties to education, including teaching university seminars and college courses on branding and marketing. In 2014, we introduced a refined version of our brandED concept to leaders worldwide through Eric's book, *Digital Leadership: Changing Paradigms for Changing Times* (Sheninger, 2014). Today, brandED is now ready for a wider, inclusive, and actionable school leadership conversation.

The first standard cited in the 2015 professional standards of the National Policy Board for Educational Administration (NPBEA, 2015) signals the need for attending to brandED leadership. It ushers in our worldwide discussion:

> Effective educational leaders develop, advocate, and enact a shared mission, vision, and core values of high-quality education and academic success and well-being of each student. (NPBEA, 2015)

I like that signal. When mission, vision, core values, and well-being are advocated and enacted, you are experiencing brandED leadership, an educator's professional stance in this new age of communication.

We're pleased to help you write your own brilliant brand-building story. Technology has ushered in transparency, enabling a "mash-up" of possibilities that can be part of your focused professional development. BrandED thinking is one of those possibilities. We look forward to seeing your brand develop in real time and online—on Twitter and Facebook; in Google Hangouts; on live streaming platforms, webinars, and podcasts; and in blog posts—as you describe your journey to building school brand. Share your school's story that defines your engaging education brand. Develop a brandED mindset and gather a like-minded, passionate team to collectively launch an innovative brandED Strategic

Plan. Invest in your own unique brandED value and professional learning plan to improve teaching, learning, and leadership in a new "business as unusual" way. No more ivory tower. Get ready to become brandED.

"THE BRANDALITY MODALITY"

No matter our level of digital proficiency, we educators grapple with the rough-and-tumble pace that professional connectivity demands in our new age. A change of leadership thinking is in order if we are to face a hyperlinked world of education. When the marvelous baseball pundit Yogi Berra paraphrased French philosopher Paul Valery's 1937 vision of the future, years before the Internet existed, he mused, "The future ain't what it used to be." (See http://quoteinvestigator.com/2012/12/06/future-not-used/ for the provenance of this saying.) So true, Yogi. We lead schools today, preparing our digitally and socially savvy students for success as adults in a future where many of their jobs haven't been created yet.

In these changing times, opening the door to branding and the transparency it brings in a digital age may make you pause. But the old-school one-way messaging behavior for leading a school doesn't jibe with our engaged, digital communication environment. A paradigm shift is in play. Recognize it and lean into it: Our community of stakeholders wants us to engage with them—starting with our students and ending with the world beyond our school. In this new inbound world of digital communication, a world where information arrives at our digital doorstep without being invited, we have to reset leadership thinking. Our stakeholders' lives are now about exchange powered by inbound social and digital forces. A new educator leadership mindset is in order: one that calls for the clear, connective, engaging concept of brand. It's time for a "brandality modality."

In today's engaging, digitally empowered school setting, stakeholders question whether schools really know best about educating their students (Rose, 2012). We have to do a better job of communicating what we do. We must be part of the exchange. It gives us the best chance at connecting with our audiences and winning support for schools. Ask Millennial parents whose trust in the education of their Gen Z kids, particularly in the area of technology, is seen as lacking (Shaffhauser, 2014). How can we share our vision and invite their exchange? How do we communicate trust and show value? Brand holds the answer.

Today's educators who embrace the brandality modality don't need to be humble. In the noisy digital world, educational leaders must proudly use stories of their schools to convey a consistent brand message about who they are and what they stand for. Because those messages can make or break us, we must be the observant stewards of the brand that our stories convey across social and digital platforms (Trish Rubin, 2016). Although our current educator demographic makeup is a mixed bag, representing Millennials, Gen X, and Baby Boomers, we can see the role of brand as a unifying tool for the generations we lead, even as decisions around the communication choice to "snap, scope, or gram" test our patience for reaching the different demographics that make up our stakeholder community (D. Ford, personal communication, May 2016).

In the pages that follow, we present the concept of brandED, claiming it as the educator's unique adaptation of the business term *brand*. BrandED is a powerful concept that is part of a progressive view of new educational directions and trends. It represents a digital "edge-dweller" persona. It suggests a mindset of continuous innovation (Monroe, 2014). The brandED edge-dwelling educator is poised for communication change that benefits students. BrandED is about providing that benefit and telling the stories around our worth.

Emphasizing the "ED" in the word *brandED* humanizes the business concept of brand, a concept that grew from the discipline of marketing. BrandED is a knowing, feeling, walking, and talking *connecting* attitude that builds on your present leadership style and brings a 21st-century finish to your presence. It is delivered using new media tools to share your clear, consistent, targeted, and sustained school narratives. These are tools that are needed in our "always open for business" world. BrandED behavior showcases the core beliefs of your school, inviting you to synthesize: to combine a wealth of important educational content with inspired thinking from cross-industry practices, creating new, meaningful, and actionable leadership communication. Call it brandED leadership. A brief look around Twitter shows the images and content of educators who are adding the communication value of brand to their work in the digital world. One example is teacher Kent Dyer and his STEAM (STEM plus A for "art") colleagues at Township High School 214 in Arlington Heights, IL. They are on a quest to create new experiences for their students. "Creativity is our future [and] the tools are digital," is Kent's proud Twitter pronouncement (@Kent_Dyer), which shows the direction of his brand as an educator. To be authentic leaders in the 21st century, school leaders must have a more expansive, informed base of content and knowledge beyond the parameters of the monoculture of public education. This polycultural behavior of knowledge sharing is what Thomas L. Friedman (2005), Pulitzer Prize–winning author of *The World Is Flat*, welcomed in his writings as a "communication mash-up" reflective of the openness and accessibility of information.

Branding behavior creates positive influence for school leaders. To be seen as authentic in online exchanges advances one's influence in powerful ways. Today's schools exist in a digital town square where people meet daily. School value is one of the most discussed topics online. People both with and without children search the Internet and consult online real estate sites to find data about their prospective local school. Trulia.com reports that 46% of Millennials surveyed want their dream home to be near a quality school. Educational leaders must be powerfully present in the digital marketing of the narrative of school value, creating a brand that speaks in an authentic voice to an audience. Adopting a brandED strategy to benefit kids helps you attain a synthesizing view, preparing you to communicate with the varied segments of stakeholders who will research, observe, and engage with your institutional brand online on a daily basis.

Today's digital and social media world is a world driven by mobile content in short form and long form, in text and video. The business communication tool of brand can inform a school improvement strategy that harnesses the power of content, of story, in this new media age. Brand is a proven tool that has resulted in trusted connections in business since the 1950s (De Swann Arons, 2011). When adapted by schools, brand becomes the beacon—the touchstone of why we act the way we do as a school, why we teach and learn the way we do. Beyond the emotional connectivity, using a brandED strategy enables leaders to set measurable goals that ensure long-term trust. As a brandED leader, guide your community to three tangible outcomes: improved school **culture,** expanded school **performance,** and increased school **resourcing.**

WELCOME TO THE BRANDED CONVERSATION

We've moved our small brandED conversation from a serendipitous first meeting onto a big stage. Little did we know in 2009 that the concept of defining a school, and the need to show a school's relevance through an engaging brand, would become as strategically important to maintaining a student community as it is now. We are educators in an age when conveying the story of a school has moved beyond being an option. Our stakeholders have growing decision-making power. In a transparent world, we must present ourselves and connect with authenticity that engages our community in a brand loyalty to our schools.

In the chapters that follow, you are invited to join our compelling conversation, our call to action about building a brand that encompasses, with power and clarity, the mission, value, and vision of your school—a story to be shared on an open digital and social media stage for your engaged community. A series of eight compelling professional conversations guides you in the process of building not only your personal professional brand but also crafting a collaboratively built school brand, one that unifies a brandED community and promotes engagement and loyalty. Labeling the chapters as conversations suggests the deep thought that goes beyond simply "trying out brand" to a dedicated commitment to incorporating brandED as a professional development experience for leaders and their organizations, one that will change the status quo of educational communication in this new age. It suggests that leaders be in a continuous conversation through reflection and sharing, in real time and through digital and social media, in order to complete their brandED journey that genuinely defines the school.

The brandED innovation starts with you and grows quickly through your strong modeling of the power of brand in your school. It grows because of your ability to influence stakeholders to be part of the collaborative endeavor of building a school brand. Thanks to the buzz of innovative thinking about brand in our modern world and the fact that everyone and everything is branded, you have every chance of succeeding. Some of your stakeholders may even ask, "What were you waiting for?"

BrandED leaders immerse themselves in conversations. First, in self-reflection, then with trusted validators, before they move outward to lead and support a brandED distributed leadership team that designs and builds a brand. It is a rich, creative collaboration of various stakeholder publics. These open conversations are necessary to communicate new processes and frameworks that will share the stories of what makes a school unique as a brand and maintain its relevance. In closing each of the eight conversations, brandED leadership tips and brandED reflective questions will support leaders who adopt the innovative practice of brandED and become its valued brandED storytellers and stewards. Join the conversation on social media using #brandEDU. Connect with Eric (@E_Sheninger) and Trish (@trishrubin) on Twitter.

From Brand to BrandED

Conversation 1 launches the journey to brandED. Leaders learn why the tenets of business brand and marketing, standards in the commercial marketplace, can be comfortably adapted in the 21st century to an educational framework. We will touch on a short history of business branding and understand the marketing discipline that shapes leaders' educational work. Readers learn about the foundational difference between business brand and the educator's adaptation, brandED, which focuses on communicating through showcasing, celebrating, and building powerful relationships that benefit the school community. Businesses focus their brand communication efforts on sales goals; a few select elements that commercial brands employ in brand campaigns can inform educators about reaching their own brandED goals. As educators, we can appreciate brand history as a starting point for our journey, but we keep the foundational difference in mind: This leadership mindset isn't about a bottom-line return. The goal of brandED is the sharing of clear and consistent messages that define our mission to educate our children.

> In this ever-changing society, the most powerful and enduring brands are built from the heart. Their foundations are stronger because they are built with the strength of the human spirit, not an ad campaign.
> —*Howard Schultz, CEO, Starbucks*

Part One: In Brand We Trust

The brand buzz is everywhere.

We live in a digital and social media world where everything and everyone is branded. What does brand mean? In order to move into brandED leadership, one must start at the beginning, with the word *brand*. Is there a "just right" definition of brand that can inform your own brandED professional leadership journey?

There are as many interpretations of the word brand as there are voices in the business community (Cohen, 2011a). A class of graduate marketing students can provide multiple versions of the meaning of brand. Those definitions might be pretty good ones because our Millennial generation gets the concept. One of the most interesting ideas about what brand is today comes from Marian Goodell, CEO of a distinctive nonprofit with a unique brand, the Burning Man Festival. Goodell claims that brand these days isn't just created, it's *cocreated and celebrated* by those who align with and promote its purpose and value (Solis, 2011b). This description of a dedicated brand process is a rallying point for brandED educators, and a place to start our journey toward a collaborative, cocreated educational brand mission.

In the business world, the concept of brand is made up of three foundational business elements:

An **image**

A **promise**

A **result**

These descriptors fit into the selling proposition for products and services that are offered to the marketplace. For example, in the case of the growth of the Burning Man Festival brand (Solis, 2011b), the **image** of an accepting society offers a **promise** of an engaged, fair "gifting economy" and delivers the **result** of a self-reliant, creative, and fulfilling city that appears and disappears each year during the waning days of summer in a remote desert area. The loyal followers of this distinctive brand savor their experience and, year after year, show repeated brand loyalty to the festival, which is the goal of any provider of a product or service.

Educators are not selling a product or service. But brand is a fit for us in a modern, digital view of professional learning and progressive school thinking. This brand is made up of three foundational school elements:

An **image**

A **promise**

A **result**

The concepts of image, promise, and result can powerfully frame a school's brand-building communication effort, but with a distinct difference from the way these terms are used in the business world (see Figure 1.1). BrandED thinking around these terms is a frame for developing your own school story: The concepts of image, promise, and result create a frame on which to build a cohesive school brand

Figure 1.1 Brand and BrandED Tenets Contrasted

	IMAGE	PROMISE	RESULT
THE TENETS OF BRAND	Promoting for selling	Satisfy a need or want	Improves: • Sales • Profit • Scale
	IMAGE	PROMISE	RESULT
THE TENETS OF BRANDED	Storytelling to communicate value	Accomplish school goals	Improves: • Culture • Performance • Resourcing

communication presence, one that leads to stakeholder engagement that brings school improvement. In schools, brand is a personification of a community. A strategically marketed brand message about the valuable work of the school is now a necessity for effective school leadership in our digital world because educators now live in a world of increasing school choice options for parents. Offering a strong institutional persona across various channels through a clear brand presence is not an option in our age of visibility. "Define before being defined" is part of the leadership agenda of visibility in a digital and social age.

TODAY'S ICONS

Brand is about visibility. Companies spend millions of dollars to get the attention needed to secure the consumer buy. There is a science to achieving that moment of brand victory, the winning over of the audience, that is focused on the first seconds of recognizing a brand, known as the FMOT, the "first moment of truth" (originally coined by Proctor & Gamble). It's the traditional face-to-face decision buyers make that leads to a product purchase (Armstrong & Kotler, 2015). As many of us know from our own buying habits, brand is a powerful part of connecting us to the products and services we love to purchase. It's the repeated exchange that leads to loyalty. Brand use is part of our daily rituals.

As more and more decisions are made online, the FMOT has now morphed into the ZMOT, the zero moment of truth (a term coined by Google in 2011). This is human decision making on steroids. In spite of powerful data platforms and algorithms, it's often anybody's guess when, where, and why "we the people" will buy. In today's exchange, the consumer has the power. In a global competition for the heart, mind, and wallet of customers, there are big winners who know how to woo and win fans. The brand champions affect us in our day-to-day lives—and the communities we lead. Think about how image, promise, and result got these iconic brands to the top in 2016. Each brand lives a powerful, clear image; makes a relevant and genuine promise; and dedicates itself to continued tangible result that keeps an audience loyal (Interbrand, 2016):

1. Apple
2. Google
3. Coca-Cola
4. Microsoft
5. Toyota
6. IBM
7. Samsung
8. Amazon
9. Mercedes-Benz
10. GE

In the "always open for business" world of online content marketing, these powerhouses are never more than a connecting click or a pop-up away on our devices. We face the deluge of visual content around these and thousands of other brands in daily life. Simon Clift, former chief marketing officer of Unilever, a powerful, iconic global company, believes that brands, even billion-dollar brands at the highest level of success, know they aren't just about what we see. Clift believes brand to be a contract between a company and consumers (De Swaan Arons, 2011). Every brand on this top 10 list knows about turning an exchange into customer loyalty. Clift's thinking about a contract implies the feeling of trust that exists in any exchange with the consumer. This same feeling should resonate with educators because schools also work to make contracts with their stakeholders that are built on exchanges leading to trust and loyalty.

Now, equating business brand with trust is a relatively new concept. The traditional world of business sales evokes a classic negative image when it comes to trustworthiness. Schools today struggle with trust issues as well and need to adapt as business has done. How did things change for business? Today's world of sales is now different because of "positioning": the perception of a brand as unique and set apart from the competition. Positioning a product on the basis of consumer trust didn't emerge in the marketplace until the middle of the last century. Suddenly, products needed to become more than *things* if they were to compete for the buy. Products needed personality. They needed to be *unique* and *different*. They needed to have a story.

Products that created stories and connected with their customers through those tales were on the way to becoming trusted "brands." Digging into brand history is the first step in making brand a part of our own educational brand development.

A SHORT BRAND HISTORY FOR BRANDED EDUCATORS

Go back a hundred years or so when all that it took to sell was to make something of good quality, package it cleanly, and offer it to people with a folksy sales pitch. Saying that your product was "the best soap" or "the best salt" got it sold. But brand has been developing on the fast track since that time.

Long before the early 20th century, clever humans were branding. Product leaders like Morton Salt and Quaker Oats heralded the birth of mass brand presence, complete with simple but powerful icons that are still around today in the modern grocery aisle. These time-tested iconic brands share the stage today with the top 100 brands of 2016 (Interbrand, 2016), including both present-day heavy hitters like BMW, Disney, and the NFL, and newcomers like Uber. All these brands have their loyal followings, but the Pillsbury Doughboy and other time-tested brands are different. They still pack a historical and emotional punch for modern customers: We trust them.

In the 1960s, brand moved beyond simple packaging. Madison Avenue executives (think *Mad Men*) created product "personalities." The Marlboro Man and Maytag Repairman began to build relationships with the consumer through the new "social media" driver of the day: the color television. Innovative communication and a new way of telling product stories gave birth to the science of brand building and the need for brand management. The golden era of TV and print advertising pushed the growth of brands that delivered new services and products to consumers, who "liked" them way before a social media thumbs-up appeared. Madison Avenue boldly tackled social issues and created campaigns to unify 1960s society, such as the Pepsi Generation campaign. Creatives successfully sold tiny Volkswagens in a time of big sedans (some with tail fins!), succeeding with a counterintuitive campaign that called the VW Beetle what most people thought it was: ugly ("History: 1960s," 2003).

Today, brand experience—the powerful concept that advances lasting emotional connection with a consumer—shapes our personal buying habits, and in this world, customer engagement through brand experience is king. Creating an experience is a continuing challenge for any brand because of today's competition. How can brands continue to keep the attention of their audience? How can a brand position itself, offer an experience, and be noticed amid all the noise? The concept of "story" is a big part of brand experience. The successful brands of today are masters of storytelling. A brand's narrative power in the exchange with its loyal fans separates the winners from the losers. Once in possession of a unique, authentic story that distinguishes it from the competition, the successful brand grows through its consistent, targeted, deliberate messaging. This is as true for classic brands like Coca-Cola as it is for newer players like Google. Each has a story that explains its reason for existence, and each brand tells the story in compelling ways to attract and keep attention.

Connecting through a unique, emotional story is why Nordstrom's department store soars as JC Penney continues to underperform. The narrative of a successful company is consistent and continually refreshed in exchange with a new social community of fans who want their own distinct stories to be heard. Today's consumers want to belong to the community. Top brands are not shouting at the consumer as they were in the heyday of advertising. They are listening and acting on what they hear, making the story fresh and relevant across many communication landscapes. The McDonald's golden arches logo is known in 119 countries, and its successful "I'm Lovin' It" slogan is a differentiator in the fast-food world on a global scale. The success of the company's I'm Lovin' It campaign is based on the connection the brand makes across cultures as it reaches diverse audiences with a simple shared message. McDonald's integrates its brand message from Japan to Brazil to London through shared human stories, which become the key to satisfying fast-food "wants and behaviors" in any culture. (Kotler & Armstrong, 1996). This brand has ranked consistently on Interbrand's list of top global brands. Mc Donald's gets there by telling its story of the brand in traditional and new-age media messages to children and parents that promote McDonald's consistent, affordable, and reliable delivery of a fast-food product. The company now shows its connection to the changing tastes of its community by expanding its offer to a more health-minded consumer. Millennial parents who played in the McDonald's ball pits as children now bring their kids to enjoy the same experience because those parents are still "Lovin' It." A customer in any part of the world knows the experience of the McDonald's brand because of the company's focused power to tell its story globally, and its ability to translate that experience into local cultures without losing brand recognition.

Brands must also be flexible to have impact (Kapferer, 2012). Apple may be the best example of a flexible brand by virtue of its being able to pivot yearly with a constant, consistent line of products. Apple appeals to its audience by telling the story of an always current, always plugged in, and always supported customer who continually embraces new ideas.

Another reason why the top brands succeed lies in the ways they quickly react to meet the changing needs of diverse niches—the segments and demographics—they serve. This is a prime lesson for school leaders in a rapidly diversifying age. Successful brand building comes from knowing audiences and focusing on what these customers want. Look at the brand behemoths. Microsoft's understanding of the community it serves, for example, recently led to its purchase of the online professional network, LinkedIn. Brand giants are tops at data collection and social listening and at using that information to drive flexible development of products, services, and relationships. In these times of big data and vast quantities of digital information, new software yields powerful metrics to inform brand managers about the needs and wants of the marketplace. Companies use information hoping to find that elusive ZMOT that will satisfy their communities. Brand winners like Toyota get their audience's attention on multiple digital platforms, using websites, social media, sales incentives, PR, and integrated marketing. Toyota devises ways to get its targets across niches to talk to the company about their needs and wants. The company connects with its engaged consumers on digital and social channels, encouraging them to share personal stories about their own Toyota buying journeys.

BrandED leaders take special note. Educators are joining the brand conversation at a unique, developmental point in brand history. Exchange today is based on a brand's clear narrative, consistent presentation, and ability to confidently engage in multiple ways with its diverse, segmented audiences. Big brands spend billions of dollars engaging with consumers, inviting us into the decision-making process. Like it or not, we are prodded and poked to be "customer engaged" (Hahn, 2014). Thanks to the Internet and social media, brands want to know us, their potentially loyal fans. They tailor stories to get our attention as potential customers. Many of our stakeholders are experienced in the online exchange that leads to satisfaction with a brand, and they seek the brand experience in all aspects of life. Transparent engagement is here to stay. And now it's at the schoolhouse door.

ENGAGEMENT EXPECTATION HAS COME TO SCHOOLS

The great news is that educators in the digital age don't need to spend millions as big business does to harness the power behind brand communication. It's a DIY (do-it-yourself) world, and that applies to the branding process. Consumer understanding of brand presence grows daily, and so do consumer expectations. Brand development, building compelling missions, and kickstarting fundraising campaigns—all are practiced by millions who own computers or smartphones. Like many others, today's savvy digital-minded school leaders can create their own powerful home-grown influence without an advertising budget and celebrity endorsements. The Pew Foundation (Smith, 2015) found that 64% of adult Americans now own a smartphone of some form, a number that rose from 35% ownership in 2011. Users connect with brands regularly and use mobile tech to connect with products and services online, from interacting with health providers to doing their banking. The brand buzz that is in our daily lives moves to a complex beat, a symphony of DIY creativity, as entrepreneurial stay-at-home moms and dads, "solo-preneur" moonlighters, job seekers, and Gen Z teens join the brand movement and search for audiences to engage with to advance themselves, to send a message, or to sell a product or service.

Schools are part of the buzz. When Millennial parents in your school community develop Web pages for the unborn, complete with naming campaigns, they are dealing in branding behavior and reaching audiences for their desired result: engagement. With the growth of social media platforms like Instagram, parents can chronicle the moments of their children's day, engaging their followers in a child's development from infancy to the first day of school and beyond. The news about student mobile use from EDUCAUSE Center for Analysis and Research (Dahlstrom, 2015) is that in 2015, the percentage of undergraduate students owning smartphones grew to 92%. That figure alone suggests the chosen direction of messaging and access for our students in this new age of engaged communication.

There have been many instances of broken trust to date. One of the most serious recent examples is the case of Volkswagen, whose genius in bringing the Beetle to America in the previous century is now tarnished by the news that it misrepresented the truth regarding emissions of its autos. This illustrates the serious component of building trust in an exchange, and it illustrates what happens when trust is broken ("VW Chairman Says Parts of Company 'Tolerated Breaches of Rules,'" 2015). The Chipotle brand, once the envy of the marketplace, has dealt with issues of trust regarding its quality control and food-handling issues (Kline, Duprey, & Noonan, 2016). Samsung is now embroiled in a digital recall of millions of phones. Trust can be destroyed in an instant in our "breaking news" digital media environment. Because trust is a foundation of teaching and learning, and of our education system, conscientious brandED thinking is a must for educators who need to build or repair trust.

Trusted brands today are doing what Mastercard's agency, the Dentsu Aegis Global Media Group, calls "riding the digital tsunami to relevance" (Dua, 2015), and the company is intense in its pursuit of the new gold standard: customer engagement. Schools are about relevance in our rapidly changing world, and they can engage with their audiences right alongside big brands through multiple communication channels: digital, social, real time, influencer, and traditional media. Schools will win when they make it their business to truly know who they're engaging with among their varied stakeholder circles. They will create a genuine exchange with these different niche stakeholder groups—kids, staff, teachers, parents, and the greater community—making their audiences trusted partners in the experience of learning. Schools that recognize the diverse, nuanced stakeholder groups that surround them, and that take steps to know the wants, needs, and characteristics of each group of stakeholders, will create brand loyalty in ways that separate them from schools who haven't yet acknowledged the power of creating a connected, trusting community.

WHAT BRAND ISN'T

You may think you know brand, but think again. At this moment, parents of children K–12 and beyond who are looking at the choices available are online looking for something different. They are looking for brand. They are seeking brand experience. Relying on the surface elements of what you think brand is will not make your school more attractive in this competitive environment. BrandED leaders must go further in their understanding and leading. These surface elements aren't brand, but you may have mistaken them for it:

- Your school website
- Your school logo
- Your school mascot
- Your school tagline
- Your school teams and clubs

Websites, missions, and mascots are not the brand of educators. They're the places audiences "touch" an education brand; they have important value to the brand experience, but they are identity outlets for the brand story and the growth of the narrative. A brand is something much bigger than these elements. The items listed are important as supportive planks for communicating a clearly articulated brand.

Today's iconic brands all have a look. Visual content communicates brand online, especially with the Millennial generation and their following demographic, Gen Z. But here's another "isn't" for the brand conversation for educators: Despite the need for presenting a consistent look, *powerful branding is more about what isn't seen.* BrandED includes exhibiting a compelling Web presence, but keep the word "feeling" in mind.

BRAND IS FEELING

The Disney brand is conveyed with more than cute cartoons and movies. The company captures the best elements of anyone's childhood in ways that create loyal brand followers, who then become brand ambassadors to their children. The best brands are the leaders of the pack because they create value that is intangible. They've made an emotional connection to the mind of the customer. In that connection lives a message that continually feeds the "wanting to connect to good stuff" that the brand brings. Take a look at an old-school Good Humor truck. Good Humor isn't as much about ice cream as it is about the delicious story of sweet summer days that many of us can relate to ourselves. Even when we buy a Good Humor product in a mega-supermarket in the dead of winter, we remember reaching for it on the street on hot summer days. The Nike swoosh captures the rush that every athlete, from weekend warrior to the NBA All-Star, feels when connected with the Nike brand experience. Anyone who proudly wears the logo of a university on a T-shirt knows the feeling associated with brand, but let's go deeper with some powerhouses of feeling. Chanel's brand mark speaks volumes to consumers about things like luxury, class, and sexiness, but of course these messages are not just seen in the design of the logo. Chanel's core brand message comes across in powerful, unseen ways that engage loyal audiences in deep, lasting exchange. School leaders have the same power to brand without a Madison Avenue marketing budget.

Creating feeling can cost nothing in a digital world. The Starbuck CEO has access to millions of marketing dollars to advertise his coffee, yet that isn't where his investment in brand value lies. Starbucks isn't just about selling coffee. In fact, Starbucks came late to advertising its brand. It didn't have to because the intangible value it brought to its loyal customers provided enough word-of-mouth advertising that the company didn't need a big marketing budget. Recently, with the rollout of new products and its move to build a luxury coffee experience with specialty-brewing Starbucks locations, more advertising dollars are spent. But Starbucks originally grew its brand from the intangible value of belonging that it brings to daily life. Starbucks launched the idea of a "third place" to belong, after home and work. That's a connection that satisfies beyond the purchase of a high-priced iced double-shot latte.

Connecting to the channel of feeling is key to building your school brand, just as it is key for our fellow business brand managers. When individuals feel that they belong to something bigger than themselves, "brand well-being" is present. One aspect of well-being comes from the feeling of belonging that develops through a trusted exchange with others who are part of a like-minded community. Distinguished management consultant Peter Drucker said, "People buy with their hearts, not with their minds" (Penhollow, 2014). People also choose education with their hearts, although educators don't generally think about a "stakeholder buy" as they lead their communities. The image, the promise, and the result of brandED fits when a leader blends the recognizable, consistent signs of a crafted brand with a genuine feeling of an educational experience. BrandED leaders, informed by the impact of experience, exchange, story, and feeling, can deliver the call to elevate education through brand. BrandED leaders focus as the best brand managers do: They make people matter by making engagement a priority. According to Maya Angelou, not a brand manager but a masterful storyteller, "People will forget what you said, people will forget what you did, but people will never forget how you made them feel." Ms. Angelou's thinking is a powerful cornerstone of a leader's brandED mindset and well worth cultivating and promoting.

PROMOTING A SCHOOL BRAND

The modern concept of brand evolved from a simple labeling of products during a communication revolution in the last century, one that touched every corner of modern life. When television became present in every home, products needed to become humanized through televised commercial stories. Brand personalities on TV screens aggressively competed for the buy. A respected voice at the time of this evolution was the father of advertising, David Ogilvy (1987), who, when observing the frenzy of the 20th-century age of selling, reasoned that "big ideas are simple ideas" (p. 195). His thoughts about defining and managing brand revealed that in the pivoting world of communication in the mid-20st century, brand was the intangible sum of product attributes, the name, the package, the price, the history, the reputation, and advertising. Oglivy's view can inform strategies for brandED leaders. Yet how do we align ourselves in the 21st-century pivot of digital and social communication with an advertising stance? How do educators create intangible brand loyalty for our stakeholders without an Ogilvy advertising agency budget? As we learned earlier from Starbucks, we don't need advertising to create a remarkable, reputable brand. We can promote a connection to community through our intangible feeling and narratives, and create a sharing experience around these stories with those we engage with daily. We must lead by "leaning into" the opportunity to use the talents of the stakeholders in our schools, the passionate brand advocates who already are engaged in advancing our school's reputation. This collaboration is key to building our message. Finding talented school brand advocates who employ brand exchange in their daily lives provides a leader a chance to grow connection with a collaborative "no cost" team in launching a new school brand strategy. Far from Madison Avenue, a brandED leader will find this goal within reach on any Main Street in any community.

The term *promotion* takes the place of *advertising* in our brandED strategy. It's the necessary adaptation that distances us from sales. Unlike advertising, promotion doesn't have to cost a thing, and it is required in today's world of education to amplify brand power. It's essential for educators to promote themselves in this digital world of connection. Who is better at sharing the school narrative of the wonderful work of the school than those stakeholders who are creating it? Kids, teachers, and staff can be the genuine voices of the narrative of success that promotes a school's brand. A brandED leader creates a culture of innovation using the power of technology, supported by multiple interested stakeholders who collaborate and commit to the brand innovation. Educators who are strategic in promotion can reach stakeholders through the tangible and intangible connection of brand awareness. You won't need a marketing department. School leaders can promote and advance brandED's foundational building blocks: image, promise, and result.

A school brandED Strategic Plan, built under an innovative leadership employing a collaborative effort, will create the essential conditions for making school promotion part of daily school life. Leaders who promote brand without the budget of a marketing executive are sound communicators. They have a sense of the needs, goals, and actions that will attract community interest in supporting the school brand. They get attention that leads to positive relationship building. Word of mouth is necessary to promotion, and the most successful school brand communicators get their communities talking. Using small communities and subgroups of interested stakeholders, schools can gradually develop a capacity to get the word out. To sustain the promotion, the creation of affinity—the good feeling that comes from the brand narrative—must be a leading part of the effort to promote image, promise, and result.

SURVEY THE LANDSCAPE: WHO'S GOT THE FEELING FOR BRANDED?

Taking on a brandED mindset is a commanding role that is suited to today's digital school leader, especially in a time when any teenager on his or her personal brand journey is pursuing the same brand elements—image, promise, and result—using social media platforms like Snapchat and Instagram. As you start your brand journey, survey the landscape and see who has got the feeling for brand. A case in point is that average teen. Granted, this teen is not as informed as a professional, but is "selling" and promoting a narrative to an audience. Why? He or she wants to matter. There's surely a lot of emphasis on image and result on that kid's part, and maybe some attention to genuine promise. Teens are sailing on the social media sea at 15, packaging and delivering personal brand value for better or worse. Recognize that their search to communicate a brand that matters offers you real opportunity. Their natural digital and social savvy and your school leadership as brand steward could make for a great partnership as you start promoting school brand. Keep your eyes open for potential brandED stakeholders who may already be positively defining your school brand under their own initiative.

One compelling school example of the support for your brand journey to result is found in an app designed by a Gen Z 16-year-old named Natalie Hamilton. Her innovative app is called Sit with Us, and it allows the mixing of students, the in-crowd and the awkward, through lunch appointments. It was launched as part of an antibullying initiative that reflects a brand of tolerance. These young digital stakeholders are sitting in our classrooms and are filled with the potential to support brand building. They may be members of your school's business clubs and traditional national organizations like DECA, a high school association of marketing students, but they can also be creative, entrepreneurially minded students as young as 15. They can be among the first to embrace and power the new school brand. You need them on your brand-building team.

Loyalty to a brand's position or its feel is the root of engagement, which marketers call brand equity. It is found in repeated exchange—face-to-face, or through digital and social means—between a brand and its audience. Behavioral habits of exchange are formed when good brand stories are advanced repeatedly, because those stories fuel good feeling and brand affinity. Think of the brands you reach for over and over and the good feeling that results from the connection.

Brand equity is a powerful driver for building a school brand. Strong brand equity rides the waves of good times and bad. Anyone who owns a Samsung phone during the recent recall is seeing brand equity put to the test for that brand giant. Brand equity comes from trust. When educational leaders earn the trust of engaged, loyal school brand fans, the fans return again and again for further supportive school experiences. An improved school community is the result. Look outside your schoolhouse door for a familiar example of brand equity. Who are those members of the community who already see the school as worthy of their loyalty? They are part of the stakeholder community, from the students in your classrooms to local small businesses. They can be the first partners for shared brand leadership as a brand is born. Their good feeling for the school is priceless, and they must contribute to brand building. Use your school calendar of events to go on the hunt for collaborative stakeholders. Meet them face-to-face. Look at your teachers as brand ambassadors. Enlist the interest of teachers who have built relationships with stakeholder parents and who still connect to former students and community leaders through their own interests. Our schools are full of stakeholders who are already using digital communication that advances image, promise, and result in their own lives.

Stakeholders are forming relationships that show their school brand power through personal sharing on social media platforms, reflecting their connection to school activities ranging from gaming to hobbies.

One case in point is teacher Arezou Taheri Montgomery. A weekend warrior as a distance runner, she uses social media to chronicle her success as an athlete along with her passion for education. Because of her sharing of her education life, many of her Facebook followers cheer her passion for teaching as much as her marathon achievements. The students and their parents cheer her on in both realms. Brooklyn professional Betty Lee is a supportive community stakeholder who has a connected tech presence in her career. As a realtor, she sees possibilities in connecting new residents to a school brand; and, as a collaborative member of the school community she serves, she is eager to grow her understanding of support through social media like Snapchat. Adam Leitman Bailey is a former New Jersey high school student who now owns his own successful New York City law firm and has spoken at his former school to inspire students about the value of building a personal brand.

Stakeholders like these number in the thousands across typical school communities. These generous, giving stakeholders have promotional value in schools. They join your collaborative design team at zero cost and bring a richness of skill and talent and their commitment to contribute to the school's success. That's how you creatively do this without the Madison Avenue budget. They join the cause to improve their school, seeing it as a social or moral imperative. First, you create the call to action through developing your own brand. Your model and commitment can be a brand beacon to others. Your effort is powered by technology, and you take advantage of the endless free resources that are available to leaders who want to reinvent and innovate.

Here's the simple map:

1. You develop a school **image** through authentic stories told from every corner of the school community, using the engaging content of your daily school narrative.

2. You purposefully promote your educator's **promise** to create the mix of messages about the mission of the school to create a type of brand harmony, a consistency that feels good, through many messaging channels.

3. You show a tangible, measurable **result**, promoting your narrative to gain resources that can sustain the school in unique ways.

Like Arezou, Betty, and Adam, your own loyal supporters will help you lead, and their energy and creativity spread the word. No marketing dollars are needed for leaders willing to innovate through interactive brand storytelling. Leaders can get the attention of their audiences through their collaborative, inclusive brandED mindset. Your supporters are out there.

STRONG BRANDED LEADERSHIP = STRONG BRAND

Marketing and brand campaigns include deliberate, coordinated steps that lead to brand awareness across many channels (McCulloch, 2000). As a brandED leader, you won't develop a campaign, but you'll move to targeted action and use the familiar structure of educational collaboration, found in the distributed leadership model, to create a shared plan. Collaboration can quickly energize your community into one that supports and celebrates the new school brand. Business brands are built to sell, and, because of that, extensive research goes into their development. They are linked to the bottom line. In schools, we are building brand through stories that show our performance value. We strive for transparency to communicate our content that shows our education success. What is key is our ability to tell the story of the school and to inspire understanding and caring on the part of others to help deliver on a brand promise that our stories illustrate. The skills and talents of committed stakeholders can power the delivery of a brand that all community members can connect with and consistently articulate.

BrandED innovation is instituted through the spirit of a shared journey. The creation of a brandED Strategic Plan guides brand implementation. A strong leadership stance by the school brand builder can move the brandED Strategic Plan, which is the result of collaborative effort, to completion. Having a structured plan ensures that there is a focal point for brand communication. A strong plan is a road map for transformation of the school's image for a positive result. The plan unifies the communication effort through strategies that sustain the brand effort. A plan weaves common threads from across many disparate supporting school efforts into a clear picture of what the school stands for, preparing the school community to face myriad pressures within the school and challenges coming from the larger world. In Conversation 5, leaders guide their community, modeling behavior and preparing the culture for being brand aware. They use a brandED Strategic Plan, built through a step-by-step cocreative process, that sets the direction for building school culture, performance, and resources to deliver the promise of the school brand. For leaders feeling the pull of initiatives, assessment pressures, expectations, budgets, aging infrastructure, mandates, directives, and concerns for the safety of students, a brand strategy functions as a unifier to aggregate a wide array of separate existing messages and programs. Imagine brand as an overarching "umbrella" under which leaders unite disparate agenda items that are part of the promise of the school that must be communicated to stakeholders. Think of the many initiatives and platforms for training, curriculum, policy, and communication that exist within the school organization. A brandED strategy can connect every one of them in one overarching message representing the good work of the school. If you're losing sleep about challenging issues surrounding your school and your ability to manage the "noise," a brandED Strategic Plan can offer a leader control: It streamlines fragmented messaging into a unified, strong brand that promotes the school's various stories of positive result.

Link your ongoing brandED effort to tangible *results*. It advances credibility with your stakeholders who want to know more than your opinion about the value of pursuing a brand presence. They want to know what is in it for them. Potential fans want feedback on growth. Brand is feeling, but stakeholders look to see results from their engagement with the brand. Results assure them that this institutional commitment is worthwhile. When leaders move the brandED conversation to a level of planning and strategy that showcases results, the stakeholder community buys in. Leaders who have gathered stakeholders to guide the innovation of a brandED Strategic Plan share the feeling of new possibilities for improved culture, performance, and resourcing. This positive spirit engages the community. Because feeling is part of the equation of successful brand and brand equity, value comes from seeing the tangible as well as the intangible results of improved school culture, performance, and resourcing. Create a plan that balances good feeling with tangible results.

As early adopters of a brandED mindset demonstrate, the strategic process of brand building allows administrators to demonstrate key functions of leadership. They promote school brand in accordance with high levels of management. In the view of the National Association of Secondary School Principals and the National Association of Elementary School Principals (NASSP & NAESP, 2013), the surest elements of strong leadership are attending to a vision of success, creating a climate for achievement, and cultivating leadership across the organization to achieve that success. A brandED leader develops effective ways to manage people and processes in a new digital world of communication. BrandED leadership embodies the same key elements of success cited by NASSP/NAESP through the development of a brandED Strategic Plan. The cornerstone of adapting brand building in education lies in recognizing the difference between business brand and brandED, your educator-owned tool for professional and organizational development:

Brand = Sales

BrandED = Showcasing and relationships

Brand expert Jason Miletsky believes that brand is the sum experience people have with a product or service (Miletsky & Smith, 2009). Value for the receiver, resulting in loyalty to the product or service, comes from the positive delivery of a provider's promise. Schools provide value every day. A well-defined school brand defined and executed in a strategic plan ensures that the brand promise is made and sustained. Even in times of educational standardization, schools can deliver on a unique promise linked to brand services that connect and engage stakeholders in valuable school experiences that will build a school's reputation beyond a test score. Create communication avenues and proudly share the results of your school's good work. A carefully communicated brand spreads the good news of academic and nonacademic success.

TALKING THE BRANDED TALK

Where do leaders tell their stories?

BrandED messages are placed wherever stakeholders are gathering online and in real time. Invite your various publics—kids, teachers, staff, and parents—to understand that the concept of brand can be powerfully adapted for education, and help them engage in the conversation. Help them recognize the value of brand in unifying a community in changing times. Encourage them to see brandED as a way to rise above business as usual, where the tendency is to do the same thing over and over for the same result. Promote the brand effort as something that provides new thinking in a new age in which our students need new answers if they are to be at their best in a rapidly changing economy. The latest group in the branding demography that schools face is referred to as "Plurals" (Hais & Winograd, 2012). Plurals, also known as Gen Z, are those born after 1997. They are called Plurals because they will be the most culturally diverse—"plural"—group of Americans ever recorded. These unique Plurals are sitting in our classrooms today, and we need to engage them.

Plurals are children of the branding world. To many of them, brand doesn't mean narcissistic self-absorption. It's simply self-expression. Brand is now present in the minds of many young teachers and students who have developed their personal brand. *Time* magazine cites that 92%

of American children have an online presence before the age of 2, starting with parents' postings of nearly 1,000 images of their children before their fifth birthday (Sales, 2016). When leaders connect their understanding of brand value to classrooms of Millennial teachers who are already living brand-rich lives on social media, they will gain early adopters, potential collaborative team members, and committed brand ambassadors among teachers and students. They will also gain the attention of those who can collaborate to spread the word about school brand. They are experts in doing this for themselves. As your school brand is built and shared, the world opens easily because of these young stakeholders. The avenues to share your message grow quickly in this new age; online and in face-to-face engagements, the word spreads. Involve the next generations.

Part Two: BrandED Matters to Today's School Leaders

Branding matters in the changing world of learning, fueled by powerful digital resources (Sheninger, 2014). Telling a powerful school story and reaching an audience have never been more possible than in today's digital world, and never more necessary for a leader to embrace in a new world of competition and choice. Early brand adopters, whom you will meet in the pages of this book, are already out ahead of the pack on digital media, and they are passionate about what they do. They are inspired by their initial success and have developed professionally in ways that make them unique compared to other leaders. A brandED mindset takes professionals to the next level, to add strategic thinking and action steps for brand sustainability.

BrandED school leaders build brand in the name of school improvement, to advance better teaching, learning, and leadership and stronger school communities. The work advanced in the area of servant leadership reinforces the importance of a having a brandED strategy. Sipe and Frick (2009) identify the following seven pillars of servant leadership:

- Person of character
- Puts people first
- Skilled communicator
- Compassionate collaborator
- Has foresight
- Systems thinker
- Leads with moral authority

The pillars of servant leadership speak to the mission of being brandED; they define leadership as something to be shared, distributed, transparent, and focused on success and happiness. BrandED does not rest on the shoulders of one person. It is a distributed, collaborative, service-oriented school improvement effort.

The marketing principle that guides business brand is its drive to build relationships. BrandED educators focus strongly on that aspect. Successful school leadership in today's digital world is fueled by connectivity. Aren't educators always building, brokering, and sustaining relationships? Focusing on relationships is a cornerstone of your leadership effort and one that supports your brandED strategy. Relationship building is a never-ending process, and in education it is not a part of a "sales cycle" (Connick, 2012) but is instead a part of an "awareness cycle." For any school leader, being relational is as important as being knowledgeable.

BrandED behavior strategically focuses on trusted relationships. Mutual trust is a core of brand loyalty in business and in schools. A great workplace is created thorough organizational credibility, respect, fairness, and a foundation of trust (Mineo, 2014). The work involved in brandED development relies on building welcoming access in real time and online so that people feel connected and happy in their work. Access is supported by people who know that the calendar isn't just about scheduling the day's appointments but also about making time for a ritual of building trust. Your purposeful strategic effort to create relationships is vital.

As you lead your brandED school improvement plan, especially through a time of innovation, the following pillars are places in which to access new connectivity for your own brand and the school's brand. In each area, work on building relationships that promote both.

Student achievement. Standardized test scores are most often used to evaluate the overall effectiveness of a school. Public relations and communication efforts focused on evidence of growth in this area and in other academic and nonacademic areas can be conveyed through social media. Doing so will help create and strengthen a school's brand presence and convey why the brand matters.

Quality of teachers and administrators. Student achievement is directly linked to the quality of the school staff. Stakeholders are often more than willing to move to towns with higher taxes that attract the best and brightest educators. Utilizing social media to convey staff statistics can build the confidence of any community, which has a positive impact on a school's brand.

Innovative instructional practices and programs. Course offerings, curricular decisions, unique programs, and innovative instructional practices play a key role in student engagement while also having a positive impact on student outcomes (Whitehurst, 2009). Unique course offerings, curricula, and programs make a school or district stand out. The publication and dissemination of this information send a powerful message related to college and career readiness and the ability of students to follow their passions.

Extracurricular activities. Extracurricular, nonacademic activities are a valued component of any school community and help develop well-rounded students. Leaders who use social media as part of a combined communications and public relations strategy spotlight these activities to gain the attention of stakeholders.

BRANDED LEADERSHIP IS "BUSINESS AS UNUSUAL"

In his book *The End of Business as Usual,* digital analyst and futurist Brian Solis (2011a) challenged business leaders to face the world of digital and social advancement. He writes of an attitude that comes with the complexity of anytime, anyplace access: a "business as unusual" leadership attitude. BrandED school leaders can adopt this attitude to power relationships. Schools, just like any commercial organization, can't operate within the business-as-usual model in this digital age. As our schools grow more diverse, they need new communication lanes. At the heart of our diverse communities is a rich mix of students, staff, and parents who want to engage. This is energizing, yet it creates challenges for school leaders today that their predecessors never imagined. Innovators like Mark Cuban and other notable business voices support this view through their own writing and teaching. "To be successful you need to see what others don't see" (Cuban, cited in Solis, 2011a). By looking through the lens of brand, you can see the opportunity that others don't see.

Creative branding thinking leads you to a unique vision of school improvement, one in which creativity leads to innovation. To borrow the classic Apple tagline from the 20th century, business as unusual gets you to "Think Different," which was a key to turning around the Apple brand. As Figure 1.2 illustrates, conditions surrounding schools today form pressures that can result in positive change. Examining the pressures opens your mind to different, new thinking in leadership, enabling you to turn perceived threats into opportunities.

The foundational pressure that brings positive change in a brandED leader's own Think Different campaign is the pressure of social learning. The online community exchanges through a wealth of content and through a wide range of voices, and it influences as it connects with our schools. Social learning is powered by available online content and tools that are free to all stakeholders. Your awareness of such resources and your willingness to incorporate them into your brand communication plan spark change.

Figure 1.2 Outside Pressures on Today's Schools

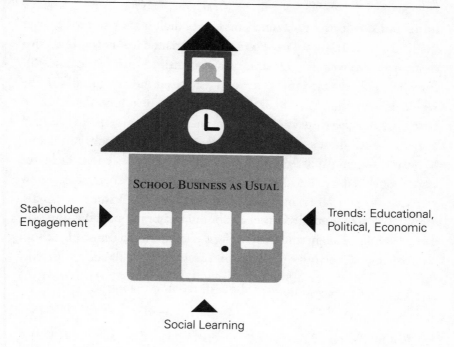

Another pressure is stakeholder engagement, but this can be seen as a positive pressure on the status quo; and again, technology powers the accelerated rate of change. BrandED leaders recognize that their stakeholders have a growing need for connection to their schools, including exchange of information and meaningful dialogue. This pressure generates a positive result as business-as-unusual leaders meet the new needs and wants of stakeholders through a powerfully built brand that can be accessed in new media channels.

Finally, in a business-as-unusual mindset, leaders can build a brand that Thinks Different about protecting the interests of the school and its achievements. The right brand makes the position of the school strong enough to mesh with the current array of initiatives and changes that affect the education of children: Trends in education, politics, and economics influence educational excellence.

This new combination of pressures—social learning; stakeholder engagement; and educational, political, and economic trends—now impact school decision making. This combined pressure did not exist at the turn of this century. The Web 2.0 world created this new mix of conditions, which must usher in innovative practice to replace the unfulfilling cycle of doing the same thing and achieving the same result. In the words of marketing guru Seth Godin (2008), "The job isn't to catch up with the status quo; the job is to invent the status quo." That thinking of a new, better status quo is part of a brandED leader's mission. A business-as-unusual brandED stance that pushes beyond the status quo is powered by the term *unique brand value* (UBV). This is new thinking for educators, but it is a business term used since the 1940s. Now, UBV is championed for use in building a brand outside the world of marketing (Eisenberg, 2016). Before you develop a brandED school strategy in your institution, reflect on your school's UBV. Ask yourself:

What are my first thoughts about differentiating my school?

What makes it a unique place for me as a leader?

Could my school community be distinguished because of its UBV?

How can I and how can other school leaders convey that value in the way brand managers have done?

When you focus on your school's UBV, try using a creative technique from the mind of entrepreneur Alp Behar. Behar suggests that leaders should not wait to make dreams come true with a bucket list for retirement. His Twitter post (April 18, 2016) says, "Every time when you have a new idea write them down and put them into your bucket. Check your Bucket every month." Adapt this "follow your dream now" attitude as a leader of brand. Keep your own brandED bucket as you journey into brand with ideas that are firing up your creativity and that reflect the edge-dweller mindset of brandED leading. These differentiating ideas help you live in an innovative stance beyond the status quo as you begin to build a UBV proposition for your school. Welcome the new ideas that brand thinking ushers into your days, and keep track of them.

Leaders develop new professional skills when they adopt the strategic thinking of brand. As Madison Avenue has shown for years, branding work is a highly creative professional activity. Advertising legend and agency owner Bill Bernbach, said to be the model for the creative characters in TV's *Mad Men* series, celebrated that creative sense of play, changed the advertising industry's way of creating content, and delivered simple but highly creative and memorable campaigns that grew brand loyalty. His award-winning campaigns included the iconic 1960s We Try Harder campaign for Avis. It was the come-from-behind story of a brand, a model that inspires many brands to this day (Petit, 2014). Enjoy this creative part of your brandED leadership journey. If you haven't as yet felt the pull toward enjoying this move toward brand, you will. This activity can be joyful and even playful as it creates exciting new opportunities for change. Creative thinking will expand your possibilities for innovative brandED behavior.

In marketing, the term *brand myopia* refers to the tendency to repeatedly rely on one tried-and-true path to an audience (Armstrong & Kotler, 2015). It never produces creative results. It's a warning for school leaders. BrandED is about new possibilities and solutions. We've all tried to fix problems using status quo remedies. How many leaders have experienced the feeling that they have a lack of new ideas and solutions to address persisting problems. Branding will break you out of a pattern, making you and the team you build ready to take on a business-as-unusual position that is anything but the status quo.

See the shared leadership possibilities of brandED. Look across your digital community. Find talented stakeholders who understand the power of digital content. Include your students, young parents, and teachers who operate in the new business-as-unusual digital and social world. This segment of school stakeholders currently forms 60% of the viewing community of the Snapchat app. Once thought only for tweens, Snapchat's demographic has shifted to 18- to 34-year-olds who are skilled at telling stories in this new high-impact way. Snapchat has already caught the attention of serious marketers and holds a world of promise for educators (Gill, 2016). In September 2016, the company changed its name to simply Snap as it gets ready to support messaging and engagement in new ways with its growing audience. (You may develop social media credibility using that newest version of the name, but many users still use the name Snapchat.)

Why not power business as unusual with the storytelling ability of these powerful and often creative stakeholders who are spending their lives as online storytellers?

BRANDED RESULTS CAN EMPOWER SCHOOLS

The day we (Eric and Trish) met, we discussed three reasons why a brandED leadership mindset could matter to schools: improved culture, improved performance, and improved resourcing. BrandED mattered as a unifying school improvement component then, and it means even more now in our increasingly fast-paced digital world of communication. We live in a world where it took 35 days for Angry Birds to reach 50 million users (it took radio 35 years to hit that mark), and in a more recent game changer, it took about a week to make Pokémon Go a worldwide augmented reality experience that attracts millions of player a day (including Norway's prime minister, Erna Solberg, who was caught playing Pokémon Go in a parliament session).

That first brandED meeting was in 2009, before the explosion of apps, social media, and transparent platforms that deliver information to the masses in an instant and enable conversations to start and grow in a few collective keystrokes by users worldwide. The pace of change has quickened since then, and it won't be slowing down soon. What has remained the same since that time is the belief that despite the intensity of the noise in the digital world, leaders can find the right channels for their messages and can weather change. Brand thinking can benefit entire school communities: kids, teachers, parents, and other stakeholders. BrandED can elevate a school's unique and valuable profile. Schools that adopt the business-as-unusual attitude see results that matter (Figure 1.3):

1. Improved **culture** shared through internal and external communication

Figure 1.3 Results: Three Considerations for Becoming BrandED

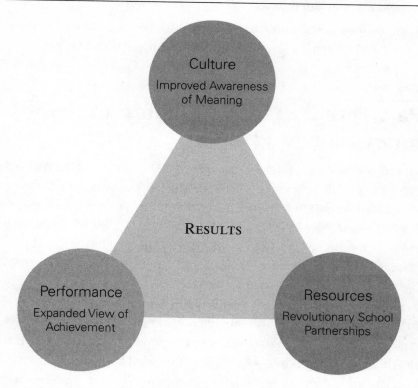

2. Expanded **performance** for students, staff, and connected stake-holders

3. Increased **resources** for the school community through internal and external partnerships

A brand doesn't appear overnight in any world, business or educational. BrandED strategy development is a collaborative creative, analytic, strategic journey. It employs a steady process, paced with benchmarks. Before starting on your brandED path and as you move into a brandED leadership mindset, you can spark your journey by asking yourself these questions:

1. What is our school's offer to an audience? What are the defining features of our district or school?

2. Whose attention are we trying to capture, and why? Who are the end users of our brand?

3. Is our audience segmented into smaller communities? Are there subgroups that we serve that have different needs and wants?

Part Three: BrandED Unifies a School Improvement Plan

The business-as-unusual direction of brandED makes identifying brand value and articulating a school promise into a shared endeavor. Building a collective brandED team will support a business-as-unusual stance. Leaders create the movement. You claim your own UBV first, and your public commitment to adopting an authentically created personal professional brand can become relatable and compelling enough to draw in like-minded stakeholders and inspire them in the institutional effort to brand. Before you take on the internal microenvironment and external macroenvironment of education, mine your own brand. Once you have created it, live it with transparency. Start to develop relationships in real time and online and test your ability. You want to become aware of which relationships are worth your investment. The fact is that leaders must make the best use of available professional learning network tools, both traditional and new age.

RELATING TO THE SCHOOL'S EXTERNAL MACROENVIRONMENT

As you build brand, look purposefully and confidently outward into the vast macroenvironment that surrounds schools today. It's the big world of content and communication where your brand and your school's brand will live, thanks to digital reach. Figure 1.4 illustrates the macro-environmental pressures of politics, economics, culture, and technology that may contribute challenges. We want our responses to the challenges to look rational, and brand thinking can help us conduct a deeper dive

Figure 1.4 Macroenvironment for BrandED

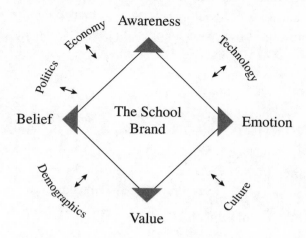

into what our school is about. The stories we can tell about our brand as we face challenges that impact our schools will help us manage both in times of uncertainty and in times of harmony.

As you move among these macro forces, it helps to find another educational edge dweller, a fellow risk-taker and forward-thinking peer whom you can trust as you build brandED. In the military, there are trusted pals called "battle buddies." You aren't in a fight, but you're on a unique, brave new journey, and it's always better to travel in twos. Choose a brand buddy who is interested in launching a campaign, or someone who is already on the road to brandED and wants to be a mentor. Find someone who can discuss the ways that policy, the economy, and technology develop your brand leadership. Become accountability partners, learn how to work together, communicate and share on a regular basis, and don't give up (Riviere, 2009).

By sharing with like-minded brand advocates, you can look for ways to deepen your brand endeavors. Use online and real-time engagements with colleagues to help focus your thinking on the ways you can distinguish your school brand as unique. Learn as much as you can through digital and social listening from schools that have found a unique way of telling the stories of their school through shared messages and connecting content. When you have a crafted school brand that you have tested with others, your emotional connection to stakeholders in the external community and your passion for leading will be evident. In the day-to-day work you do, include the story of your own journey. The community will believe in the brand you've built if you are transparent. As you get to work on your own professional brand, use it often as you build new relationships in your existing circles as well as in new ones. Try out your brand in many ways, both personal and professional. In every meeting, include brand thinking. Ask colleagues about the term; see what they know, and learn how they think being brandED can advance a school community. Brand is based in communication, so talk to everyone about this idea. Someone like Brad Currie can help you find the words.

A BrandED Short Story: Brad Currie Gets the Word Out

Brad Currie is the dean of students and supervisor of instruction for the Chester School District in Chester, New Jersey, and the founding partner and chief information officer for Evolving Educators LLC. He is also an author, blogger, and presenter who shares his passion for branding in education because he firmly believes in the way it can transform culture on a global scale (B. Currie, personal communication, March 30, 2016).

Branding in the educational world is all about getting the word out and creating a positive image of all the great things taking place in classrooms, schools, districts, and organizations. Case in point: Brad's son's teacher does an outstanding job of branding her classroom learning experiences through Twitter. Using the handle @MrsMooreFRSD, she shares what is happening in class with stakeholders on an almost daily basis. It's a win-win for all involved, on several fronts. Parents can rest easy knowing that their child is in good hands and that learning is at a high level; Mrs. Moore can shed light on all the amazing learning experiences that her students are a part of day in and day out; and students learn that what they are doing has importance beyond the classroom. Right before dinner, Brad will check Mrs. Moore's Twitter feed to see what learning experiences took place in class on that particular day. For example, one time Mrs. Moore tweeted out pictures of students participating in a rock lab. That same night at dinner, Brad was able to have a thoughtful conversation with his son about the different types of rocks that he learned about. Because of Mrs. Moore's approach to branding her classroom, Brad and his son, Cooper, can feel proud of what was accomplished in class and know that those accomplishments are being recognized on a social media platform.

There is no doubt that branding in the educational world is contagious and is directly correlated to promoting the success of all students. Often, Brad will blog about the awesome things that are taking place with the students and staff at Black River Middle School in Chester. For example, he visited Jackie Epler's (@jdepler2) sixth-grade language arts classroom, where students were using an interactive presentation tool called Pear Deck to persuade their classmates to read a certain type of a book. The inspiration he felt from this particular lesson caused him to write a blog post so that others could see how technology can transform learning spaces. Putting this sort of thing out in cyberspace serves several purposes. First, it gives credit where credit is due: to the teacher for creating this wonderful lesson and to the students for having the skills to make an interactive presentation that engaged their peers in the topic at hand. Second, in writing a blog post about this best-practice learning experience, Brad shows readers that the school is doing some remarkable things. Word then starts to spread about how innovative Black River Middle School truly is, and that if those students can do these

(continued)

sorts of things with technology, then so can we. As Currie puts it, "Branding helps people reflect, learn, promote, and understand what is possible." It also cultivates an image and mindset that Black River Middle is a place where innovative learning experiences happen on a daily basis.

Brad lives by this motto: "Promote, promote, promote and when you think you are done promoting, promote some more!" The amount of positive information a person can put out for all the world to consume is infinite. Too often, negative stories are associated with our classrooms, schools, and districts. Fortunately, the tide has turned with the evolution of technology and social media. Now more than ever, educators have the opportunity to connect, collaborate, consume, create, and curate. Sharing can be thrown in there as well. The more that educators share best practices, the better their educational profile becomes. Over the 5 years that Brad has been a connected educator on platforms like Twitter, he has seen many such opportunities arise. For one, he founded #Satchat, a weekly Twitter conversation for current and emerging school leaders that takes place every Saturday morning at 7:30 EST. Brad was also fortunate to write a few books because of the people he knows and respects within his Personal Learning Network (PLN). These accomplishments have become a part of Brad's own educational brand. Through the work that Brad has done, particularly with educational technology, he has painted a positive picture in people's minds of the kind of things he can do as they relate to helping learners, teachers, and leaders move forward.

The final destination in Brad's journey on the educational branding train takes us to a company he formed with his business partners, Scott Rocco and Billy Krakower. Evolving Educators LLC, founded in 2014, takes great pride in providing relevant professional growth opportunities for educators. Looking back at how he built up his personal brand in the education world, Brad aimed to replicate that same success with his new company.

Through planning and holding successful educational technology trainings, the Evolving Educator brand has grown tremendously over the past several years. Word of mouth, coupled with a strategic social media presence, has placed Evolving Educators on the map. The company's website, www.evolvingeducators.com, makes clear the brand that Brad, Scott, and Billy are trying to establish. From the Tomorrow's Classrooms Today Conference to Google Apps for Education Training to the countless speaking engagements around the country, Evolving Educators wants to maintain a positive brand presence and be at the forefront of innovative professional development.

BrandED leaders like Brad connect and share across channels as they grow their brandED community. The forces that school leaders face—culture, economics, society, and policy—will be easier to manage with a strong school brand (Armstrong & Kotler, 2015).

STANDARDS AND BRAND BUILDING

Standardized testing is one of the main macroenvironmental forces that educators live with every day. Creating the narrative of brand among the negative stories of standardized testing from the external community can be a challenge. But brandED can help you tell your school story in ways that communicate the good work of your school in this environment. You can reach beyond a test score and use the business-as-unusual thinking of a brandED leader to illustrate the promise of a school, a promise that is expressed beyond a single sitting during a spring test evaluation and that showcases the authentic learning that your school provides. The culture of defining a school's value exclusively through testing can be changed using a brandED mindset to promote the academic and nonacademic stories that show a school's worth and value to a community. Collectively, brandED leaders with an inclusive mindset for defining education could change the culture of using tests as a sole measure of value. A leader who adopts a brandED mindset can model a powerful way to shift current thinking about the quality of education.

Political pressure is one of the macro forces that can be managed with a brandED stance. A district or school should never be branded solely by a result on a standardized test. Your brand can value results that demonstrate capability, including national or state standards, but this is a score-driven marketing approach that uses limited data to describe the school brand. BrandED leaders think bigger and choose academic and social norms to measure as they value performance in a more expansive way. Stakeholders can collaboratively identify data found in the unique stories of your school's mission and purpose. These are narratives that show measurable pride in the educational experience. These are real tales of individuals and communities engaged in learning. A variety of academic and nonacademic content shows the performance of the school in various ways. Attention to brand found in the stories of what is good in a school illustrates a belief in children and teachers, in their growth of pride in their work, and in the celebration of their innovative thinking or the recognition of problem solving. These stories invigorate the brand image and contribute to the school's value as a unique brand. The school will find its distinguishing story in the difference it brings to the task of learning. It's not the brandED approach to strive to be like everyone else. Brand identity is unique.

MICROENVIRONMENT AND THE SCHOOL BRAND

Communicating a UBV supports improvement efforts in the local microenvironment as well. This is the close community beginning with staff, teachers, kids, and parents, one that moves to include the relationships that are built from within, which strengthen the UBV (Figure 1.5). Your focus on brand in your school microenvironment won't upset the balance of the bigger ecosystem of state and federal mandates and of politics and economics. It can only help you develop success.

Figure 1.5 Microenvironment for BrandED

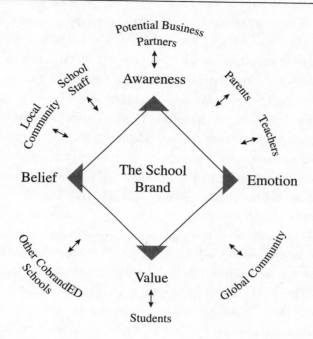

Schools exist within a microenvironment of inner structures that identify, create, and promote messages (Armstrong & Kotler, 2015). A school with a unique brand—one that shows awareness of its brand mission, that values going beyond the status quo, and that taps into the emotion of learning—has achieved harmony in its microenvironment. A brandED school promotes itself in an exciting and connected community. With a focus on a strong brand narrative in the brandED school microenvironment, what is exchanged with the outside macroenvironment makes your brand unique.

A commitment to giving value in credible, innovative ways helps school leaders face challenges to education. Telling the story of the school and educating your community to share the school's UBV helps enlists them in what Seth Godin (2008) calls "the tribe." Creating a unique education tribe is one way to quickly achieve the awareness that leads to building your school's UBV. As the tribe convenes, narratives are of great importance to the brand. The good work of the tribe, the content that you share through many digital and traditional channels, connects to sustaining a school's continuous improvement.

Look at brands that are the best at creating brand messages that connect. Winning brands make the communication flow between brand and audience easy and frictionless. The exchange is harmonious, and people are loyal. The Disney tribe, according to Seth Godin, operates on the simple message, "Make people happy!" Virgin's tribal brand basic is, "Never see obstacles, only opportunities." Tribes who identify a measurable core belief celebrate value together, and that emotion builds more loyalty.

In an education tribe, creating stories and showcasing across channels will indicate success and well-being in ways that scores on a standardized test can't begin to capture. Seth Godin's tribe metaphor captures the connected feeling of brand that gives schools new ways to define and express their worth. BrandED schools can creatively offer real-time demonstrations of authentic learning that teachers create and students value. Schools can champion their students' range of social, civic, and academic achievements and celebrate the school's UBV. What is shared on websites, blogs, and social and digital platforms can communicate a school's value in ways that engage stakeholders emotionally with the brand. Highlighting the evolution of new programs, resources, and curricular adoptions from a storytelling perspective inspires those involved in the endeavor. Honesty and a genuine sense of transparency result. Sharing the stories of new curricular changes through the experiences of those engaged in learning makes the connection to the brandED mission of the school.

The building of a tribe for your school's brand sustains positivity. Tribes are powerful in brand management, and when leaders form communities based on shared well-being, you find a tribe that is happy. Their narratives inspire continued confidence and loyalty among stakeholders. Your strategy distinguishes and promotes the value of your school as much as a company brand does for its consumers.

BRANDED CONTENT FUELS STAKEHOLDER CONNECTION

Storytelling is foundational to your brandED strategy. The story of the school is continuously communicated through narratives of your UBV. Educators' storytelling—in real time, through word of mouth, or online in digital and video promotions—is communication of the most authentic and powerful kind. It's a form of content marketing that prevails in business. Using this type of brand content in education can be marketable as it engages communities in your brand messaging on a wide stage through digital and traditional channels. The school experience produces rich content that can be described and shared in original forms and then saved and archived and even used again and again through repurposing to send a robust, consistent message of brand value (Armstrong & Kotler, 2015).

The emotional power of your stories creates brand loyalty for your school. Leading brands like Coke, Nike, and Apple communicate with their loyal Godinesque tribes with crafted stories and engaging personal narratives. The best brands use platforms like Instagram, Twitter, Facebook, Pinterest, and Snap in ways that engage and that offer value. Whole Foods has 1.7 million followers on Facebook, and not because the company only thinks about selling to them. Whole Foods thinks about "showing" how it values its followers' healthy lives. A big brand like Target learned to be global as it grew its market, yet it still acts locally. It shows its customers around the world that it values relationships. One way that it tries to show its connection is through affinity, meaning the caring it shows about its customers outside of a buy. Target offers that value connection when it sends online local traffic updates to customers in their local communities. This creates brand engagement and value beyond a sale price.

Be aware of the positive stories that abound in your school community every day and your need to promote them in connection with your school mission and brand. Use new channels available for sharing that help build your presence with the community. In school districts like Baltimore County Public Schools, leaders share unique stories of their schools' core values and highlight examples of teaching and learning that establish relationships. They harness the power of story.

A BrandED Short Story: Ryan Imbriale and the BCPS Art of Storytelling

Ryan Imbriale, Baltimore County Public Schools (BCPS) executive director of the Department of Innovative Learning, understands how important the art of storytelling is to the development of a brandED mindset. "In today's social media–rich society, marketing and showcasing the work of a public school system is as critical as the daily operations of teaching and learning" (R. Imbriale, personal communication, April 12, 2016). In this world of instant access to platforms like Facebook and Twitter, if you don't tell your story, someone else will (Sheninger, 2014). Ryan feels strongly that school systems need to be ahead of the message and ensure that the story being told is accurate, timely, and compelling. BCPS, under the leadership of superintendent Dr. S. Dallas Dance, is a leader in brand building and marketing.

One of BCPS's most successful approaches is Team BCPS Day, an annual event held in January, designed to rally the entire community around supporting public education. Since its inception in 2014, Team BCPS stakeholders have been asked to photograph themselves wearing blue and to send or post on social media those photos, as well as photos showcasing BCPS history. The district encourages all current, former, and future students, families, staff, volunteers, partners, and community members to join the party and show their support by participating in special Team BCPS Day activities. Imbriale stated, "Team BCPS Day 2016 yielded more than 3,000 tweets, reaching 2.3 million unique viewers, resulting in the hashtag #BCPSBlue trending in the middle of the day." The power in this annual event is that it celebrates pride in BCPS and an understanding of public education's vital role in the community.

BCPS has been bold to brand its initiatives and highlight the work through multiple media outlets. Two examples of this are the school system's Passport and STAT programs. The Passport program, dedicated to second language acquisition, is designed to ensure that every student becomes proficient in a second language. BCPS is currently implementing a Spanish-language instruction program in elementary schools county wide. It is one thing to implement the program, but BCPS is also not afraid to open its doors to outside visitors and showcase the program with videos and onsite visits (www.bcps.org/academics/secondLanguageAcquisition.html).

The same is true of BCPS's initiative on transforming teaching and learning, known as Students & Teachers Accessing Tomorrow, or STAT. STAT is the multiyear transformation of BCPS into a complete 21st-century technology learning environment to prepare globally competitive graduates. As Imbriale puts it, "BCPS is first redesigning core content curriculum to redefine what instruction will look like in a blended learning environment, while placing a stronger emphasis on critical thinking and analytical skills." BCPS realized early on that in order to address such a massive transformation, communication was critical. School system leaders developed what they refer to as their "Eight Conversions: A Strategic Framework for Transformation" (www.bcps.org/academics/stat/STAT-Flyer.pdf), one of the eight essential elements being communication. By highlighting communication, the system has put a focus on clear messaging around the initiative.

BCPS has communicated the STAT message through a comprehensive multimedia campaign. STAT's Web presence allows for anyone to learn more about the transformation of teaching and learning. For example, the STAT page on the BCPS website (www.bcps.org/academics/stat/) serves as a place to get news and information on the overall program; the Lighthouse site (lighthouse.bcps.org) specifically targets those interested in the

(continued)

"pilot" schools that are the first schools to launch the program. Imbriale says, "The Lighthouse site is unique in that it serves multiple purposes as a professional development tool and as a storytelling site." Both of these websites rely heavily on social media, using Twitter and blog posts as the foundation for sharing information "from the ground." The Lighthouse site, specifically, is populated with blog posts from students, parents, and educators. In addition, the STAT website has news stories from local media, and videos that have been produced both in-house and by external partners.

One important aspect of BCPS's communication approach is its acceptance—and endorsement—of social media. According to Imbriale, "The system does not shy away from Facebook, Twitter, Flickr, or Instagram, but rather encourages school faculty to tell their own stories and share classroom successes via social media." These posts demonstrate a key understanding: that social media has become vital for daily interactions. Meeting stakeholders where they are and sharing the district message are critical to success. To help document the story of BCPS's transformation, the hashtags #BCPSLH and #BCPSSTAT are heavily used to pull together and connect all of the schools' journeys. Many times, these small social media snippets are expanded on through posts from stakeholders on the BCPS blog Deliberate Excellence (deliberateexcellence .wordpress.com).

To best meet the unique needs of all families, BCPS developed an innovative Parent University program to offer workshops— both in person and online—on such topics as technology, special education services, behavior management, and financial planning for postsecondary educational opportunities (www.bcps .org/parentu). By interacting with the community in multiple venues, BCPS reaches more stakeholders, engages those stakeholders continually, and gains their confidence. The outcomes help establish that BCPS is a trusted partner.

BRANDED SCHOOL IMPROVEMENT: CULTURE, PERFORMANCE, AND RESOURCING

Innovative student performance, both academic and nonacademic, takes the stage every day when schools share their brand's inspiring content. Defining the success of a school community and reporting the value of daily student performance are linked to a passion for education. Storytelling expands the definition of performance beyond a test evaluation. The Baltimore story proves this point.

Telling stories and showcasing student work create brand awareness in a community and thus engages fans. Your brand's strength depends on the authentic content you share with your stakeholders. Showcasing brings return on investment (ROI). In business, ROI is about the bucks, the net return divided by the cost of the effort (Armstrong & Kotler, 2015). The ROI for schools is not about money. It is focused on achieving the well-being of a school community through the connecting, defining message of brand. What makes the effort worthwhile for educators isn't dividing profits but more meaningful "shares"—sharing their content with the community in a way that builds relationships that in turn improve school culture, performance, and resourcing.

THE BRANDED STORYTELLER-IN-CHIEF

One of the foundations for brandED leadership in the digital age is to become the storyteller-in-chief (Sheninger, 2014). Take control of the narrative of your school with a brandED stance. As you advance to a strategic plan, understand the value of presenting clear, compelling content in your role as an educational leader. The wealth of content at a school's fingertips, once identified, curated, and shared, will power your brand movement forward.

One strategy to harness these powerful narratives comes from communication consultant Carmine Gallo (2016). Gallo, Steve Jobs's speaking coach, reminds us that stories are free, priceless content that can educate and bring desired results. He presents six ways that storytelling creates value for an audience: it can (a) inspire, (b) motivate, (c) educate, (d) build brand, (e) launch movements, and (f) change lives. Looking at those powerful categories of content, brandED leaders can see the range of possibilities in getting the word out about their schools. Using the framework of Gallo's six types of story content can be a step to identifying content that promotes what's right about your school. Find content on your own and through your stakeholders.

Educators are among the strongest communicators on the planet. Becoming the storyteller-in-chief may be a new stance, but it isn't a sales job you are taking on. Think of it more as *persuading*. According to Daniel Pink (2012), persuasion is nonsales selling. With brandED thinking, we message through our telling. It's a form of persuading. Our stories help build support and grow relationships with stakeholders; those relationships bring mutual trust. This is a business-as-unusual stance that helps you promote value as a storyteller-in-chief.

A storyteller-in-chief forms a collective team that is focused on communicating content—original and curated stories—that can reach many different publics so as to sustain the brand. Guided by the range of stories that Gallo's model presents, your diverse, talented, passionate team of stakeholders can find and curate the narratives of the school for messaging. The storyteller-in-chief sees the development of narrative content as a part of the school improvement plan. As you have started to survey your community landscape, it's not too early to begin to enlist a team, your brandED collective for shared brand leadership. Your collaborative team of teachers, staff, administrators, kids, parents, and other key community members works to identify the brand's image, what it will promise, and the goals and result of the effort. Part of the job of the collective is collecting and curating stories, narratives, and conversations that show what is worth reporting to the community about the school brand in daily action. Keeping emotion and connection in mind, these are the stories of feeling that show kids learning in unique and meaningful ways. The genuine stories that schools craft for various publics promote who we are as educators. We can win grassroots support through our narratives. We can open up the world to others beyond our borders to educate our students. We can even improve on our school's resources through our storytelling capacity.

THE MACRONARRATIVE AND MICRONARRATIVE FOR CREATING STORIES

As leaders journey from brand to brandED, they adapt brand information to their school situation. One common thread that brand and brandED share is the power of story. Leaders commit to the never-ending narrative of promoting and sustaining school brand. Just as the iconic brands have shown, telling stories of the relatable day-to-day moments connects a tribe. A common thread of experience shared through crafted brand content makes people happy. It also informs and engages a community. In the stories of a school, audiences see the consistent, tangible result of their investment in their school community. As with the legacy business brands, our stakeholders can admire and appreciate the school brand value as an anchor to building a core tradition, a legacy. BrandED's reason for being is to improve the long-term development of schools. Developing a legacy attitude with a brand commitment will enlist support for what the school brand is promising and delivering every day.

In the lead of the brandED strategy, the storyteller-in-chief personally models the value of brand as a tool for communication in the digital age, and leads the call to action, promoting the school's value on websites and across other school-sanctioned platforms. Narratives both large and small are valued as tangible evidence of the school's worth. Stories come in different sizes and hold different purposes, but simply said, they keep the engagement going. Sharing through big ideas, called macronarratives, may convey important information related to issues and policies and help the brand navigate in a "frictionless" way. For example, a school's new homework policy is an example of a needed macronarrative for the community to embrace. Smaller stories, micronarratives, found in both text and video, mix with the macronarrative across channels. Micronarratives come from every edge of the school community and are told in the engaging voices of the community in digital and social exchange. The mix of messages and stories creates even more brand value. This is a public commitment, demonstrating the school's transparent effort to engage with a community on many interesting levels. The power of storytelling is essential to brand development of a school community where the remarkable ideas and actions of that community can define success in new, exciting ways.

Conversation 1 Tips

- **Check out** brands in the marketplace that resonate. Find the brands that have your loyalty and examine the influence of brand feeling on your own choices.
- **Create** a short brand history slideshow of your favorite legacy and new brands. Include global brands. What do they have in common with a potential school brand you develop? Keep this presentation for your first public meeting.
- **Assess** your school's current website through a quick "brand walkthrough." Does it have a unifying message; a unique brand value (UBV); and a feeling, something emotional that tells the story of a unique brand?
- **Challenge** yourself to draft your school's image, promise, and result on the back of an envelope or on a napkin, and share with a colleague.
- **Explain** the difference between brand and brandED to a colleague and how defining a school brand is important in today's digital world.
- **Identify** a value of servant leadership that could connect to a professional brand you will build.
- **Adopt** a business-as-unusual stance for your development of brand by examining the range of stories that your school can present to the community.

Conversation 1 Reflections

Before holding public conversation around why business brand tenets inform educational leadership, think about these questions:

- How is digital transparency breaking down the barriers to sharing for school leaders, and will it help deliver results?
- How can the big idea of business brand inform my own professional leadership growth?
- How have I shown loyalty and trust with the brands I value? How do I engage with them in ways that I want my stakeholder community to engage with my school's brand?
- Do I understand my role in a "nonsales" sales effort as an educator? Can I use persuasion related to my personal professional brand and my school's brand as a vehicle to create stakeholder relationships?
- Do I have a sense of what my school's UBV may be? Have I thought about my own UBV?
- Can I find the brand ambassadors who can share the storytelling vehicles for brandED?

In the Zone for BrandED Innovation

In Conversation 2, we create a bridge to innovation using a brandED mindset to help educators master their most important communication messages and position themselves to engage with new brand power. A brandED change process, with its focused transparency, lives in the very public eye of a school community. Because your brand innovation is launched under the watch of stakeholders in this transparent digital age, you must develop the confidence to display a new brand mastery that inspires others in the journey. The call to become brandED requires you to get in the zone for developing your own brand and the brand of your school, with a capable attitude that projects the benefit of becoming a brandED community. Like other original ideas and innovations, brandED introduces a new culture, complete with a language and frameworks. (A glossary at the end of the book supports learning the language of the brandED leadership tribe.) We suggest that you create a zone for your development using an innovative, business-as-unusual approach to leading change, exploring how innovation is effectively managed with a close eye on human behavior in a social media age. The innovative brandED school model of communication is based on brand tenets that unite the internal organization and external stakeholders in a whole-school adaptation of a communicative, authentic brand. A collective community cocreates a new brand that transforms the way a school communicates its worth.

A foundation for this educator collective mindset, for becoming a brandED community, is not rooted solely in business but grows out of an understanding of human behavior in our fast-paced digital world. Much of the change process around introducing a brand is based on understanding people: social psychology. When you are leading brand change in your organization, the inclusive participation of the community is important. Find your like-minded brand-savvy people. Enlist their awareness in a brand journey, inviting their engagement through your emerging brand mastery. Growing purposeful internal and external stakeholder connections will make you a stronger leader in the zone of brandED implementation. Understanding how to manage change is vital, especially in brand adoption, which relies on open social and digital exchange among parties and their continuous, productive engagement through active messaging. In response to the complexity that modern digital life may hold for communicating, a brandED leader looks to incorporate simplicity, safety, well-being, generosity, and even happiness within the brandED change process.

Leaders themselves must model their new, open behavior across the transparent digital landscape. An engaging leadership brand style, built from an understanding of human behavior and focused on relationships, builds capacity within the community to be in the brand zone and to collectively change a school organization for the better. A brandED leader knows that recognizing the latest trends in behavior and social interaction is connected to implementing a relevant school brand. Leaders inform the brand direction using up-to-the-minute knowledge of human behavior as they first design and promote their own brand and then lead the journey toward a school brand strategy.

A brand is about belief. Demonstrate your brand with clarity as a brandED leader. With belief established, inspire a community to collectively embrace brandED change. A most important job in developing brand is to get in the zone for building a school's image, promise, and result.

> #Digitalschoolleaders can create unique #brand value to support excellence seamlessly w/out the 3 martini lunches! Right, @NMHS_Principal?
> —*Trish Rubin (2009) [Twitter post]*

Part One: The Psychology of BrandED Innovation

This is a world of powerful brand evolution.

The Apple brand, which was Interbrand's Top Brand of 2016, is an evolutionary case in point. Apple didn't focus just on computers as it muscled to the top; it was far from being brand myopic. It became number one by casting its eye in other directions: the world of phone communication, photography, wearable technology, televisions, and mobility, to name a few of Apple's ventures out of its own industry comfort zone of making desktop personal computers. Apple used its understanding of human behavior, of psychology, to innovate. It built its business on living its unique brand value (UBV) every day for as many different people as possible and increasing value based on its understanding of the behavior of its customers.

As another example, Facebook announced in 2016 that it is getting into the transportation business through a patent application for ride sharing that will connect to Facebook groups and events (Murphy, 2016). Innovative thinking results when disparate industries and cultures begin to inform each other and partner around human behavior, decision making, and the psychology of a buy.

Just as the big brand builders have done in their search for connecting marketing messages to their audiences, you can evolve as a brandED leader who will message a community about the positive value of your school in new ways. First, tell your story and demonstrate your brand mastery. Then lead your audience to define and endorse the stories of the school. Adopt a brand-curious attitude. From the start of your journey, use the power of your browser to investigate a range of human behavior related to communication that can bring positive result for brandED school change. Start picking up signals from neuroscience, decision-making science, and behavioral economics that can help you manage innovation. Seek knowledge of current developments in media, technology, and even the study of artificial intelligence (AI). These are but a few topics that will connect to school brand conversations that you launch with your collective to get them into the brandality modality. Your devices connect you to sources that are rich with current information, questions, and advancements that can influence your school brand. Dig into research and practice daily within these fields and other areas of your choosing on any of your screens. Generously share what you find as you demonstrate your new brand of connectivity. Ask questions about what you discover and start conversations as you look for other brand-savvy thinkers online and in real time. Lead educators can quickly Google topics, scanning them for a few minutes a day, seeing how the ideas connect to education issues. Even something as distant from education as the new self-tying Nike sneaker can have implications for a school community: Special needs connections? School athletic sponsorship? Makerspace lessons?

Your awareness of what's happening outside your school door across industries, agencies, and topics has never been more important. Appear connected to what is affecting behavior in our world as you lead a brand community effort. Build a personal database of your own ideas and of the links and stories from across current areas and others that connect to your mission of brand development. Use the content to promote school interest in brand—memes included! True brandED leaders understand trends that impact their stakeholders' moods and activity. Trends can drive a brand conversation that identifies the position of a school in the news of the world. Tech, academic, social, relational, and political trends influence brand development and execution.

This brandED approach to trend awareness tracking is adapted from communication and media agencies that are picking up signals that influence human behavior every day. BrandED leaders can adapt this progressive thinking as they build their brand strategy. A case in point regarding the power of trend awareness is found in the thinking of the sparks & honey advertising agency. Big brands seek the agency's services as culture strategists. The strategists help companies create up-to-the-minute brand relevance, but brandED leaders without a marketing budget can mirror these trend spotters using databases of engaging content that support their school brand. Imagine how many brand ambassadors a leader can gather by starting a "trend scout" program among stakeholders, especially young stakeholders. These digital natives naturally look across the social and digital landscape every day. Invite these scouts into your network to share stories of behavior, found through trend spotting, that impact education locally and globally and inform a developing school brand. With the increasing number of platforms to follow marketing trends, educators can explore and be informed about brands and marketing behavior that can build their appreciation for innovating with brandED. Appendix G provides support in that effort, including the N2N app of sparks & honey that updates a user each day about world-shaping trends.

Topics from psychology are woven into the development of brand in the 21st century and have been useful to the marketing community. These topics can help you create your brandED profile. You will see natural connections for leading and plenty of resources that can be adapted to your school role as you build a knowledgeable brand presence. Investigate brand and marketing updates, scan tech development, and search for leadership tenets. Explore the different generations in your school through the study of demography. Scan behavioral economics, training innovations, and digital trends. You don't have to do a deep dive to keep yourself informed. No course registration is required. Through 1- to 2-minute reads of content-rich posts and articles on trends and current developments found on Twitter and Facebook pages, or on free apps like

Flipboard or Medium, you can update yourself across industries in fields related to brand. At the touch of a button, these platforms aggregate the buzz of the modern world into areas for your thought and sharing.

Checking in regularly on management association and industry blogs and webinars can develop your brand leadership vocabulary and knowledge. Resources come from a quick keyword search in YouTube, where the world of basic elements of marketing and branding can advance your brand mastery as a brandED leader. Currently, the growing numbers of free massive open online courses (MOOCs) have benefited people who want to learn on their own time and on their own schedule about how to lead and innovate in the areas of marketing and branding.

Those of you wanting a deeper dive into marketing can use a search method that may take you to surprising connections. Interactive marketers call this exercise a "longtail keyword hunt" using three or more powerful keywords. For instance, launching online relationships for your school brand with potential partners may be a new social behavior for you to adopt. Try typing some powerful words into your browser— for example, school/resources/education/relationships/partners/brand/affinity/innovation. Spend a few minutes looking at the results of the search, and you will no doubt be able to bookmark potential connectors beyond your usual searches. Content, websites, thought leaders, and processes will spark your brand thinking after a longtail keyword hunt. At your own pace, you can begin to build the online connection to partners found in your searches. Test out your new behaviors as a brandED leader in search of relationships and cocreators. Be curious about the worlds of connection and relationships as these topics power your brand efforts. Ask yourself whom you can connect with as a thoughtful partner, and be selective in exploring online contact with these possible partners. As you will see in later conversations, there is a method to taking this road to connection. Start by simply building brand awareness as you explore new topics and the communities associated with them. As you master your own profile as a brandED leader, keep educating yourself with a personal warehouse, your professional database of content, from the many worlds that inform you about human behavior. Keep the direct line to your conscious mind open to learning across industries to build your growth as a connected brandED leader.

READY TO INNOVATE

A brandED educator mindset is informed by the discipline of marketing. Your own research online expands your knowledge and comfort with brand. You will see that branding shares marketing's connection to psychology. Understanding psychology and behavior is part of brand development for the business marketplace. In the educator's workplace, the need for understanding behavior is also important. In the 20th century, Daniel Goleman's work served to connect educators to behavioral thinking, including the concept of emotional intelligence. Today's brandED leaders have several new expert models that can inform their brandED leadership journey. You may have your own favorites from your academic studies or from your reading of current pop culture. It's time to connect what you already know to your growing brand awareness and incorporate the inspiring thinking of influencers for your brand development journey.

One current leader, a professional whom Malcolm Gladwell described as his favorite thinker, is organizational psychologist Adam Grant. Dr. Grant lives his UBV, which sets him apart in his field. As a top-rated, chaired Wharton School management professor, Grant is distinguished among his peers. He creates an engaging, generous persona as he leads *Knowledge@Wharton* which introduces the most powerful business ideas and the people who are creating them to an interested community of learners beyond the walls of the Wharton School of Business at the University of Pennsylvania.

Grant is a recognized strategist and the author of *Give and Take: Why Helping Others Drives Our Success*. His research touches the tough world of business, revealing a powerful way to leave behind the status quo of corporate organizational behavior. His studies of business organization through the lens of applied psychology move institutions beyond the status quo, bringing "extra credit" for organizations (Grant, 2013).

Grant's unique work can give brandED leaders a perspective that they can adapt to their school community's innovation. He suggests that changing the status quo of an organization can be powerfully achieved through introducing and modeling "giving behavior." This idea is of particular note in a sea of research about human activity in the workplace.

Grant's studies show that individuals in organizations who recognize the role that giving and generosity play in their day-to-day work help bring the extra credit of effectiveness to their daily work lives. The result is evidenced in a stronger community and more productive activity related to the business bottom line. BrandED is an innovation that takes a community beyond the status quo. Exploring this idea of giving behavior can enrich brandED leaders as they lead change. In his newest book, *Originals: How Non-Conformists Move the World,* Grant (2016) describes the thinking of nonconformists who create a new world through their business-as-unusual thought and innovation. Thinking like this can get leaders into the zone for becoming entrepreneurial, a characteristic of unique brand development that can distinguish educational leaders. Entrepreneurial presence and giving behavior are bridges to your brandED leadership mindset and can lead you into the creative world of entrepreneurial behavior, one that is outside the status quo of most schools. Understanding the value of a "giving stance" in leadership can bring authentic, productive change to the community of educators.

BrandED leaders know that human behavior figures into introducing change. Transitions are uncomfortable. People, especially veteran educators, may resist innovation. The concept of brand, coming from a business perspective, may look suspect to some in the school organization. Using branding principles and management tools to impact school culture, performance, and resourcing is a nonconformist stance for educators and is something of a hybrid idea (Horn & Staker, 2015). If resistance arises, having tools to develop well-being can ease the transition. The adaptation of brand thinking into a school context invites a coexisting view that's been missing in the relationship between business and schools. The business tool of brand, a tool that we experience in our daily lives, can support new cooperation.

In our brandED model of giving behavior, leaders promote well-being. The business of school improvement is led by modeling generosity with time, expertise, and thinking as a means of improving the organization. This is part of a giving stance. BrandED leaders also welcome nonconforming, innovative thinking as they build their strategic plan. In return for modeling generous and giving behavior, they will see increased loyalty in those participating in the journey to develop the school brand. In addition, effectiveness in delivering the school's brand message increases when leaders adopt a giving stance. A successful brand leader is goal oriented in service to transparent communication and focused on brand building as a benefit to the community. BrandED leaders are givers. They understand that their generous leadership and their giving way unite the entire school community. Leaders who present their value in this innovative way offer their stakeholders well-being rather than roadblocks during times of change.

Grant (2014) develops more efficient and effective organizations through implementing his model of "giving behavior." This model recognizes the need to work purposefully to create generosity in professional settings, generosity that advances others in organizations. Grant's model can inform a journey of change that is brandED. Developing your own professional leadership brand with his tenets establishes the foundation of authenticity, generosity, and trust needed for creating the school's brand.

UNDERSTAND BEHAVIOR, UNDERSTAND BRANDED

Continue to use psychology to get beyond the status quo. Understanding of human behavior is needed to guide brandED's business-as-unusual stance. As educators, we draw on the power of psychology and human behavior in solving daily school challenges. Today's lead educators, thanks to the wealth of expertise found across our screens, look to the work of psychologists to inform their professional growth during times of innovation. In addition to Grant's model, the work of Stanford University's Carol Dweck (2007) on the concepts of fixed and growth mindsets resonates with educators. Her theory of intelligence is something brandED leaders can embrace as they take on a personal brand that is founded in a belief in themselves.

Cultivating growth and the belief in the ability to change a fixed mindset may be part of enlisting help to innovate. A leader may honestly break out of what Dweck refers to as a fixed mindset in order to lead change. Seeing oneself as a brandED leader, as a giving, generous, and accepting innovator, may require a leap. There are many leaders who have overcome their fear of being transparent and open, especially through new technology. How leaders empower others to recognize their own professional brand can be supported through sharing this evolution out of a fixed mindset to a belief in the ability to learn and improve. Getting clear about moving beyond an individual's fixed mindset and inviting that person to grow will create an energy for success that can inspire individuals and invigorate community efforts.

As leaders prepare to innovate, turning to the field of psychology informs their professional path. Behavior, specifically human decision-making behavior, is related to persuasion, a skill that is essential in innovating for change. Remember the First Moment of Truth (FMOT, mentioned in Conversation 1) as it relates to buying behavior? FMOT behavior occurs in education as well. School stakeholders must "buy" into our educator decisions—the adoption of ideas, the prioritizing among budget items, the persuasion for school tax levies—are but a few topics for the decision-making process that school leaders face as they enlist the support of the community. Stakeholder decision making, the FMOT, impacts educational leaders every day through community behavior, both online and in real time.

Knowing your way around decision making, human behavior, and organizational psychology can make you a better brandED professional. Your community of stakeholders is already out there demonstrating behavior in the transparent digital and social world, creating their own educational decisions, having their own Zero Moments of Truth (ZMOTs). They are expressing their own original ideas and opinions related to the school community in real time and online, some of which may be inaccurate. In the 2016 national election, we experienced a ZMOT phenomenon: the fake story. Digitally savvy leaders keep their eye on how stakeholders may be buying into those questionable threads of ZMOT conversation. Leaders bring their voices into the conversation to guide. A leader must have the protection of the truth at top of mind. That is a powerful reason to launch your brand strategy. Educators can take control of defining the message of the school.

Digital decision-making behavior is made evident by anyone in your community who has a Twitter handle; Facebook page; blog; Snapchat, Instagram, or Periscope account. Those who study the act of decision making, such as behavioral economists, inform us that digital decision making in online communities moves us closer to using our comfortable social norms as anchors that tap more into emotions and feelings about brands. We bump up against a world of influencers once we are online. An example is found in the instant message, which can hasten a buyer's decision making (Goodwin, 2016). The same emotional decision making can be found online around educational conversations ranging from where to buy a house in a particular geographic area when school-age children are in the mix, to online debates among parents about school zoning. Digital buzz makes the ground fertile for innovation of strong brand thinking as thoughts in relation to a brand's value are shared daily, and influence abounds at the stroke of a keyboard. A leader informed by an understanding of the psychology of human behavior in the digital world can more successfully guide the process of building a brand by keeping in mind **image, promise,** and **result** as they relate to decision making. Developing proof points of content about these elements is necessary. Through these proof points about the school brand, brandED leaders keep an eye on consistency in the message of the brand, and monitor content that illustrates the stories of the brand narrative. The trustworthy image that the brand promises creates a more satisfying result for schoolwide communication. Understanding the nuances of human behavior and the role of digital and offline engagement with brand makes your brandED leadership role stronger, more focused on building a solid **image** of your school and on identifying the

promise you want to deliver and the **result** you publically want to celebrate and sustain.

THE DIGITAL BOOKSHELF FOR BRANDED THINKING

As a brandED leader, be open to learning from diverse, polycultural voices. You must educate yourself as a trend spotter and knowledgeable brand voice. The online world of influencers and their networks are yours to access and share. For example, Malcolm Gladwell, author of the *Tipping Point* and *Outliers,* shares insights in those books that can further develop your success as you lead. Check into the work of social scientists, applied psychologists, and social-minded journalists. Joining Gladwell on your digital bookshelf of Twitter or LinkedIn blog posts might be Daniel Pink, Thomas Friedman, Steven D. Levitt, and even creative retail expert Paco Underhill. The work of Dave Kerpen, a social media–savvy entrepreneur with an eye on organizational behavior, is a must on your shelf to develop your entrepreneurial muscle, as is Time Inc.'s media guru, Scott Kerr, whose Twitter feed @scott_kerr offers an addictive daily global window on the innovative world of design. Kerr's content is inspiring on any day and is worth checking out and sharing with your stakeholders as you build your brand-savvy mastery.

Build your own inspiring team of experts; enlist a superstar bench of brilliant trend-spotting digital influencers. To use a sports metaphor, make them your personal team of utility players whose thought leadership can support and anchor your growth process. Through online search that leads to interaction, you can build relationships that become important to your own brand presence, and you may even find a brand supporter for your school as a result of a relationship you develop with a superstar influencer. Consult a cadre of digital masterminds from across industries and disciplines and keep them as your virtual mentors. In many cases, it is even possible to develop a true relationship with a potential mentor online if you have an authentic attitude that may lead to offline support. By following an engaging Twitter feed and retweeting valuable content, you can come to the attention of thought leaders and begin extending value to them through your retweets, which may result in the leader following you. That opens the door for respectful exchange. The opportunity to be your authentic self leads to trust when a thought leader follows your sincere messaging.

Understand human behavior online as well as offline. Exploring online relationships across fields of industry and scholarship is a crucial task for today's tech-aware school leader. Live in the Friedman mindset of a "communications mash-up" of information about human behavior through your access to excellent online content of those mentioned, and keep searching out new experts and influencers through your digital social research. Be curious about all sorts of trending topics: personalized learning cars, the world of virtual reality, the impact of gaming on education. You will connect to others online who are thinking about these topics too, people who can become part of your growing network. BrandED leaders are students of change; they are passionate about learning and connecting to new thinking. Developing online relationships that come from this bold thinking will bring benefit to the school. Thanks to online communities like Twitter and LinkedIn, leaders can choose their own virtual mentors that fit the personal professional brand, and connect with them closely online. The free tools of connection on social media allow you to build relationships with those you respect, enabling you to build your performance.

One such mentor for brandED leadership who can join your team of content experts speaks to the well-being of people in organizational shift. Martin Seligman (2012), one of the top five leaders in the field of positive psychology (Srinivasan, 2015), introduced powerful thinking and practice around the study of human behavior and happiness. Seligman was primarily influenced by Abraham Maslow. Maslow is a familiar name for educators, but his research is also foundational for marketing and brand due to its relationship to the study of behavior (see, for example, Maslow, 1998). His Hierarchy of Needs (Figure 2.1) both impacts buyer decision making and informs the educational

Figure 2.1   Maslow's Hierarchy of Needs

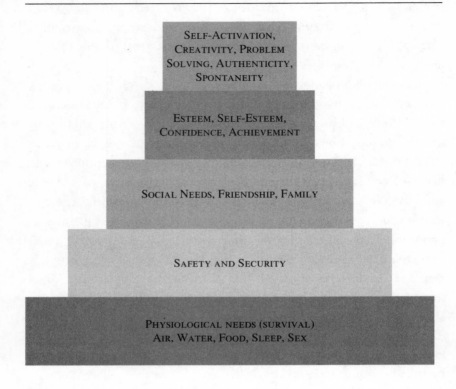

community about the decision making of a learner ready to engage (Gunelius, 2014). Seligman's work and Maslow's views on the concept of well-being can help support brandED leaders who are ready to innovate.

THE PSYCHOLOGY OF A CREATIVE BRANDED LEADER

Successful brands advance new marketing concepts by integrating distinct, creative messaging that relates to specific human needs. Marketers survey needs and then dig further into human wants to find what people actually crave in an emotional way that can go beyond a basic need. Connecting to a consumer's driving want is the sweet spot for a sale. Look at the cost of a second of Super Bowl advertising. Companies vie for the distinction of having the most remarkably creative commercial. Millions are spent on messaging that can hit the right note in presenting a need, such as telling time, and then showing a brand's solution that uniquely satisfies a want of the target audience for a timepiece. Think: It's not just a watch that I need—it's a Rolex! To yield the best results in the search for marketing creativity and the connection to wants, many corporations have begun to rethink human behavior and are integrating once disparate company offices, moving away from departmental "silos" and requiring more sharing and contact among departments. Times have changed on Madison Avenue because of the power of the consumer: There's a new digital- and social media–savvy audience that knows what it wants and is demanding new creative brand presence from advertisers. Although culture, strategy, technology, and management tools are important in generating effectiveness in the 21st century, creativity and innovation are what drive this organizational success in many business sectors (Agbor, 2008). Madison Avenue has made creativity a big priority of the shared internal mission to satisfy wants.

Creativity is central to a school leader's job as well.

Sir Ken Robinson's popular TED Talk video (2006) on YouTube may be a good starting point in your study of creating an innovative culture. He speaks about the creativity that is absent from schools. Robinson claims that there's a flattening of student intellect as a result of standardization. "Where is the creativity?" he asks. BrandED and the creativity involved with the building of a school brand can be a starting point for taking on that question.

THE CREATIVE VALUE OF RELATIONAL BEHAVIOR

Branding success is based on creativity. The majority of relationships educators create should be means of benefiting the school through new types of creative partnering. Leaders who adopt this behavior as a creative leadership endeavor will be successful. Increased happiness results in the community if leaders creatively form genuine partnerships and sponsorships. Being a brandED leader means using your own brand to strategically pursue powerful relationships. BrandED leaders set relationship building as a top professional goal, and execute that goal in a mindful way. They cultivate creative relationships on a daily basis. With a nod to business guru Tom Peters, launching your brandED strategy means that you, and members of your brandED team, will be building your own brand and thinking relationally with new passion for forging creative connections that benefit the school. Reach personal branding guru William Arruda cites in his blog that according to Peters (1999), building a professional brand is done through connecting that's "10% vision and 90% execution." How is this done? Before you take a step toward a brandED strategy, before you build your brand, take Tom Peter's management advice: "You have to develop a Rolodex obsession, building and deliberately managing an ever-growing network of professional contacts".

Don't wait. Start looking for connections right away. Plan to creatively open windows to relationships in all directions. Reach beyond the schoolroom door to find where your new partners are waiting. The combined energy of a team of brand-savvy educators engaged in reinventing school brand can get their creative juices flowing, just as can any collection of Madison Avenue creatives. A range of creative school brand ambassadors can build bridges and connections to external partners. Give your community the power to engage as brand ambassadors when you demonstrate your own creative brand. Share the message that the brand is being developed as a giving effort, one that will raise the culture, performance, and resources of the school. Demonstrate a brandED mindset and modality that engage and get them sharing the word about this innovation in their circles of connection and influence.

As the leader of the effort, you model your own relational power creatively, continually showing your brand mastery. The relational behavior you command grows your connective power. Use the power of the food and beverage industry and its development over the last 20 years to guide you. The best chefs inspire because they each demonstrate their creative brand. They win the respect of their peers and the loyalty of their followers by showing mastery through their relational behavior.

Relational behavior isn't just for five-star celebrity chefs. It is an essential part of the business of education in this new age of creative connection, and it is a requirement for modern school leaders.

A new vehicle for moving beyond traditional partnering and into creative relationship building is the visual world of live streaming. BrandED leaders can check into the streaming app that connects to Twitter, called Periscope. Periscope, which is quickly growing a following in the educational community, allows users to transmit live video recordings of themselves to Periscope and Twitter followers. Because Periscope is owned by Twitter, it automatically links to your Twitter account. Users get a notification anytime the educators you're following do a live transmission. There is even the option to archive the video feed, which keeps valuable content accessible to educators. In its latest move, the Periscope app has launched a 360-degree camera attachment that makes for even more engaging visual content.

School leaders are looking at a whole new niche in our stakeholder community: the digital natives who have grown up creatively building their worldview through screen time and are primed for connection. Their future will be rich with digital connection that calls for increased ability to move creatively in both traditional and real-time engagements. Today our Gen Z students can meet and connect to people as soon as the computers boot up or they turn on their smartphones. When they do, hundreds of new people are in your schoolhouse! Endless opportunities now abound to provide a global bridge to discovery that sparks learning and relationships.

Leaders can model this creativity and inspire their digital stakeholders. Adopt the saying "You never know!" as you focus on the full range of 21st-century relationship-building possibilities. Open yourself up to developing new daily routines that push your relational creativity and extend your network. Using the brandED leadership tools detailed in Conversation 6, you can advance your connective behavior in ways ranging from the traditional to the innovative. Simply picking up the phone to offer a favor, talking to someone new on Twitter, or asking a person you trust for a referral to someone new may be a creative use of your time as a relational leader. Later that day, joining a Twitter chat or participating in a Google Hangout can take you to a new experience in creative relational activity. This behavior is all in service to brand and creates a daily mindset and ritual.

As you take on more commitment to connecting, you will be sharing your school's story and starting to build relationships that expand your network for your school's advancement. Pursue this "you never know" attitude in both real-time and online connecting as a creative call to the serendipity of establishing relationships. Look across generational lines and connect with Boomers, Gen Xers, Millennials, and the youngest generational demographic, Gen Z. Sample new platforms and apps to make your connections. Start slowly with these new sharing platforms or pace yourself at a faster rate. There is no one way to test these new channels. Be an early adopter. Join in with the goal of growing confidence and engaging to benefit your community.

Show up as a "listener" first. This listening soon turns into engagement and participation in online chats, which can get you moving toward building interesting professional relationships on a global level. These new relationships can become what marketers call "affinity partners" for your brandED efforts. Creatively target these partners. Get to know them and find the common element they share with your school brand. What's the affinity connection that will pull them into a genuine exchange? They can connect more easily to a crafted school brand and help you build your school's resources through their own network of connections. Historical evidence shows that the great American networker of his day, Ben Franklin, used the affinity model to create relationships, and as a result, he was "pulled" by his connections into partnerships that advanced not only him but also, later, our young country. The book *Pull: Networking and Success Since Benjamin Franklin* (Laird, 2006) is a robust read that can only make one wonder what that leader extraordinaire would have done with a smartphone. As you build your leadership brand, push yourself as a creative brandED leader to create affinity in the spirit of Franklin, and your growth will be remarkable.

Part Two: Tools to Inspire BrandED Innovation

> Well-being cannot exist just in your own head. Well-being is a combination of feeling good as well as actually having meaning, good relationships and accomplishments.
> —*Martin Seligman (2012)*

A TOOL FOR CREATING THE BRANDED TONE: PERMA

BrandED leaders collaborate with their internal and external communities as cocreators of brand. Seligman's book *Flourish* contains a model that supports your brandED effort as a lead educator who builds relationships and powers accomplishments. His "human dashboard" is a working control center for brandED leaders, bringing stakeholders charged with developing innovation into a state of well-being that creates brandED change. Applying Seligman's elements in a collaborative team process evokes a shared productive personal and professional commitment to a successful brandED school innovation.

Seligman's dashboard describes five elements that create professional well-being and that will be important touchpoints for brandED leaders as they show brand mastery within these elements and inspire well-being within a team that is getting into the zone to create change. Presented in the acronym PERMA, the keys to well-being are *positive emotion, engagement, relationships, meaning, and achievement* (Seligman, 2012). Your enlisting support for innovation depends on, your engagement with others around a belief. Your energy powers success. Individuals are invited into an enhanced state of positive emotion and focus as they engage in a brandED innovation. In pop culture terms, this state is often called being "in the zone." This concept is rooted in psychological research. The zone is what Mihaly Csikszentmihalyi (1990, 2004) described as the psychological state of "flow": a time when individuals are completely involved in a purposeful, creative activity; a state in which people are so involved that nothing else seems to matter. The experience is so enjoyable that people will continue to engage in it even at great cost, simply for the sake of doing it. This is where a brandED school movement begins: with a leader dedicated to creating flow that results in a brandED plan, by marshaling the energies of a diverse and collective community.

A brandED leader uses a PERMA mindset to build the community of flow during innovation by using Seligman's dashboard model. The dashboard illustrates the commitment of individuals to new thinking that results in highly engaged participants in a change movement. Leaders who build their own brand will experience flow and can describe the process and behavior in launching a brand with new brand ambassadors:

Positive emotion—optimism. The energy of the new pathways for communication for a school in the digital age introduces the unifying and invigorating opportunity that a crafted school brand can bring to the school.

Engagement—being in a state of flow. The brandED leader works to convey the benefit of raising the profile of a school. Innovative brand thinking creates a connecting excitement. The sharing of the narratives of the school community goes beyond the sharing of the limiting report of test scores in a local newspaper. Telling the story using voices raised across the community illustrates the new awareness of the value of brand culture, performance, and results.

Relationships—connections both internal and with stakeholders: The brandED leader models the value of being relational. The leader envisions the connected world of exchange that inspires exterior partnerships and sponsorships that benefit all stakeholders. A connected internal organization that values relationships within the school community is essential.

Meaning—belonging to and serving something bigger than oneself. The brandED leader challenges others to innovate. Opening the door to new ideas from every stakeholder connects the tribe.

The school community becomes a committed group that holds a shared affinity and authentic connection for the new school brand.

Achievement—pursued even when no positive emotion, no meaning, and nothing in the way of positive relationship may result. Most people will sense a contagion—brand just feels right. The brandED leader strives for meaning in the brand innovation. In some cases, people achieve flow by focusing on result for result's sake. Leaders understand the varied ways people view achievement. They welcome a broad definition of achievement when it comes to brand and include all views, even of those who reach the brand goal simply for the sake of experiencing achievement.

Through self-reflection, leaders master a personal brand experience by moving through the PERMA model themselves. Before building a team, ask yourself whether you are in the flow for innovation. Are you positive minded? Are you ready for engagement? Are you primed for relational behavior? Are you ready to launch the new meaning that makes a school connected?

Once you've committed to leading a brandED movement, use the PERMA tool to build confidence and well-being among collaborators and to engage them at a high level of interest. You want your team to commit to developing the school image, promise, and result with joy and energy. What they create will be embraced by all stakeholders in the brandED school community. BrandED leaders communicate a shared culture and high-level performance that are part of being in the zone for creating a brand in a collective effort. The leader brings the message that a **culture** of coexisting around a shared belief and a spirit of **performing** are mainstays of the collective work. The brandED adaptation of the PERMA model features this need for shared understanding of culture and performance for success as a team of cocreators. The model suggests the relationship between the leader and the stakeholder team, who are building commitment to a cause using the PERMA touchstones in an exchange The interaction between leader and stakeholders is a two-way street. As a leader, you guide and support the creativity of your

Figure 2.2 A Dashboard of Well-Being for Modeling and Leadership: PERMA

Adapted from *Flourish: A Visionary New Understanding of Happiness and Well-Being*, by M.E.P. Seligman, 2012, New York, NY: Free Press

team. Your judgment is important, but you share the leadership as a brand is built. BrandED school leaders use Seligman's dashboard to show how the culture of belief and the standard of creative performance in the development of brand help their team perform as well as any Madison Avenue design team, as they work together in a shared model of distributed leadership to craft a new school brand. PERMA offers leaders a framework, language, and map for facilitating the support of a district-wide change (see Figure 2.2).

A BrandED Short Story: Alexis Bonavitacola Leading Through Change

Dr. Alexis Bonavitacola is a progressive educator who is in the flow. She's been responsible for ushering in large curricular change for several districts, from the West Coast in California to numerous schools on the East Coast (A. Bonavitacola, personal communication, September 2016). Brand thinking touches her work in tangible and intangible ways. Implementing meaningful change is a passion that allows her to further a district's brand, conveying to its stakeholders through innovation what the district values. Her purposeful approach to education is characterized by her inquisitive leader stance. Her close study of research and her innovative, artful practice blend into a leadership brand that uniquely reflects her commitment to innovation. Over her 20-year journey, Bonavitacola continually seeks opportunities to be a change agent as she builds her career. She believes that visionary administrators are responsible for their own constant learning and researching. Her own vision for learning has been "teaching the whole child" as she has both introduced and developed programs for learners. For instance, implementing the International Baccalaureate Middle Years Program in Cherry Hill and Hoboken, New Jersey, and St. Helena, California, has allowed her the foundational experience of bringing an innovative educational change in collaboration with a committed stakeholder team of fellow administrators, staff, teachers, and parents, who join in this innovation for the benefit of children.

Bonavitacola knows that although change is necessary to reach and teach all learners, it is never comfortable. A positive stance is called for when moving initiatives forward. Her work in building collaborative teams that are committed to strong culture and high performance reflects the elements of Seligman's PERMA model. In the case of IB, successful implementation of an IB Middle Years Program included recognizing the power of meaning in teaching and engaging the whole child. Her understanding of human nature and behavior and her support of staff moved the adoption of this innovation. Promoting relationships is part of the work, and she demonstrates a unique, engaged level of communication.

Whether preparing the next generation of teachers or developing the work of those teachers she supervises, Bonavitacola

(continued)

knows that trust and communication are essential parts of the collaborative leadership process. Innovation is based on developing conversations that are "brandED" by nature. Educators must dig deeply and explore how they are invested in an innovation. Leaders must strive to connect in their learning communities and stay rooted in what is meaningful in the district. At the same time, we move forward to support the educational needs of children. All of this is part of creating the innovation.

With a brandED eye on the well-being of her teachers, Alexis advances her work in a safe space. She describes school districts in terms of the metaphor of a family that tends to relationships and builds the personal and social aspects of education, securing the path of an innovation. She knows that's why the word of mouth spreads about good schools. These schools are families of learners. Teachers want to work in those schools. If brand is image, promise, and result, her work throughout her career makes her a brandED leader. In every community she has served, she's built a unique educational experience for students and teachers through studied, consistent, and innovative change. Testing the power of innovating through online learning, she brings the same brand engagement and safety to the courses she teaches.

As Alexis has managed change that has benefited students through both large-scale initiatives and new programs brought into a school district, what has always worked for her for close to 20 years—and what has worked for successful brands since the invention of the World Wide Web—is cultivating leadership capacity in others. Her model of belief in people spreads across a community. The evidence of positive change is both exciting and necessary to sustaining any change process. Alexis focuses on supporting the well-being of her team and their commitment to positivity and meaning. In her view, successful leaders model the way through any innovation. They own an ability to be approachable and to walk the talk of change.

BrandED leaders are authentic in their own professional brands, they build relationships, and they approach change in a way that supports stakeholders. Alexis Bonavitacola looks immediately to teachers' need for positive emotion and the need to bring well-being into the change process. For large-scale change, she has provided necessary resources and supports of time and materials to help the teachers see meaning in their efforts. Leaders have to do their homework before taking on innovation. What has always been key for her was thinking of change in terms of relationships: What systems are needed to make this change successful?

When innovating, brandED leaders need to recognize the psychological implications of change; and they turn to psychology to help those who feel the fear. Attending to the PERMA dashboard is one way for leaders to move supportively through change.

As Bonavitacola points out, with any new educational change, teachers who felt successful at their craft may begin to feel vulnerable and fearful that they will not be successful. Parents may not understand why things have to be different, especially if their children are succeeding in the moment. Students may not be willing to move out of their safe zones of learning. To bridge the transition between old and new, it is invaluable to recognize the success of the community and use this as leverage to move forward. Strong leaders have a genuinely generous nature, and they engage—they don't invalidate people. They look at what has been successful and build from that stance, making room for meaning on the road to change.

Leaders like Bonavitacola will always seek new learning, launch initiatives that focus on innovative learning, and bring people together in the name of kids. They use their understanding of human behavior in service to the whole child.

A TOOL FOR SETTING THE BRANDED DIRECTION: SWOT

Leaders of the school brand effort find frameworks and systems to support their own change, as well as their co-creators' growth. As a school leader developing a brandED plan, you have a great deal in common with a business brand leader planning a campaign. Business leaders know that assessing the status of an effort prior to beginning to raise awareness is key. As an innovative leader, you are reinventing the school through a brand lens, so just as brand managers do, get a sense of the journey ahead by taking stock of where you are in the current moment. Prior to leading a new initiative, you can use an adapted version of a well-known business tool to take a snapshot of where you perceive the community to be in its current brand situation. Using this adapted tool may reveal important data that helps you understand the status of your school and how to position your own leadership brand, which you will create in Conversation 3.

Every business brand journey includes the use of this tool, an activity known as a SWOT analysis. In conducting a SWOT, the **s**trengths, **w**eaknesses, **o**pportunities, and **t**hreats to brand success are stated and examined (Figure 2.3). The SWOT activity is done in the very early stages of development of a mission so that the brand strategy can be assured of success (Armstrong & Kotler, 2015). Adapted for educators, a SWOT analysis is a chance to understand how you perceive your school community and can help you articulate a brand that addresses the current state of the organization. Especially interesting to leaders will be the opportunities for growth that they identify, which can be used as tangible measures of brand success, and the threats that are challenging the school. Making those threats a target and finding ways to see opportunities in those challenges may strengthen the school's brand. A SWOT analysis can serve you well in your initial reflections about both your personal brand and your school's. A SWOT process conducted with frankness yields valuable information about the current state of an organization and directs decision making. Once the analysis is complete, it forms a direction for leaders as they take on their personal brand, as they can more clearly see themselves serving the needs of the community.

As business managers have found, putting yourself through your own SWOT analysis can even further inform the building of your own brand. Why do a personal SWOT? A SWOT analysis may goad you into real action as you advance your own brand in real time. Honestly assessing

Figure 2.3 SWOT Analysis for BrandED Development

"POSITIVE ANALYSIS"
MATCH STRENGTHS WITH OPPORTUNITIES TO COMMUNICATE BRANDED

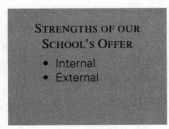

STRENGTHS OF OUR
SCHOOL'S OFFER
- Internal
- External

OPPORTUNITIES FOR
SCHOOL'S OFFER
- Relationships
- Environment
- Local and Global

"NEGATIVE ANALYSIS"
PUSH TO ELIMINATE OR OVERCOME WEAKNESS AND THREATS TO BRANDED

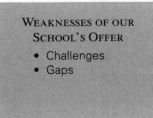

WEAKNESSES OF OUR
SCHOOL'S OFFER
- Challenges
- Gaps

THREATS TO
BRAND WELL-BEING
- Microenvironment
- Macroenvironment

Adapted from *Marketing: An Introduction* (12th ed.), by G. Armstrong and P. Kotler, 2015, Boston, MA: Pearson

your strengths and weaknesses and reflecting on any opportunities or threats that are present in your leadership style can help you assess your capacities before you build a professional brand that you own as the brandED storyteller-in-chief. If you do decide to take this on, think about your goal for implementing a brandED innovation. Set yourself on the path of being the best brandED leader you can be by conducting a SWOT analysis. Gains in self-knowledge and personal leadership can result.

A simple tip suggested by those who study behavior is to look at threats first. For example, as you try to grow your own brand, you may see "changes to the way schools are funded" as a threat to your ability to implement change, or "resistance to change on the part of staff" as a roadblock to your leadership. As an opportunity, you might notice "technological advances like blogs, social media, and webinars" as a way to develop yourself professionally with a minimal investment of time. Another tip is to share your SWOT results with someone you trust to get feedback.

Keep the SWOT in mind as you form your brandED team. You may suggest that every member engage in a SWOT analysis to familiarize himself or herself with this process of reflection and assessment, especially if the collective group will create a SWOT for the school community.

When developing a personal SWOT, people reflect on strengths that define them: education, social position, resources, networks, caregiving, personal characteristics (for example, "respectful" or "faithful"). Weaknesses might appear as risk-averse behavior, inflexibility, fear, intolerance, and such characteristics as "focused on myself." Opportunities might include availability of resources, ability to keep positive, and resilience. Threats may appear as weak job advancement, inability to balance demands, limited time, and inadequate resources. Moving through the process in a self-directed activity allows the individual to reflect with honesty and self-assess. The awareness that results can lead to action. The SWOT is completed as a private activity. Many companies that have used this model find that working through the challenge on a personal level prior to engaging with a group serves to benefit the work in an organizational SWOT endeavor.

As a group convenes to build a school SWOT, they use their reflective experience on a bigger stage. Leaders can refer the brand builders to the figures depicting micro- and macroenvironments that surround the school (presented in Conversation 1) and examine them through discussions about the strengths that the school owns and displays. The discussion is led as an examination of the way the school positions itself with parents, teachers, students, staff, and the local community, and determining each element as it fits in the SWOT can stimulate close reflection. Additional attention to external forces—political, economic, cultural, policy, technological, regulatory—can bring these bigger influences into the discussion of how the brand should be designed and articulated. The SWOT analysis can serve as a snapshot of the district. Actually, the opportunities identified during a district or school SWOT analysis can serve as a reservoir of worth for the ongoing development of the school brand. A forward-thinking team can plan for turning opportunities into future strengths as a "next step" to maintaining a school brand. Further, the SWOT activity sharpens the work of the brandED Drivers presented in Conversation 4 and is highly recommended in the development of the team.

Part Three: BrandED Reputation Management

Before you launch your brandED strategy, keep in mind that you are going to act as the "brand manager" and lead protector of the brand. In Conversation 8, you'll learn that developing your role as steward of the brand is key to sustaining the authenticity of the brand promise. Before you develop your brandED Strategic Plan, consider the importance of a transparent communication effort and be prepared for the response such openness brings. Having a strong brand counteracts the stress of things that happen outside your leadership control, such as community feedback in forms that weren't possible before digital channels were created. Lead with an eye on showcasing the reputation of the school before others might end up hurting that reputation, either intentionally or unintentionally.

Transparency brings positive connection, but as today's leaders know, their world is filled with expectations. Sometimes these challenge the leadership landscape, and you must think: "Am I going to be ready to handle the pushback of all sorts, from casual comments to legal ramifications?" Make sure that your brand presence is informed by your understanding of the community—these people and businesses are your audience. Let them know you care. Start creating the connection to the social world through hashtags that can build strong discussions about the good things going on in your school. Promote those hashtags so that others can use them. The people who use them and engage with your brand can be the people who will promote the school in tough times.

In this simple way, leaders build strategic partnerships and become aware of their supporters and those who aren't yet on board. Before you set the stage for your school brand strategy, promote your own brand and look forward to managing the brand you are about to build. Consider that there may be times when your school or district's reputation, or your own reputation, may be challenged. The connectivity you engage when building your own brand is deeply connected to managing that brand in times of challenge. Good brand thinkers are always ahead of the curve, thinking about "What if?"

"WHAT IF?" AND BRAND REPUTATION

Investigate the world of reputation management. Don't wait until you are in a crisis and have to go into a reactive mode with the local news team at your door. Crisis management is part of the PR world that business brands handle on a daily basis, and in our changing world, schools must do the same. "Brand reputation management" consists of the monitoring of conversations and the gathering of feedback about your organization (Walkin, 2013). As you develop brandED activities, make attending to reputation a public effort. Get the word-of-mouth discussion going about developing and using brand as a tool for school improvement. Work toward having the community embrace the branding effort by creating a team that reflects all stakeholders, and begin to tell the stories of the brand that you are building. Do it in real time and with the online channels you have at your disposal.

Educators are used to starting with "the end in mind" to plan for curriculum success. See the end of what your brand will stand for and work backward, forecasting any threat that may challenge reputation. As a brandED leader, you are thinking about risk reduction in a fast-moving digital age. It is crucial to have a plan for guaranteeing the quality of communication so that the school brand always looks strong. Even when called into question, a clear brand presence can sustain threats to any product or service. This is true for education. Provide updates on progress toward any of the positive initiatives that are connected to your brand. Search for content that illustrates brand passion, which can be used in times of challenge. Manage your brand reputation by getting the support of people who have good digital reputations and good networks, people who understand how to communicate. You might even consider doing an audit through searching on Twitter using hashtags or on LinkedIn through groups. Find people who are active online who reside in your school community's geographic area. This search may find an "outlier" who hasn't connected to the school community but is an active member online. This is an informal way to gather data about the team you are trying to create.

Find your bloggers and community activists and add them to your list of possible members of your collective. Find your media gurus in-house who may further educate you because of their brand awareness. You may be surprised by finding someone in your organization who has expertise not on the radar. A crossing guard with PR background could be in your midst. Be alert. You are operating as the storyteller-in-chief as you share your story of why brand matters, but you are also the brandED steward when considering reputation.

BRAND MANAGEMENT IN THE DIGITAL AGE

Your digital footprint is a portrait of who you are as an educator, leader, school, or district. Make sure it conveys your true values and work. In an age where billions of people have taken both their personal and professional lives online, you'd better be cognizant of your digital footprint. With each Facebook post, email, Instagram photo, comment on a blog, YouTube video, Skype call, and the like, you are leaving a trail that can be seen, searched, or tracked. Basically, all of your activity on the Internet leads to the creation of a digital identity: a footprint.

If you have that covered, you might think that you have everything under control, right? Wrong! Your digital footprint is formed not only by what you post but also by what others put online about you.

There are two main classifications for digital footprints: passive and active. A passive digital footprint is created when data is collected without the owner knowing, whereas active digital footprints are created when a user, for the purpose of sharing information about himself or herself, by means of websites or social media, deliberately releases data. Educators who have embraced a brandED mindset understand how important their digital footprint is to them.

It can seem daunting to keep tabs on both the digital footprint that you are actively crafting and what other people are creating and posting unbeknownst to you. Here are some free tools that you can begin to use right away to track both your active and passive digital footprints.

Google Alerts (www.google.com/alerts) This free tool allows you to monitor the Web for content that you specify. Set up alerts for your name as well as that of your school, district, or business. When I (Eric) was a principal, I had an alert set up for New Milford High School so that any time content specific to my school was shared on the Web, I could either read or react if necessary. Now I have alerts set up for different iterations of my name, including Eric Sheninger, Mr. Sheninger, and Principal Sheninger. Each day, I receive an email from Google with news of what people write about me on the Web.

Mention (mention.com) Mention takes monitoring a step beyond Google Alerts. It allows you to monitor any keywords related to you, your professional brand, your school or district, or anything else you want to monitor. The alert settings are much more robust than those of Google Alerts. You can set it up to monitor not only the Web (news, blogs, videos, forums, images) but also mentions on Facebook, Twitter, or an array of other social media services. What is even better about Mention is the variety of ways you can access and be notified of new alerts (website, Google Chrome extension, desktop application, and apps for iOS and Android).

Tweetdeck (tweetdeck.twitter.com) and Hootsuite (hootsuite.com) These two applications not only enhance your Twitter experience but also allow you to create different columns or categories on your dashboard. Each column or category in a sense becomes a search based on the keywords you identify (Twitter username, your real name, hashtags, school or district name, and the like).

The aforementioned tools will greatly assist you in tracking your digital footprint, especially what other people post about you. In addition, a brandED strategy employs some commonsense tips to help you actively create a positive digital footprint. When posting content online, always

1. Keep it professional and focus on your work
2. Remember your role within the school and/or professional community
3. Think before you post
4. Be consistent
5. Own an empowering view of engagement

Perception is reality. With a strategy comprising consistent content production and technology monitoring tools, anyone can create a positive digital footprint. The choice is yours as to what you want your reality to be on the Internet. Don't roll the dice and let others dictate this for you.

Conversation 2 Tips

Establish a giving nature, based on your developing knowledge of current psychology, as a focal point for your brandED leadership development, and create systems to support stakeholders during change.

- **Recognize** the range of tools that support brandED leaders as they prepare for distributed leadership; these tools come from the fields of psychology, economics, leadership, technology, business, and so on.

(continued)

- **Understand** the PERMA model to identify ways to use *positive emotion, engagement, relationships, meaning,* and *achievement* as a model that creates well-being among your stakeholders and advances your brandED innovation effort.
- **Conduct** a brand SWOT analysis on yourself. Identify your own brand's strengths, weaknesses, opportunities, and threats in terms of your leadership of brandED. Before leading a school brand SWOT analysis, suggest a personal, private SWOT for your team members.
- **Ensure** the reputation management of your unique school brand with a plan that starts with positive storytelling from across the school community, using platforms that let you gather support through online hashtags and face-to-face conversations.
- **Connect** to future brand ambassadors from across the organization—kids, staff, teachers, parents, and the greater community of partners—as you search for members of your brandED team and as you build relationships.
- **Monitor** your digital footprint from the start: Manage your brand today with an eye to the future.

Conversation 2 Reflections

You will be holding public conversations around the idea that branding principles and brandED leadership tools will set the stage for *culture, performance,* and *resourcing* gains. Think about these questions:

- How does the field of psychology inform me as I create a brandED leadership stance and build support for this change?
- How can I create a genuine feeling of trust, acceptance, and even happiness among my community of stakeholders before taking on an innovative brandED approach?

- What does my existing network look like? Can I consciously make the attempt to build relationships so that innovation will be welcomed? Do I need to know more about creating relationships for brandED success?
- How do I present myself and my brandED mastery in a transparent way in this digital, social, and online world? Do I need to create a more powerful and authentic self in public profiles?
- Can I use information—the most current trends and signals—from a range of communities, such as social science, economics, media, technology, and business, to employ new strategies of thinking and action for brandED leadership?

Developing a BrandED Leadership Presence

In Conversation 3, leaders claim brandED as a critical part of their own professional development by crafting their "personal professional brand" that will inspire and guide the collaborative brand mission for school improvement. The school leader invests in the role of storyteller-in-chief of the brand and models the business-as-unusual mindset, moving beyond the status quo and taking on an innovative "edupreneurial" spirit that inspires a community of stakeholders to a cocreate a whole-school brand movement. Leaders who are aware, intuitive, and comfortable with their personal professional brand are educators who have done the work of building brand awareness in a dedicated personal way, blending an authentic personality with a distinguishing educational persona. Through introspection and testing, brandED leaders communicate a growing brand mastery that gains genuine followers and supporters who become new brandED ambassadors.

This leadership journey to brandED brings an innovating, engaging focus to schools. We live in a creation economy. Let's be at our creative best for our schools, starting with our leadership selves. Brand development is work. It isn't about a quick fix or short answers. Anyone can put up a website and open a Twitter account, but it takes creativity, smarts, and perseverance to create a school brand that will live authentically on those platforms. Looking at the acceptance of today's creation economy, we know we have others who want to share the passion for the work of brand. Happily, in this creative environment, anyone with a smartphone can help us tell and share our positive school stories. A storyteller-in chief with a personal professional brand presence can lead the way.

Cocreating the story of the school brand is part of being in the creation economy, an ecosystem that grows more powerful each day through new digital sharing platforms. Change feels satisfyingly possible under the leadership of a confident brandED leader who can unify stakeholders and guide them through the complex world of engaged communication.

> Be genuine. Be remarkable. Be worth connecting with.
> —*Seth Godin, marketing/branding thought leader*

Part One: A "Personal Professional" BrandED You

Do yourself a service: Create your own brand.

Amazon CEO, Jeff Bezos, uses the term *personal brand* when he points out that your personal brand is what people say about you when you leave the room. In the brandED adaptation for educators, leaders will be authentic in building their *personal professional* brand. As a brandED educator, you claim that stance by crafting a brand that combines the best of both aspects of your persona. You blend the most powerful and complementary aspects of your personality and professional presence in a personal professional leadership brand that fits your online and offline presence. Before you take your steps toward image, promise, and result on a schoolwide scale, develop your own unique brand value (UBV) to power your institutional effort, and commit to living it every day as a model. And as noted in Conversation 2, do it sooner rather than later, before someone else does it for you. In an article that focused on the need for becoming a brand personality, business guru Tom Peters (1997) referred to this activity as building "Brand You." He is still blogging on www.tompeters.com, citing 21st-century thinking that supports the need for a brand presence. Peters's Brand You is a call to action for educators to shine their light, to promote what makes them uniquely different and, at the same time, what makes them approachable.

Your personal professional brand reflects your true core. Unlike a "selling" brand personality, a brandED personal professional brand envelops you in a trusted, communicative presence in service to your school. Some call it a brand personality; some call it a brand tag or profile. Call it whatever you like, but create it. Work hard on self reflection and self-assessment. Refer back to your SWOT analysis and give a voice to your UBV. Any brand is only as good as the perception the audience has of its value. You want your personal professional brand to resonate with your stakeholders. The result of your development of "brand you" is a product that can communicate, attract, and engage with your community in a new way.

When you introduce the concept of brandED to the wider community, you must already have your own values, mission, and vision articulated. You must be living your educator brand. As the storyteller and steward of brandED, you must be ready to model the process of developing a "brand you vision" for those on your team as you launch your institutional brand strategy. Your model needs to be strong enough and authentic enough to bring connectivity to your mission of developing an institutional brand. Your brand mastery grows as you live it. Demonstrate your brand daily and talk about your belief in the process of building it to benefit your community. You must support the growth of your early adopters who see your brand and "get it." Your "ambassadors," your team, can experience the power of a "brand you" through your example. Help them recognize the value of creating a personal professional brand on their own and offer to help them validate theirs. The experience prepares them for developing a school brand for the community.

OWNING A "PERSONAL PROFESSIONAL BRAND" AND AN "INSTITUTIONAL BRAND"

Chapter 7 of *Digital Leadership* (Sheninger, 2014) recognizes that hesitancy on the part of educators new to the concept of branding oneself and branding a school is expected. If you haven't engaged in branding behavior, be assured that the two separate brand elements of your personal and professional life align for a complete brandED leadership profile. Promoting your UBV hasn't been a part of preparing for your career as an educator, and it's an exciting proposition to be in charge of creating this product for yourself. See this as a necessary form of professional development in our 21st-century digital world.

Thinking about your unique value to a school may not be easy to take on initially. Some may feel that bragging and the self-promotional sharing of successes have no place in education. It's not true. The time has come to awaken to the need to define ourselves and our institutions through brand. Brand presence needs to be part of a professional improvement plan for leaders so that they can guide brand building into the "must do" column for institutional development. Ignoring the world of communication that is defining your school puts you at risk. The educational world is more competitive now. A well-defined educational brand keeps you and your school relevant to stakeholders who live in the sharing economy that social media has created. Educators share. That's in our DNA. We need to share our truest story through our brand. Now more than ever, it makes sense to embrace this promotional trend to benefit our communities.

One rallying cry for brand is expression. Educators don't all do things the same way. Original and innovative thinking is now becoming the norm for educators in a digital world where new ideas spread to the point of viral adoption. There is natural UBV that distinguishes each of us, and we must craft our UBV for ourselves in order to guide our followers. The proof of our brand will be found on blogs, websites, Twitter feeds, Facebook pages, and Google Hangouts. Innovation abounds online for educators. Lead Learners distinguish themselves online, showing, "Yes, I not only want to do it *this* way but also want to share it!" Telling the story of "This is how I do it" fosters growth for educators. The success that results is a powerful part of professional branding for educators that in turn builds the positive perception of schools.

The need to build a positive brand presence begins with you and your recognition of brand value as a tool for school improvement. As soon as your brand is developed, it touches the community. Your sharing of this persona will result in attention. Your brand will get people talking. When it comes time to turn to branding the institution, your own brand will motivate and inspire your staff and coworkers as well as colleagues nearby, and even may reach across the globe. Your brand success is amplified in a way that others can appreciate, connect to and replicate. Your personal professional brand tells stakeholders what you stand for as a leader. It inspires others to create their brand, and powers the creation of a school brand. From logos and mascots to tweets and hashtags, a positive brand presence tells the real story of a school. The positive brandED school presence begins with you. It clearly articulates to stakeholders what to expect from your district, school, and you as a leader. This promise builds not only precious support but also invaluable relationships.

CAPTURING YOUR UNIQUE PERSONAL PROFESSIONAL BRAND

The work of professional brand building at a personal level is highly reflective. Start with a core belief. Ask yourself what you stand for and who you are, and try to reduce the belief to one word to get started. Find one word to communicate the feeling of your brand. CBS journalist Lee Woodruff, the wife of the nearly fatally injured reporter, Bob Woodruff, has a personal brand of *resilience* that she brings to her complete brand image. All her work, and relationships are informed by one word that came out of living through trauma and then inspiring a national wounded-warrior community.

Finding your own one-word brand may not come as clearly to you as it came to Lee Woodruff. To create a flow for this activity, challenge yourself and write a one-page reflection on your prospective brand. Put it away for a day, then edit it to a half page. Take another day and keep that half page in mind as you go through a school day. Go back to that page and see if you can't identify one word that encapsulates your stance as you move through a typical day. What are you trying to convey? Many of us know that the Volvo brand comes down to one word, *safety*. Imagine the sorting out it took to identify that one distinguishing word that has become an iconic hallmark for that company. Spend some time finding your one word. It is at the center of your educator brand.

TRYING OUT YOUR PERSONAL PROFESSIONAL BRAND

With your one-word identifier established, you can move more deeply into branding yourself. How will you further communicate this word? Where can you share this one-word presence? Which digital platforms are you comfortable with as you begin? Where can you demonstrate your one-word brand offline? Are traditional channels easier for you? Keep in mind that face-to-face sharing of your one-word brand can happen over the course of any day in casual and professional moments of your workday. Early "brand you" adopters have tried these brand activities on for size:

- Use your brand in one word in meetings and in introductions as you share the idea of brandED.

- Share your journey of developing your brand. Take on the tool of SWOT analysis described in Conversation 2. Include your one-word brand. Share the SWOT with your peers and trusted advocates to discover more about brand you.

- Talk to student stakeholders in classrooms about your brand word and ask them to come up with their own one-word descriptor. Encourage teachers to use this in their classroom instruction as a way of getting to know their students.

- Add your brand word to existing school channels, such as in announcements. Include it in your email signature.

- Choose a social media outlet (Pinterest, a blog, Twitter, Instagram) to communicate that you are in a brand-building process, and highlight your one-word brand in posts, even as a hashtag (e.g., #spark #amplifier #learner).

When you set up a profile around your growing brand persona on any social platform, be as careful as if you were writing a will. This isn't skywriting that fades. These words last. They should communicate powerfully. Building a brand allows you to reveal only what you are comfortable with sharing to an audience. Your authentic self can be presented in a way that isn't intrusive. As educators set up profiles, some include personal references and other don't. Find your comfort zone for this new transparency. Let your profile reflect your core values and the values of your school or district.

As you add your brand to more digital platforms, make sure that your personal professional presentation looks and sounds consistent. Before you take on a full profile on LinkedIn, experiment with the short profile that is part of the range of social media platforms. Start with Twitter or Instagram. These offer a bridge to promoting yourself more openly as a brand persona, yet because they are quite limited in text, you can easily build on your one-word brand with a few key descriptors. Use the same defining elements in every profile so as not to confuse your audience. Be consistent in your identifying hashtags. Use the same photo across platforms. Change your look? Change that photo! Keep checking in on your profiles quarterly to make sure they represent you, and make updates. You don't have to share your favorite color or where you spent last summer as you build your brand on LinkedIn, Facebook, and Twitter. For credibility, use real details and facts that are appropriate for the platform. Use what you think will define you. Add some personality and a human touch that can form connection with the audience. Reference hobbies, books, movies, sports, or family life if you want to enhance your profile. Kevin Carroll, a New Jersey principal you will meet in the next short story, has a model Twitter profile. He can be your guide. Kevin shares his genuine voice by specifically stating that he is the author of his posts.

> Principal @WaldwickWHS (NJ) I am passionate about learning, education, technology and leadership. Father of two amazing boys. #OwnitWHS My tweets are my own.

THE LEADERSHIP RETURN ON BUILDING YOUR BRAND

BrandED educators have an opportunity to create a new leadership presence for themselves. Build on what has worked for you to date, and focus on new aspects of leading that come from your understanding of brand awareness. The positive response you receive from audiences who engage with your personal professional brand builds rapport, which is important to sustaining your brand. The more connectivity your unique brand brings through engagement, the more you can demonstrate authenticity and build trust for developing a whole-school brand. The increased connectivity with stakeholders that brand building brings will show you a return on your investment. The time you put into the effort of crafting a unique, connective personal professional brand becomes part of your continuous professional development. Personal professional brands may come down to one word, but they are continually refreshed around the connections that attention to brand brings. The active development around brand always brings new discoveries and fresh thinking.

Introspective questions can prompt this new thinking as you further elaborate your professional brand. Ask yourself, "What can I do for others as I share who I am?" Think beyond your own needs; think about generosity, along the lines of Adam Grant's work (discussed in Conversation 2). Keeping in the flow of the Seligman (2012) dashboard elements described in Conversation 2—positive emotions, engagement, relationships, meaning, and achievement—helps you toward being genuinely perceived as a trusted innovator.

The pace for developing a personal professional brand will vary among leaders. After recognizing brand as a valuable leadership tool and creating early signals about personal professional brand, you may be comfortable taking your personal professional brand "on the road" for a test drive. There is not a strict timeline for that moment. When you are clear in your core message and feel confident in sharing this for the perception of stakeholders, the time will be right to begin building brand mastery. Your new leadership brand can be quickly displayed through visual communication. Videos, pictures, and infographics can be found on free platforms and used to visually represent your brand on the digital and social channels you select. If you are ready to be transparent, you can share your brand in an instant, and you'll reap the returns quickly. Your community is engaged and perceptive online—and they are welcoming engagement. As you begin your journey to storyteller-in-chief, you start with your own narrative. Your brand well-being—the strong appearance of your persona and developing mastery—is visible to anyone who sees your own personal professional branding process unfold, and you will gain not only "likes" but also new leadership respect from across the community of stakeholders.

A BrandED Short Story: Stepping Into Promotion

Kevin Carroll is an early adopter of a personal professional brand that continually powers his brandED leadership and genuine commitment to the development of his New Jersey high school's brand. This Waldwick High School principal, known as @WHS_Principal on Twitter, messages across ever-evolving channels, communicating and engaging with his stakeholders every day.

(continued)

Through Kevin's principal's blog, he builds pride and community. Using text and video highlights of the stories of his #WarriorNation, Kevin promotes his growing school brand in a personal, inviting way (K. Carroll, personal communication, 2016). He's a natural at promotion and sees the activity as a leader's responsibility, one that is absolutely necessary for administrative professional development in the 21st century. With confidence that comes from a strong personal brand, Kevin creatively engages beyond his school website and his principal's blog. Innovation continues through his staff blog (Flipped Faculty Meetings), an engaging school YouTube channel (www.youtube.com/user/WaldwickHS), and his ventures into the Periscope streaming community.

Look for Kevin using his UBV to launch each school year through his engaging videos. A principal on a skateboard giving a school tour? That's this energized brandED leader in action. At the root of Kevin's commitment to brand is his mission to create relationships. Building connections and engaging the community aren't a one-way sales mission. In true brandED educator spirit, Kevin finds that promotion of brand can lead to enriched, reflective thinking that yields new ventures into social, digital, and face-to-face communication—all wins for his stakeholder community.

Kevin sees the power of brand everywhere—even in the physical design of his school. He sees material elements that can support sharing and communication. Beyond his schoolhouse door, he builds his personal brand at conferences, spreading the word about Waldwick High School and sharing what #OwnitWHS is all about. Kevin Carroll models a risk-taking stance that challenges the idea that schools change slowly in our new age. One look at his back-to-school archives online, and you will be inspired to build the best personal professional brand you can and to take it on the road to highlight your loyal community.

BRAND YOURSELF FOR AUTHENTIC PERCEPTION

Building a unique brand around yourself is about discovering your value. If you chose to invest in a SWOT analysis as a leader, you gained insights that inform your brand development. You recognized your strengths and opportunities that can inform your professional value. The SWOT can help you find your unique voice. It is your signature, one that you want people to respond to in a genuine exchange. Because the first impressions of a brand are often hard to change, avoid being misunderstood. Find "validators" as you create your personal professional brand. You don't have to run a focus group as business brands do, but get feedback. Ask the validators—close friends, colleagues, and family members—to help you focus on yourself so that you can promote yourself confidently. This may be uncomfortable, but it's a necessary part of conveying capable brandED leadership.

In *No One Understands You and What to Do About It,* Columbia University's Heidi Grant-Halvorson (2015) lays out the challenges of being perceived by others. Without careful thought and study, we tend to imagine that people perceive us as we see ourselves. Not so. You'd be surprised to know how much of who we think we are is actually lost when we communicate with others. According to Grant-Halvorson, "Perceivers make automatic, effortless assumptions on the basis of your behavior" (p. 60).

Find the confidence to move to the next level of growth. Think about forming a plan for brandED. When you adopt this more strategic mindset, your strategy comes from your own consistent brand that you have crafted carefully. Return to the PERMA model in Conversation 2 and see brand in connection to developing the elements of well-being. Are you confident in your "brand you product" as a component of leadership presence? Will it inspire well-being needed to create followers for your work? An accurate perception of your brand is vital to growing brandED on a schoolwide scale. Push further to find your core and ensure that you are perceived as you want to be viewed. Help yourself into that confidence by writing down four nonnegotiable elements about yourself that are going to be part of your personal professional brand. Seeing it in writing makes an impression. Share these statements with your validators to check the fit.

Having a brand helps you manage your own reputation as a leading educator as you guide your institutional brand. Commit to maintaining brand daily, online and in real time. How to add to your growing confidence? According to recognized brand expert William Arruda (2013), branding starts by figuring out what *you* want to do. You have to find your passion. Define a passion for your education life and your life in general as you begin, and make those passions clear in your new brand profile. The best way to bring that passion to the public is through a mission statement about yourself as an educator.

FIRST STEPS FOR RELATING

Recent findings from the Harvard Business School (Zenger & Folkman, 2015) address the need for leaders to recognize that how they are perceived by those they lead may be different from how they perceive themselves. That is a disconnect that negatively effects organizations. What perceptions are already out there about you in the community? Are they reflective of your core brand? How can you build a more connective and authentic perception so that any potential disconnects in perception do not create negativity around your brandED effort?

As you become more aware of the personal professional profile you want to share, think about how this brand will build relationship success. You must focus on creating messages that resonate with future partners.

To create a persona that will be clearly perceived, challenge yourself to write a very short mission statement that you will use for your public networking. A mission statement in business is defined as "a statement by the organization regarding its purpose and what it wants to accomplish in the larger environment" (Armstrong, 2015, p. 39). This is a first step to building a mission: Create a short statement introducing yourself and your school's purpose. This is not the introduction that business-people present in their elevator pitch. Your introductory brandED mission statement pushes you to reflect: What is your professional purpose? What do you want to share about your school brand in the larger macroenvironment of education? You are telling a short story on your feet when you say, "I'm [name and title], and I'm dedicated to collaborative partnerships for a school that is dedicated to [purpose]" as you introduce your brandED self; you are not selling a product.

Perception of your brand becomes clear as you build relationships for your school with a remarkable brand mission statement (Figure 3.1).

Once you have reflected and created a short statement, tighten up your first thoughts by working on this exercise. It results in an invisible compass for yourself that can guide you day to day.

1. Write a short, two-line mission statement that will introduce you in professional and personal settings. Be plain spoken, not lofty or full of eduspeak or jargon.

2. Include whom you want to serve or how you want to help. Use some prompts to stimulate the development of your mission statement: Whom do I serve? What do I believe? What's at my core? What's my responsibility in being a good steward of my school brand?

3. Sketch a strategy for introducing this mission statement to your colleagues in real time, also ensuring that it can be shared digitally

4. Test the statement on validators and those who will form your collaborative brandED team.

Ready yourself to use your mission statement in a real-time handshake or a virtual one. To see if you've created a fitting brand, go back to the field of psychology. Keep perception and the *primacy effect* in mind, meaning that stakeholders' first impression of you will be the most memorable. Your brand will be continuously perceived in digital and real-time engagements. But it also continuously forms a first impression

Figure 3.1 Elevator Speech vs. BrandED Leader Mission Statement

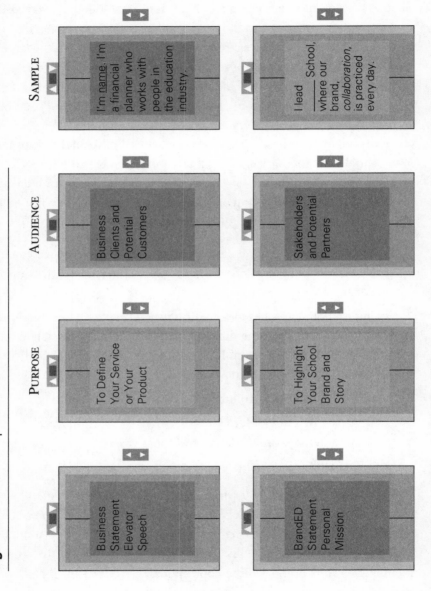

	PURPOSE	AUDIENCE	SAMPLE
Business Statement Elevator Speech	To Define Your Service or Your Product	Business Clients and Potential Customers	I'm name. I'm a financial planner who works with people in the education industry.
BrandED Statement Personal Mission	To Highlight Your School Brand and Story	Stakeholders and Potential Partners	I lead ___ School, where our brand, *collaboration*, is practiced every day.

for many stakeholders online and in real time. Get feedback on the primacy effect of your mission statement. Are you conveying yourself accurately in an instant? As you work, do some simple math and make it your goal for the following equation to be true:

$$\text{Your self-impression} = \text{How people perceive you}$$

You need to make that equation true for yourself first, before taking on the school brand in this equation. Feel confident in your work toward creating a solid personal professional brand that represents you.

Continuing your brand transparency journey, you may want to approach the digital landscape and pick out some virtual "real estate": identify a domain online where you can actually register yourself with a name, either your own, if it's available, or with an authentic brand descriptor. A search on Twitter can introduce you to other educators with creative brand handles, such as Megan M. Allen, 2010 Florida Teacher of the Year, known on Twitter as @Redhdteacher. Your handle helps you identify yourself to the tribe you will be building. If you want your voice to reach out through the social media professional landscape, be ready with a few pieces of brand collateral that describe who you are in a transparent way. A mission statement is one of them. Complement that text with some photos. As you develop a brand flow, you'll grow your brand presence and relate to stakeholders across many channels with a genuine message. More adventurous brandED leaders may even consider the "real estate" of an online portfolio that shows further leadership personality. Leaders can create a brand presence on storytelling publishing platforms like Canva, Visage, Storied, Atavist, Fabl, or Dunked. Posting photos and written content that shows your personal professional status, including your mission statement and other relevant artifacts, helps elevate the authentic perception of "brand you." As you develop a brand flow, you'll grow your brand presence and relate to stakeholders across many channels with your growing knowledge of sharing your genuine leadership brand.

GROWING VALUE IN YOUR BRANDED SELF

You've grown your personal professional brand from one word to a short mission statement that can be part of your online profile and face-to-face networking. Now you need to value that statement through continual use. A brandED mission statement is a piece of professional marketing collateral that will signal your commitment to your own brand and help you inspire others' growth. You can repurpose your personal professional brandED mission statement in a variety of ways. As you move to forge new relationships, you need an engaging introduction for yourself and your school or district that you will use as you build your network. Remember, we are different from businesspeople who wield elevator speeches. Educators go deeper to show their passion for their school and work as they form connections for their schools. Keep marketing thought leader Seth Godin's advice in mind when he tweeted out, "If you can't state your position in eight words, you don't have a position." He charges us to be clear. Getting your mission statement into eight words may be a bit of a stretch, but work to distill it down to what drives your passion as an educator.

Work from the giving, storytelling perspective of brandED and create a bank of short mission statements for your personal professional brand. Remember to ask yourself, "How do I want to be perceived?" Remain in the flow for building your personal professional brand using additional brandED perception builders:

1. Email your trusted colleagues and tell them of your personal professional brand journey. Include your one-word descriptor and mission statement.

2. Invite validators to a follow-up in a conversation about brand. Do this repeatedly to comfortably establish your brandED narrative.

3. Place your short brandED mission statement in the signature of your email and refresh it as you grow as a brandED leader.

4. Check for consistency as you start any sharing of the brand across multiple platforms.

Part Two: Be the BrandED Storyteller-in-Chief

You've committed to a personal professional brand-building effort and have an initial personal professional brand presence, and you have delved into your passion for education by developing a mission statement. These steps will move you toward institutional brand building with the team you have selected to help you define the institutional brand image, promise, and result. A professional test of your new brand occurs when you begin to gather dedicated ambassadors for your effort as a brandED team. Your brand must inspire supporters to create the school brand and lead the strategy to implement it. When you share your brand and tell your story, you are ready to lead as the storyteller-in-chief.

THINK "BRANDED LEAD"

The title of CBO, chief brand officer, reflects a relatively new business role, someone who oversees the total brand and marketing mix for a company (Gunelius, 2008). The brandED adaptation of this role is found in the title storyteller-in-chief, which fits for schools. In this role, a leader employs a distributed leadership model for school development. Unlike the CBO, a brandED collective works as a team of stakeholders in a shared leadership process. This supports what Jahana Hayes, 2016 National Teacher of the Year, describes in a CBS TV interview as needed "community service" to schools. Stakeholders from the community take on the shared role of service providers to the school (King, Rose, & O'Donnell, 2016). A brandED collective creates that form of community service as it builds a school brand. The distributed model of leadership is a match for brand building. A Bain & Company article cites this collaborative leadership activity as one powerful way to fight against fragmentation of school improvement efforts (Bierly, Doyle, & Smith, 2016). As the brandED storyteller-in-chief employing a distributed model, you define, embrace, orchestrate, and model attention to brand consistency.

In the macro-environment of mandates for your school community, there are many initiatives that can be sheltered by an overarching strategy. BrandED is a unifying endeavor, which makes it a match for shared leadership activity.

UNDERSTAND THE ASSETS OF A BRANDED COLLECTIVE TEAM

Innovation thrives in a climate that removes the fear of failure. Your skill at using your personal professional brand and your actions as storyteller-in-chief will support your search for a team. As you form this collective team, put fearlessness on the list of qualities shared by your early adopters. The words of Thomas Edison say it all: "I have not failed. I've just found 10,000 ways that won't work." Have the courage to accept that the road to brandED might not be without its moments of challenge. If you have done an honest SWOT analysis, you are prepared for that occurrence. Model acceptance for the team you are building, and in designing the collaborative, seek others who have the quality of acceptance and tolerance. Allowing people to have the safety of failing is vital, especially when no one at the planning table possesses a master's degree in marketing. That won't matter, because you have shown how a brand can be built, and the combined talents of those you draw together will create harmony. BrandED leaders quickly learn that they don't need an MBA to develop a brand plan. A collaborative stakeholder team possessing diverse brand assets can produce the desirable brand-building result.

In business, internal divisions provide particular assets, such as data analysis, creative content, financial acumen, technological support, and communication power, which are necessary when a company sets to the task of building a brand. Business internal departments work together to develop a product. In a brandED adaptation, we focus not on the sale of a product but on the systemic delivery of a narrative of the school, a new form of qualifying our value to an audience. We can use the model of a team possessing a range of desirable assets to convey that value to stakeholders. Our collective team isn't working in separate divisions; brandED unifies. We work collaboratively to build and deliver a school brand.

Adapting a successful process of business brand development to fit a collective educator team is based on finding early brand ambassadors who have the high level of skills and talents that also exist in Madison Avenue creative branding teams. Our school stakeholder community is full of talented individuals who may be capably using these skills in service to their personal or business brand development. Go on the hunt for your diverse team. The desired assets listed in Figure 3.2 can lead you to your dream team for brand development that would make a marketing manager proud. These individuals will be the first group in the community to get "up close and personal" with the personal professional brand you have built for yourself. Survey the range of assets that people bring to a brand project. You can determine more assets, identify more skills, according to your own leadership situation, but Figure 3.2 identifies some necessary skills that can guide you as you begin your search process.

Figure 3.2   Assets of the BrandED Collaborative Team

Human Capital Assets	Social Capital Assets	Brand Assets
Business Experience	Tolerance for Risk	Networker
Social Awareness	Culturally Savvy	Curiosity
IT Experience	Social Media Savvy	"Non-Sales" Seller
Builder	Diversity Minded	Presentational
Global Perspective	Collaborative	Public Relations
Manager	Relational	Authentic
Content Creator	Targeted	Psychology
Visual Content Creator	Forecaster	Design
Relations	Giving	
Communicator	Well-Being	
Assessment/Benchmarking	Trusted	

Some of the people you seek for your team may be your validators; others may be new stakeholder "finds." The group collectively brings a variety of needed communication and branding skills. Some offer unique value in human capital, the hard skills that supply the brand messaging, the communication skills of writing, editing, journalistic ability, and copywriting; technology and digital acumen; administration skills; and management ability. Some prospects possess social capital, the soft skills that help develop relationships for delivering the brand message: community awareness, networking ability, well-developed relational ability, and influencer capacity. Finally, there are those who possess natural branding capital and marketing savvy, who have either worked in positions that required marketing experience or have been entrepreneurial. You need a rich mix of all of these skills for the team. As you build, enlist people who are digitally competent and those who are social media savvy. Find the wordsmiths. Find people who are comfortable with face-to-face communication, people who can analyze, and people who can express feelings and are strong presenters. Create a team that has many complementary dimensions. A collective for brandED is a bit like a mosaic. Put the pieces together as you build a team whose members can inspire each other with their unique abilities. Find collaborators who are open-minded, inquiry-based thinkers and who see that a school brand can be the unifying voice and connecting message for many school initiatives. Your brandED strategic team is collaborative of leaders who use human, social, and brand talents to create the brandED Strategic Plan.

THE BRANDED LEADERSHIP COLLECTIVE

Your collaborative is a design team—a set of diverse, unique brandED colleagues from across every segment of your stakeholder community, starting with the kids, who are the reason why we advance brand. The group will grow in confidence to become ambassadors who extend your personal professional brand and who design the school's brand. They collaborate around an exciting innovation, a brand journey for school improvement. They have a broad range of skills and styles for navigating the relational, traditional, and digital channels. Inspired by your own brand and leadership, they will be in the zone with you. Your mixed team of creative and analytical people will bring the image and promise of the new school brand to the community. These early adopters of brandED engage the school's "audiences" by creating a compelling school brand and strategy that demonstrates **value**, that connects with **emotion**, that communicates an **awareness**, and that translates into **belief** in a brand. No matter where the school is in its development, the recognized brand tenets of value, emotion, awareness, and belief set the stage for creating the school's most important brand **promise**. Your team will be responsible for the internal development of the brand and the external communication of the core school brand effort.

CONSOLIDATING FOR A STRONG BRAND MESSAGE

As your collective's work begins, you will want to tell your personal professional brand story and describe the crafting of your own brand. Share your "mentors." Introduce the virtual influencers mentioned in Conversation 2, your digital bookshelf that shaped your thinking about brand. You present the unifying message of brandED as an overarching message, a promise, that fits an entire community—in effect, what experts call a "parent brand" that is an umbrella encompassing the school's true brand message. Bringing groups together for consensus is challenging, especially when many disparate programs, initiatives, and projects already have fragmented the school landscape. To assure understanding and embracement among potential members of a community, it is important to recognize the common thread of a brand as it brings together a community around image, promise, and result.

To make the move toward a strong brand profile and honor the stakeholders who will bring different assets and perspectives to the conversation and who can create a unifying message, brandED leaders explain that a strong overarching school brand allows the community to fit many initiatives into a parent brand, what the school stands for. Businesses have done this well for years; they have used the common brand attributes of a parent brand and connected them with the brand community in a way that honors their needs.

Car companies, for example, are brilliant in using this model. The Ford brand is familiar to all as an automotive power. Ford's "parent" brand is comprehensive in the world of autos, with an overarching theme of toughness and the spirit of the USA. Under this umbrella are different sub-brands, such as family cars and trucks, that carry Ford's brand to different segments of the audience. Every model works out of the Ford company's promise of a reliable brand, but each segment has its own story and profile as a connected sub-brand. Think like an educator's Henry Ford as you design a school brand with one symbolic brand message that can unify your disparate school efforts.

In Conversation 4, your collective team designs a promise that benefits the school, one that reflects all stakeholder voices. Your team develops positioning, the perception of the school brand throughout the segments of the community, that helps connect stakeholders to the brand. Developing a strategic plan will include identifying segments of your community. You must know your stakeholders and be able to describe them. This knowledge may eventually lead to small tailored messages that fit the sub-brands of school activity helping in the transition to an institutional brand. This personalizes the brand and puts it in close contact with the range of audiences that perceive the brand message. These threads are connected to the overarching school vision: Anything from inquiry-based teaching and portfolio assessment to character development, antibullying programs, and teacher assessment can connect to the parent brand, and the stories of those initiatives contribute to the brandED narrative presence. In short, all school efforts must connect to the core brand's image, promise, and result.

A consolidated, strong brand message needs support from the start. Stewardship, the maintenance of the school brand, will be woven into the mission of designing the brand. Under your guidance, the team will build with an eye toward joining you as the "protector of the school brand." Team members proudly develop, share, and showcase the brand in online, print, social media, and word-of-mouth channels. The brandED team not only builds and monitors the magic of the brand image but also will seek ways to target and measure the impact of identified brandED goals that are developed in the brandED Strategic Plan.

A BrandED Short Story: Robert Zywicki Shares the Magic

Meet Dr. Robert Zywicki. This innovative superintendent of the Weehawken Township School District in New Jersey knows that it's all about the students he serves, and he has built a personal professional brand presence that attests to this belief. Building relationships with the student population of school stakeholders, he leads from a personal professional brand perspective, one that he shares with the entire community (R. Zywicki, personal communication, September 2016).

Zywicki's personal professional brand is powered by his authentic brand positioning. As the father of four, he places himself in the shoes of the parents of his students and promotes his personal professional brand from the foundation of being a father. He believes that this approach goes a long way in building trust across all stakeholder segments. Trust is the foundation of any successful brand campaign. When he sets a target to know every one of his students, he does this with the eye of a parent. He is the protector of the brand and a conscientious steward. It comes naturally for Rob to embrace and build relationships, whether with the president of his board or the parent waiting at the door of the schoolhouse. He works every day to prove his resolve. Reading his school's mission statement and seeing the collected hashtags that embody the vision of the

(continued)

school make it apparent that there is strategy behind the "brand-EDness" of his efforts to connect.

> The Weehawken Public School District is a progressive, student centered community of learners in pursuit of collective and individual excellence. To this end, we will implement systems and structures that ensure all students will achieve at their maximum academic potential, develop values that embrace civic responsibility and hone skills to adapt to a dynamic global society.

Rob believes in accessibility and openness as he creates change, and his brand reflects this. Follow him on Twitter, Instagram, and LinkedIn, where he demonstrates his commitment. He reaches for digital tools to move beyond the school walls, knowing that not everyone in the community is sending students to him. He shares his own brand and that of the Weehawken School District with the greater community, locally and even globally.

When Rob engages with the community, he employs his personal professional mission statement and carries a business card that shows his interest in connecting in digital and social media spaces. This relational behavior is seen in the presence he advances in his community as the storyteller and steward of his school brand. Through his engaging blog, The View from Liberty Place, he consistently builds and promotes his leadership presence. The blog is a powerful showcase for his school's brand presence, providing a newsfeed and updates to the entire community. Transparency is on Zywicki's list of communication priorities, and he advises fellow school leaders to demonstrate that transparency in digital time by opening a blog. In real time, his brand is demonstrated in public open meetings and forums. In both online and offline communication channels, Rob demonstrates his expanded version of our suggested one-word brand; in his case, it takes two words: *rigor* and *relevance*.

Rob is strategic in his thinking: He holds himself accountable for results through a strategic district plan that weaves the values of rigor and relevance throughout curriculum, policy, and management decisions. By doing so, he's built and maintained the connection to improved culture, performance, and result that is the essence of a brandED community. Rob says that it's simply about "sharing the magic." Open communication has brought this magic, but his work internally and externally to build relationships shows that the magic comes from a focused dedication. Rob continually looks ahead. New partnerships with universities, and collaboration with nonprofits like OCEARCH (a marine tracker that monitors and studies shark behavior), are results that have brought new richness to Weehawken's curriculum development. The magic happens both in school and outside of the school, thanks to Zywicki's belief in the Weehawken brand, which is one of the foundations of his personal professional mission to the district and guides his developing school brand.

SETTING THE COLLABORATIVE TABLE FOR THE SCHOOL BRAND

Like the brandED leaders in our short stories, Danny Meyer, the successful Shake Shack CEO, speaks passionately about brand engagement. His experience with brand building can inform your own journey as a school leader. His organization is focused on delivering the highest level of customer service. There's a good reason for his company's growth. He teaches his internal team to deliver on brand promise every day. His attention to value, emotion, presence, and belief is tested worldwide. When Meyer's Shake Shack opened in South Korea, his team successfully served about four burgers per minute to his tribe who waited for hours in line to enjoy his renowned Meyer service experience. His success isn't based on magic; it's based on relationship building and on providing a consistently satisfying, valuable experience for his audience. In his book *Setting the Table: The Transforming Power of Hospitality in Business,* Meyer (2008) speaks about the intense drive he has to provide hospitality that goes beyond the scope of business as usual. For Meyer, who debunked the idea of "the customer's always right" as a service mantra, setting the table means creating human connection. His take on service innovation isn't just for restaurateurs.

Meyer's business is built on a few tenets that can directly apply to school brandED leadership. He stresses that organizations have to clearly "know their purpose" and must be able to articulate it to their audience; that isn't an empty activity for his company. All of his employees know why they are in the Shake Shack organization. His internal team observes a second valuable tenet: "Everybody has each other's back." He provides a recognized brand image, and delivers on the promise of providing value to customers. The successful result is rooted in the ability of his internal team to perform at a high level and "to care about each other" as they work together. Meyer puts employees first and understands that when those who serve feel valued and know why they are there, it makes a difference in the service they provide. He enlists the right people onto his internal team and "unleashes" the leader in all members of the group.

BrandED leaders can adapt a bit of Meyer swagger as they assemble their innovative collaborative team that will create a true brand strategy. Like Meyer, use the assets of a brandED collaborative as you deliberately set the table for brand thinking and activity. Find the right people, help them understand why they need to be there, and create affinity so that they care about each other as they collaborate in the zone to create a brand, Commit to developing your internal brand ambassadors. Here are some Meyer-like questions to pose during the first meeting of the complete team:

- Where are we as a school community?
- Why are we here?
- How did we arrive at this point?

- Where could we be if we were "better"?
- How can we get to our new goal?
- What do we need to do to get ready to be the best school possible?
- What ultimately do we want our school brand to convey?

Listening is a most important part of collaborating with the brandED team. Listen to stakeholders as they talk about where they are now, and hear them as they imagine what the school community could look like in the future. They must talk about how it feels to be part of the school's evolution in this digital age of learning. Talk about the **purpose** of the school by talking with the people who are in it every day. What motivates the staff in school every day? What are the kids' purposes? The parents' purposes? The answers to such questions brought out to the public are tied to the brand momentum. They create energy and meaning for developing the brand and awareness of the importance of brand in the school.

Many business brands have missions that can also be part of public conversations. Engage stakeholders in conversations around the school's "big idea." The Revlon company's big idea is a case in point. In a scholarly article on the power of feeling that conveys brand, the authors note how Revlon's big idea connects to emotions: "When Revlon sells perfume, it sells more than the tangible product. It sells lifestyle, self-expression and exclusivity; achievement, success and status; femininity, romance, passion and fantasy; memories, hopes and dreams" (Sadeghi & Tabrizi, 2011, p. 699). We can certainly identify a school's big idea with more authentic connection than a company that's selling beauty products. Why? BrandED leaders own a genuine education heart. We can connect authentically to the emotions that charge our belief and build a promise that distinguishes us based on intangible as well as tangible brand attributes. Thinking about what the school is passionate about fuels the identification of a big idea that will be part of building your school's brandED Strategic Plan. Stakeholders who have a sense of vision and purpose can position school brand in a strategic way.

GETTING OUT AHEAD: COMMUNICATING AS THE STORYTELLER-IN-CHIEF

Leaders who work purposefully and publicly on building their own relationships early in their brand effort offer a new view of transparency to parents and staff. Showcasing the interest in building brand is a genuine form of reputation management. Don't build your school institutional brand alone. First, get out there ahead of the formal team-driven brand-building effort. Create connections and relationships that will make your innovation work. Both internal and external stakeholders need to be aware of the existence of any new plan. The public conversations, questions, and searching for new relationships are important touch-points for communication during brand innovation. The mission—to become a responsive, transparent brandED community through a strategic planning process—is shared early with the community. Get the brandED word out

What educational leader wouldn't agree with the words of David Butler, the head of innovation entrepreneurship for the corporate king of brands, Coca-Cola, as he points to the necessary value of communicating your innovation:

> Forming informal networks, both internally and externally, is key. It's really important to build relationships across a company. In the same way, it's equally important for the company to authentically connect with the community. Being very open and honest with what they're trying to do is key. We've found that once we built this bridge, we've been able to count on a lot of help from the community (and vice versa). As the relationship grows, so does the trust. (Balmaekers, 2014)

On the road to brandED development, school leaders must adapt that business mindset to their growth efforts—they present their own brand value publically and work to make their brand communication change process open and transparent.

In communicating the innovation of brandED internally, you can use another leadership tool called Radical Candor, advanced by Kim Scott, a former Google employee and sought-after management coach, to keep communication focused through consistent and accurate storytelling. The concept of Radical Candor, inspired by Scott's boss, the formidable Sheryl Sandberg of Facebook, focuses on showing leaders how to both "care personally" and "challenge directly" (Scott, 2016).

As an innovating educator, you can adapt this model to keep the brandED internal conversation consistently flowing with the external community. Keep messages about what your brand is about and how it is being developed on the school's radar. Be transparent in giving feedback. School leaders can adapt Ms. Sandberg's process that inspired Ms. Scott's own thinking. Be consistent in communicating the school brand as it is formed through the efforts of your brandED collaborative team. Once brand is built, through transparent cocreation, be confident. Celebrate it, communicate its worth, and don't be afraid to address situations when the emerging brand story is being diluted or misrepresented.

Radical Candor is not a public thing (Kosoff, 2015). It's supportive internal feedback that is delivered face-to-face by those mentoring the new effort. In schools where clear and formative feedback in teacher assessment is present, where assessment programs like Charlotte Danielson's or McREL exist to establish better evaluation feedback, leaders may integrate this direct form of feedback into their brandED professional development. BrandED leaders can aim to use clear feedback with staff as another communication tool to ensure that brand consistency is present and internal brand understanding is clear. Giving feedback helps the internal organization advance the communication of brand to external stakeholders. Once a brand is identified, it is the responsibility of the internal team of a school to know the brand and deliver it daily. Much as we saw in the Danny Meyer story, the internal structure supports the messaging to the public. Brand communication is part of a teacher's improvement plan in our digital age.

Brand power flows through the school community. A brandED leader listens to the voices of the school brand family—kids and parents, teachers, and the community—to show caring about the brand of the school and how it is maintained:

- Convey regular and clear messages about the evolving school brand to every segment of the audience.
- Gather grassroots feedback through brand ambassadors and collective members to quickly get information about the brand as you roll it out.
- Use more formal ways to listen to brandED implementation: surveys, social media listening, or brand town halls.
- Invite the team and other stakeholders to communicate at new levels of transparency as they listen for evidence of the brand and then identify, produce, share, and showcase the school brand across traditional and digital channels.
- Build ongoing relationships for potential positive partnering.
- Be consistent in the message about the value of being brandED. Each member of the community must be able to answer why it's worthwhile.

When you create well-being around the power of brand in a trusted climate, your audience will form a strong attachment to the big idea of your brand. The feelings and emotions that are part of brand development are the glue that sustains positive school impact. The end goal of your brandED strategy is brand loyalty among all stakeholders. A community devoted to an authentic unique brand is powerful. It is a tribe. You may recall that such community power was shown on a global scale in 1985, when Coca-Cola changed its original formula, resulting in historic brand backlash. Even though the company was transparent in its decision to change the brand formula, it totally underestimated the attachment fans had to the original Coke. Maybe you were one of those who pushed back. That's the kind of loyalty you want to result from your brand-building effort. You want your tribe to speak. In the end, Coke was forced by its own tribe to change the formula back—in 79 days! This is the type of community you want to be engaged with for the long-term life of your school brand, a community in a state of brand well-being and harmonious flow. You want a tribe that knows and passionately loves your school brand, a community that you and your team serve with pride.

ENGAGING AN AUDIENCE IS CRUCIAL TO BRANDED LEADERS

As the school brand emerges, school leaders must be vigilant about what marketers have discovered in the last decade. The powerful 21st-century game changer for true brand awareness: engagement of the customer or, in the school equivalent, audience engagement. We don't serve customers in education, but we have an audience of stakeholders, and we have to let them know that they matter. When you meet with your school collaborative to create the school brand, include discussions about the school audience by asking a few pointed questions:

- Who makes up our audience? What do we know about them?

- How do we positively engage our stakeholders in the story of our work to help schools succeed? What are the innovative ways to make audiences trust the unique school brand we offer?

- Are there differences in the segments of our audience that we must be aware of in our work? How are these audiences' needs different? Do they perceive our school presence differently? How do we approach them through consistent, tailored messages?

The answers to these questions are essential to brand messaging. You must truly know your community and on a deeper level, a level that reveals their need for engagement. Thanks to the social and digital world, we get more data on a daily basis about our community than ever before. The image, the brand created by the school for an audience, is based on authenticity and trust and must find its home in the hearts and minds of the stakeholders. Your brand must engage people positively in your community of teaching and learning. Schools are in the service business in the year 2017. Knowing the stakeholders who are in a trusting exchange with you is of prime importance. Take time to find out who they are by using offline and online channels to listen to the conversations that surround the school. Engaging with stakeholders in well-developed strategic messaging and responsive exchanges is key. The behavior of your stakeholders as consumers will make this job of knowing them easy.

Today's school audiences are "spoiled" by digital communication. They have free 24/7 communication access to brands they depend on in their lives. Our stakeholders are people who are used to being courted: seen, engaged, mentioned, and liked in their own daily brand experiences, online and in their real-time lives. BrandED leaders recognize that serving these digitally driven engagement realities is part of their job description in a digital age. Leaders must respond to these needs with transparency. They must invite the audience into brand awareness, partner with them in brand development, and enlist them into brand loyalty. As they do this, successful leaders find ways to make stakeholders feel connected and engaged. Make rapport building that leads to deeper relationships part of early conversations about brand. As you build your team of brand builders, identify people who know that relationships must be built and valued. Enlist individuals who know how to do this, and offer support to others who want to grow in this way. It's important for leaders to stress the need to provide engagement and connecting, and not to be seen as distancing to stakeholders in this age of connection.

The more that leaders connect to the emotional benefits and well-being sought by school audiences as they become aware of brand change, the more that schools can deliver on their genuine promise. A school promise that articulates tangible and intangible attributes that benefit the community will power a brandED effort. The collective team works to ensure that the school brand can be engaging for stakeholders each day. The audience can't be kept in the dark; these stakeholders must see how a brand sustains the school's mission, vision, and values.

SCHOOL DIGITAL TRANSPARENCY LEADS TO REMARKABLE PARTNERING

Partnerships are of tremendous importance today. The visible result of a thoughtful brandED strategy can attract school partners; transparency engages audiences. Storytelling and messaging improve the prospect of increased resourcing opportunities. Consistent relational behavior presented through digital content will grow a brand's access externally and make partnering possible. BrandED plans use the power of digital and social connection to locate and connect to resources and sponsorship partners. A strong brand presence can ensure that potential sponsorship partners will take notice of a school's story that is consistently told online. An active and well-rounded online presence shown across social media platforms is a digital storytelling footprint for connecting to partners. Once a leader adopts a personal professional brand and presents a profile that reflects authentic leadership, the leader's presence opens the door to connection.

As a crafted school brand becomes an essential part of the school's operations, projects to reach sponsors become reality. The school brand sparks a creative effort to seek valued new relationships. A strong brand presence can grow contacts in many ways. A well-defined school brand can be linked to volunteer appeals and to social responsibility efforts by the many external associations and businesses that look to show their ethical responsibility to children and schools.

Beyond business opportunities to partner, a connecting brand can further the engagement of alumni in exciting ways, capturing their brand loyalty and helping them remain connected to the school brand they have experienced themselves. On both levels, having a brand that touches people's emotions is desirable. Social media and digital tools play a role in getting the attention of sponsors. With an investment of a few minutes a day, a school community can tell its brand story to the world. New advances in storytelling platforms are being rolled out in quick succession. The recent development of new video platforms, including the Instagram addition of video to its popular Instagram Stories, offers more ability for schools to present themselves—to broadcast their brand—and gain attention for partnerships. In a few months, new features will surely abound to make the storytelling experience more connecting. Schools must follow this trend to attract attention of sponsors and partners. The strength of the strategically built school brand makes launching successful audience partnerships a reality in this vibrant visual world.

"Tribal" thought leader Seth Godin (2008) points to the need for leaders to make a brand "remarkable" and so memorable that people are talking, remarking positively about the brand on a regular basis. People have to talk glowingly about your brand in order for it to be sustained (Giang, 2012). BrandED leaders, along with an energized team, must cocreate what is remarkable about the school. When people are repeatedly remarking—sharing, liking, positively commenting, and promoting the school's story—potential partners notice. They want to be connected. Through a strong brand presence that uses every avenue to tell your school story, resourcing opportunities can increase.

CREATING A DEEPER BRANDED LEADER MISSION STATEMENT

As you feel more connected to the personal professional profile you are sharing, and look to being more remarkable as you lead, think about growing your developing personal professional brand to advance further relationship success. You are heading for an entrepreneurial stance as a leader. You can go deeper with your vision of a mission.

Find a quiet moment. Create a more in-depth reflection of your mission statement by writing a leadership statement that expands the essence of the short mission statement you crafted earlier. This will be a more developed statement that personalizes the experience of living your new personal professional brand as you lead. Because brand building is a process involving continued awareness and expression, even as you are beta testing your own new brand, continue to work on your brand development. Continued self-reflection is necessary. Build a more authentic BrandED leadership mission statement as you reflect on questions such as these:

What am I learning from developing my brand?

Is my professional purpose changing as I guide the community?

What do I now want to accomplish in the larger macroenvironment of education as I become a brandED leader?

A deeper perception of your own brand becomes clear for you as you build more and more new relationships. You will understand what's working and what people are responding to. Developing a remarkable, reflective brand mission statement, one that captures your passion and vision, can grow your professional power. When you compose that statement, this activity completes your journey, from coming up with a brand word and developing a brief statement to crafting a full reflection of your mission at this moment. Invest in this activity and find places to share this thinking. The more robust reflection builds your persona beyond the short social description you may use in meetings and at public events to test your personal professional brand. The leadership mission statement goes beyond the public but limited text profiles that you place online. It signals your own valuing of continuous brand development. This brand-building leadership activity enables you to connect with the core beliefs that you will live by in the transparency of a digital world. Extending your personal professional mission statement can extend your brand into a vision for what you want to be in your promotional role as brandED leader and storyteller-in-chief.

The exercise yields a core of brand beliefs that function as an invisible compass that can guide you day-to-day into your future. To accomplish this,

- Write a longer mission statement, with goals that are real and relatable.

- Find an influencer or peer who possesses brand qualities that complement yours, and identify how you would incorporate these qualities into your mission.

- Expand on why your goals are important and describe what they stand for in terms of image, promise, and result.

- Synthesize what you have learned from your virtual team of experts into thoughts about the new understanding and presence you are creating.

- Identify what new learning you want to undertake to sustain your brand.

- Say what your passion is, and set a goal for sharing that passion on a new, far-reaching scale.

- Revisit these questions with a deeper focus: Whom do I serve? What do I believe? What's at my core? What's my responsibility in being a good steward of my school brand?

- Find digital and real-time channels through which to share this mission statement.

- Refresh the statement quarterly and test it on validators.

Part Three: The BrandED Leader as "Edupreneur"

> Your work is going to fill a large part of your life, and the only way to be truly satisfied is to do what you believe is great work. And the only way to do great work is to love what you do.
>
> —*Steve Jobs, cofounder, chairman, and CEO, Apple*

Becoming a brandED leader is something you will love doing. It's based on belief and satisfaction, two critical tenets of brand. As a brandED leader, you'll naturally have something in common with all entrepreneurs: They do what they love, and brandED leaders do the same. Entrepreneurs are dreamers, but they also are doers. Entrepreneurship may be missing from your educator's resume, but taking on a brandED perspective will change that as you experience the rush of an entrepreneurial mindset. It's professionally exhilarating to be brandED, especially at a time when education is dealing with image problems. According to the recent white paper "Teaching the Next Generation," unlike Baby Boomers and Gen X college students, many Millennial college graduates do not see our education profession as viable (Hiler & Erickson Hatalsky, 2014). They characterize it as restrictive and regard it as a profession that attracts average people. This is neither flattering nor true. There are myriad examples of creative, innovative practices that fuel education. That's why brandED can be a call to our youngest educators. The idea of being average fades with a brandED mindset that is fueled by an entrepreneurial, educational spirit—the spirit of an *edupreneur*.

Brand strategy invites educators to take on innovative behavior that impacts their organizational culture and improves schools. This exciting new trend is taking root through disruptive innovation in the workplace. Google rules in the corporate business space with its contractual charge to employees to be innovative and entrepreneurial. The company's "20% time" policy, which encouraged employees to spend 20% of their time thinking about anything at all that might help Google, was credited with bringing many new Google products to market (He, 2013). BrandED leaders who behave in the disruptive ways of entrepreneurs are in step with organizational thinking by advancing original, innovative ideas that bring measurable results (Trish Rubin, 2016). An educational leader inspired with an approach like brandED can tap into creativity and can power start-up juices in the organization that benefit the school.

Pursuing an excellent brand strategy as a leadership goal opens the door to edge-dweller innovation. Consider the MIT Sloan School of Management's model, the Six Building Blocks of Innovative Culture, as a measure for your edupreneurial brand. The model advances a six-point framework that bolsters your culture for innovating, focusing on organizational values, behaviors, resources, processes, success, and climate (Rao & Weintraub, 2013). These are all elements to consider for innovating and for building your own brandED strategy with your creative team. Reflect on your edupreneurial positioning as you create brandED change. Check back to your leadership mission statement and your reflection on your growth. There's nothing average in this thinking. In his most watched YouTube video, the great Steve Jobs pointed to the top innovators of the world who lived passionately through innovation, despite being called the "crazy ones" (Jobs, 1999/2013). BrandED leaders can join the ranks of innovators like Ford, Einstein, and Jobs.

Act as an edupreneur. Model your newly minted personal professional brand, a brand that you continually strive to have perceived as an authentic leadership brand. This edupreneurial persona, one based on openness, can creatively cultivate new relational value and garner trust among members of your community. Your new personal professional brand grows your school's loyal fan base as you make connections and keep communication top of mind. See what's worked for successful entrepreneurs who've met their own goals, and find a fit for your continuing brandED professional development:

> **Surround yourself with inspiring people.** Relationships matter to edupreneurs. Do this in real time through face-to-face associations and with your closest validators. Use the wealth of TED Talks, webinars, and YouTube content online to get inspired. Follow the hot topics in leadership, communication, and relationship building. Start to follow them online. Connect to Mention and Google Alerts to get tailored feeds and information about those key areas you need in order to increase your own edupreneurship.

> **Get feedback every day.** Talk to people about branding and the innovative climate for school reform. Share how applying a few powerful select business strategies is empowering your school leadership. Test the waters on social media with thoughts, quotes, and content that match the topics you are advancing. See the results from your tribe.

Ask questions. Don't be afraid to ask questions about the new direction you are setting as a brandED leader. Get feedback. Be curious and search for answers. Leverage social media or go with face-to-face conversations. Just ask!

Find happiness. Entrepreneurs work out of a passion. So do edupreneurs. There is joy in innovating.

Connect to a brandED buddy. It's better to have a colleague than to brand yourself and your community alone. Your brandED buddy is your closest validator.

Build your personal professional brand. Work to present yourself with a unique authentic brand; UBV is a key to edupreneurship.

Celebrate every brand benchmark for your school. Talking about big and small tangible accomplishments is part of communicating value. It's the small moments that create big data, the proven results and gains with the community that can complement test score reports and expand the idea of value.

Be a continuous and curious learner. This is a no-brainer for educators. Continue your study in the manner of a trend spotter. Look out—online, in apps, or through print resources—for the latest trends and research in leadership, pedagogy, initiating school change, technology integration, and whatever other tropics inspire you. Search outside your own educational backyard to learn from other disciplines. The digital world allows us to see thousands of bits of information that can be woven into new creative thinking for growing our unique edupreneurial brand.

Work to expand your network. Grow your relationships upward for your community with "reach targets," the great people you aspire to meet with whom you can share the school brand and engage for support. Grow relationships downward with those good people that complement your network. Build relationships with service providers who help students. Talk to bus drivers, crossing guards, security staff—anyone who provides support to the community—about the school brand. Finally, network horizontally with your peers and other leaders in real-time associations, and online through hangouts and chats. Invite them to share their thinking and content about education brand. Promote brandED relationships so that deeper connections can form, leading to cobranding exchange between yourself and other leaders.

Be a writer. Take the time to write about your efforts in becoming a brandED leader. Making visible the thoughts and reflections that are part of the journey can be the first-draft thinking that starts you on the way to sharing your personal professional brand.

Be persistent. Entrepreneurs have the will to carry on; with that same spirit, edupreneurs don't give up. We demonstrate our persistence on a community-wide stage. Belief is an essential part of brand development. Be the chief believer in your school brand by becoming the storyteller-in-chief.

Be patient. Entrepreneurs who are successful have a tendency to wait. Some entrepreneurs are actually procrastinators of the highest degree. Edupreneurs brand at a pace that can ensure their success. Don't rush the process. Focus on the work of your students, staff, and district. In time, the results of your brandED strategy will come to fruition.

Take your brand confidently into the public eye. Use as many channels as you are comfortable with as you promote image, promise, and result for a brandED strategy.

Conversation 3 Tips

- **Plan** for promoting well-being as you develop your innovation with the spirit of an entrepreneur. Psychology continues to play an important part of brandED leadership as you enlist support.
- **Identify** assets that are needed for a brandED change process. Build a brandED collective that possesses a varied set of needed talents for communicating brand.

- **Start** to set the table for change with a fervor for service to the community. Model and develop commitment to being relational and to creating trusted partnerships. Start internally by building relationships with your brand collective.
- **Adopt an edupreneurial stance:** Just as entrepreneurs do, take on calculated, informed risks to break new leadership ground with brandED thinking.
- **Dig into innovation:** The edupreneurial spirit of brand can further an entrepreneurial culture in your school community as you model transparency and draw support for the brandED innovation.

Conversation 3 Reflections

Before holding the public conversation about the need to develop a personal professional brand, think about these questions:

- Have I taken enough time to deeply develop my own personal professional brand presence? Does my management style need to become more representative of my brand ? Am I ready to communicate my new personal professional brand and lead an institutional brand development process?
- Have I shared my new brand with enough trusted people, such as a brandED buddy, or enough validators to check on my brand authenticity? Can I build trust during change and innovation?
- Am I clear on my role as a brandED leader? How will I recruit a brandED team collective? How will I guide the first public conversations about brandED?
- Have I embraced the spirit of entrepreneurship that fuels a brandED strategy and creates a culture for innovation?
- Am I ready to be an edupreneur and create change with my personal professional brand?

Developing Your BrandED Strategic Plan

Conversation 4 marks the formal beginning of the design of your school brand. This is the "roll up your sleeves" time for institutional brand development. Without the hefty price tag for the development of a campaign, your brandED team works creatively using its unique persona and combined stakeholder assets to build the school brand under your guidance. In meetings that feature select tools adapted from the creative world of marketing, the team moves through the step-by-step construction of a purposefully crafted school brand. In the pages that follow, the storyteller-in-chief is supported in guiding the effort. The team works out of a framework called the brandED Drivers. The group's efforts result in a public vehicle, a commitment to school improvement through the development of a brandED Strategic Plan, which is central to the delivery of the school brand, in service to improved school culture, performance, and resources.

> Unless you have absolute clarity of what your brand stands for, everything else is irrelevant.
> —*Mark Baines, global CMO, Kellogg Company*

Part One: The BrandED Drivers

It's time to work on the brandED Strategic Plan.

You've developed your brandED leadership presence and have gathered a design team. You have presented your personal professional brand with transparency. It's time to make brand building a visible process for the entire community of teachers, students, parents, and partners. This is an exciting, innovative part of your new leadership stance as you become both the storyteller and steward of brand development. You are communicating brandED value and guiding the community to sustaining school brand success.

The process of developing a brandED plan is a natural adaptation of the business brand-building process. It has a distinctly different foundation in the reason for its existence, far from the business world of sales. The brandED Drivers help you with the design for cocreative thinking around a strategic brand plan. The brandED Drivers guide the activity of a commitment to school improvement through brand. The drivers are not about not making a sales quota but about making a statement about school quality that can be perceived and celebrated.

You have developed confidence in your ability to facilitate thinking and judgment around brand development. You will set the time to begin brandED Driver conversations. Be prepared to guide the effort by creating smaller patterns and professional brand rituals that develop the muscle for being a brandED leader. Your own repeated testing of your brand helps you build your brandED leadership. Once the "flow" in your day-to-day use of your brand is established in a few daily targets, you will have the confidence to show your community the power of your role as brandED storyteller-in-chief and steward.

DAILY TARGETS CONNECT TO BRANDED DRIVER LEADERSHIP

Genuine engagement and transparency in an ever-changing digital world result from being a focused brandED leader. As in the development of any brand, a long-term plan is needed to assure a brand's maintenance. You will practice stewardship of your own brand early through maintaining daily targets that keep awareness of the promise of the brand strong among the community of stakeholders. Before setting into the activity of developing the institutional brand using the brandED Drivers with your team, look for ways to establish brand awareness every day. Weave the image, promise, and result of your emerging school brand innovation into all meetings where you present your personal-professional brand. Promote the activity of development of brand to the community through daily postings on select digital channels and platforms. Through photos and videos, stimulate engagement by sharing the process of development and a few stories of the brand in action in your school, using the voices of your team.

Set a daily PR goal by promoting the innovation of brandED on your feet, telling stories of brand to stakeholders in face-to-face settings in addition to digital and social opportunities. In these daily meetings, share the consistent messages that brandED can unify many existing and future school improvement efforts. Brand attention improves culture, performance, and resourcing, and that dedicated effort to build brand across the community is always on your radar. Think of internal and external resources that are available. Enlist the help of educators who are posting content on sites like *Edutopia* or *Huffington Post.* Do a search on any state's educational administrative site; look at websites for superintendents' and principals' associations. A short read of their blog content can be repurposed for your own connection to initiatives you are growing. That strategy alone connects you with a community of leaders who can be potential brand buddies.

Be an edge dweller and forecast. Imagine what accountability in your brandED strategy-building process can look like if you set a few specific, measurable, and attainable outcomes to show the power of your branding efforts. Daily targets may include

- Making the time in your schedule to promote your school brand and be consistent in the messaging

- Reinforcing the brand message in quick posts using a variety of social media tools

- Engaging a variety of stakeholders in two-way communication about the brand in real time and online

- Creating and curating authentic content to share that aligns with your vision, mission, and values
- Incorporating hashtags for the branding effort to be used across multiple social media channels

STARTING THE DRIVER CONVERSATION FOR YOUR BRANDED TEAM

Before introducing the drivers, promote your own edupreneurial spirit to advance brandED creativity, which can serve as a model for your community. You will have developed your own story of connection. The tips on the following list can aid you in launching your effort. Be advised that your storyteller-in-chief judgment about the development of brand will lead your team. Explain to the collaborative team that they are encouraged to take creative risks, even fail. Their bold spirit to achieve a unique school brand will be welcomed. As you begin the work of development,

1. Present your own brand-building experience.

2. Introduce the history of brand, discuss the relationship of brand to brandED, and share winning strategies of some of the best brands.

3. Gauge the group's collective understanding of the concepts of audience, perception, engagement, and digital and traditional messaging. Take a deep dive into the team's personal experience with brand to prepare them for their creative school brand-building experience.

4. Give the team personal experience by having them create their own individual professional brands in one word and write their own brand mission statements.

5. Have each team member do an individual SWOT analysis to create connection in the early stage of team brand building.

6. As you introduce your team to the work of branding, use language that frames brandED to bond the tribe. The words *image, promise, result, vision, belief, emotion, value,* and other powerful brandED terms found in the Glossary can unify a team's direction.

As marketing managers know, there's no strict formula for brand creation. Frameworks like the brandED Drivers guide a brand-building process, yet this is a highly personal and unique experience for each team. Your agenda for introducing your team to the journey of brand building reflects your passion for the project, your personal brand-building experience, and your goals for the crafted school brand.

Without your modeling, a brandED team will stall. A brandED collective gets into the zone by catching the edupreneurial spirit from the team's energized brandED leader. Charge each team member to become an edupreneur, to be open to the creativity of the branding process. Build in time for reflective team conversations based on continuing inquiry. They are a necessary, collaborative component of the brand's success. Remember, your team is equipped with a range of valuable skills for the process. Get to know them through their own brands. Be ready to listen. Inspire them to build. The brandED Drivers featured in Figure 4.1 will be your road map to inspire brand development.

BRANDED DRIVER ONE: PROMISE—MAKING THE COMMITMENT TO BRAND

Identifying the school's **promise** is the first brandED Driver. We are prompted to identify our audience and what they need and want. We craft our promise to ensure that we give stakeholders what they value, and define our commitment to them in the exchange as brand partners.

An attention-getting example of promise is that of LeBron James, who promised Cleveland that he would bring "one trophy back to Northeast Ohio." He gave the people what they wanted and needed. He knew their pain and crafted a transparent plan to deliver. He made good on his promise when he helped the Cleveland Cavaliers win the 2016 NBA Championship, and it wasn't easily delivered. LeBron was dedicated to the promise, and crafted his plan to achieve that result.

Figure 4.1 Drivers of BrandED Value

DRIVER 1	DRIVER 2	DRIVER 3	DRIVER 4	DRIVER 5
PROMISE	STRATEGY	IDENTITY	BUSINESS AS UNUSUAL	ENGAGEMENT
"Positioning"	"Goals"	"Connection"	"Innovation"	"Loyalty"
How does our audience perceive us?	What end do we have in mind?	What channels are available to tell our story?	What kinds of original thinking will we advance?	How do we continually bring value that creates and sustains loyalty to our brand?
What does our audience need and want?	How do we behave as builders of the brand?	What are our priority lanes for messaging?	How will we demonstrate our commitment?	How do we maintain brand presence in real time and online?
	Do we measure our brand in select measurable and attainable goals?			How do we stay relevant to our audience?
Answer leads to the setup of select goals	Answer leads to identifying brand messaging channels	Answer leads to innovative behavior	Answer leads to sustained community adoption of the brand	Answer leads to checking back to positioning

Handwritten annotations:
- (EOS) monitoring
- want 2 come back / parents them / parents wants / In a smaller setting
- Graduation / kids improving
- 7 Behavior Issues
- Ch 13 / Guest Speakers
- Emails / Call parents / TEXT
- model/us / Showing up / Being Appropriate
- communicating / Listeners / what's going on? / Ongoing Training. / Caring.
- NEED structure / want our Help
- Graduate / Transportable
- out SOS / Signal / a week event
- over all group
- Bringing outside Stevko Wildner
- They ask us what to use N need

How the brandED leader presents promise

Together the team articulates the school brand promise with a passion akin to LeBron's. According to brand guru Brad Vanauken (2015), "The brand promise is the most important part of the brand design. A brand must promise a relevant, compelling, and differentiated benefit." The brandED school promise is made with an eye on the future, and it is linked to establishing brand loyalty. A brand promise is about benefits, not features, and should differentiate the school in ways that are extremely important to stakeholders. Your team must believe that the school is capable of providing the benefit in ways that show result. Benefits are connected to value, belief, awareness, and emotions. Knowing the stakeholder audience is of prime importance to developing a strong offer, a steady promise. Guide your team with your own experience of setting your brand in motion. They must know the persona of their stakeholders in order to create a connecting brand promise.

The promise offered should be "evergreen," to use a marketing term; that is, it needs to live a long life and stand the test of challenging times. School promises must embrace bigger issues than simply raising performance on a test. Evergreen promises are created out of the essential core belief of what a school community will value today and in the future. LeBron's promise was *tenacity.* Schools who think in an evergreen mindset are developing promise around big and deep core issues, such as tenacity. Schools can use deep connectors to community, such as *access, tolerance, equity, diversity,* and *expectations,* as part of their school brand promise. Just as Mr. James demonstrated, promise is powered by communication. His visible commitment to tenacity was on display daily.

A school leader guides the process of brand building by uniting the minds and hearts of stakeholders around core beliefs. For LeBron, it was the belief in the community he led and the tenacious commitment he made to the journey to a championship. The promise went deep. James's promise was powered into tangible action: words, demonstrations, and hard work. His focus was on delivering a collaborative promise that stakeholders could share. All members of his community understood the commitment and believed. Communicating as a brandED leader means that you elevate the core belief of a school's existence into a promise that binds people and programs. Weaving an evergreen core of tenacity, equity, and high expectations into your brand saves it from becoming a quick fix, a superficial nod to brand. Using a powerful and connecting core in developing a promise and then communicating it every day in digital and traditional channels keeps the tribe together, bonded and engaged.

How the brandED team creates promise

The mission statement is the school's first visible promise to its audience. It creates the initial contract for the exchange. From there, positioning statements, a new logo and website, taglines, and other features that continue to promote the school brand and elaborate on that promise can be developed and shared across digital channels. Creating the mission allows all stakeholders to contribute their view of the core identity of the school.

In articulating the promise—the mission statement for the school— the team should consider these questions:

> What are the **attributes** of our school community? What do we want the audience to perceive about us that sets us apart?
>
> What are the **benefits** that are supplied by the brand of our school? What do we want the audience to appreciate as we work to meet that promise?
>
> What are the **beliefs** that we stand for as a community? What values do we bring to our community and want to share?

Conversations around promise are conversations about the school's vision, purpose, and big idea so that the mission statement reflects the core of the school message.

Team members work to identify the school's distinctive difference. They may want to develop bullets that show benefits and run them by their own trusted colleagues and validators, reporting back to the group about the response. The school's unique brand value (UBV) is at the heart of that promise. Once the promise is crafted, the team can move toward developing the mission statement (Appendix A). A mission statement tells the world what the school publically stands for as an organization that is built on a brand promise. The mission statement is a deep dive into claiming what a school offers and what results the school will bring to the community. A classic example of a mission statement is that of Southwest Airlines: "The mission of Southwest Airlines is dedication to the highest quality of customer service delivered with a sense of warmth, friendliness, individual pride, and company spirit." It is interesting to note that this statement was written in 1988! It would be high on the approval list for social scientists, as it exudes well-being. The airline was ahead of the curve in delivering a sustained promise. Most businesses are playing catch-up with their mission statements and have gone through a series of rewrites. Intel's most recent mission statement looks very different from its 1995 statement. Today, Intel promises, "This decade we will create and extend computing technology to connect and enrich the lives of every person on earth" (Ferrel & Hartline, 2014).

School examples that capture the spirited intention of these successful business messages while adopting a stance that's more inclusive of education stakeholders might be short and targeted, and may even speak directly to the audience. For example: "The mission of [school name] is the dedication of engagement with every member of the school community as respected individuals while capably developing them to their fullest as individuals and participants in society today and tomorrow."

New 21st-century mission statements are necessary for all schools, and we (Eric and Trish) challenge you to be different in developing unique statements. Before you create your own mission statement, look at businesses, nonprofits, agencies, and other schools for examples of what makes a mission statement resonate. In the case of large school districts adapting brand thinking, consider useful extensions that personalize individual schools' value connect with what the district brand delivers. These extensions may be found in individual schools that create what is called a *positioning statement*—a statement under the umbrella of the big idea of the district brand, a statement that is individually crafted to address specific school promises that support the overarching district mission. These statements honor the "parent brand," the inclusive umbrella, of the district mission statement, but address the individual school's positioning of its unique social role in educating kids in the district. Writing positioning statements for disparate segments of stakeholders helps individual schools stay in synch with an overarching district brand while projecting their own UBV that fits for groups like parents of children with special needs. The positioning statement can speak to a specific group of school stakeholders across channels of communication: emails, newsletters, and messages from the school. See Appendix B for more information on crafting positioning statements in support of the unifying, umbrella brand of the school that is created through the brandED Strategic Plan.

Before moving to the second brandED Driver, the team will determine the powerful mission statement as a transparent commitment to a crafted school brand promise. Included in the discussion are beginning dialogues about how the brand is shared online and offline through the words, stories, and testimonials of stakeholders.

BRANDED DRIVER TWO: STRATEGY—A PLAN FOR MEETING THE GOALS

In working with the brandED Driver **strategy**, your team moves to identify clear and decisive goals to commit the brand to a school improvement effort. The strategy for brandED implementation is based on three tangible results: improved school culture, expanded school performance, and increased school resources. Teams find measurable and attainable brand goals in those areas.

How the brandED leader presents strategy

Applaud the effort that has resulted in articulating the brand promise. Use the new mission statement to inspire goal setting. Lead the team discussion around these strategic questions and develop your own:

- What goals will support our promise and show the result of our mission?

- How can we set goals and objectives that improve culture, performance, and resourcing through our brandED effort?

- What do we want to stand for as a brand in each of these areas?
- How can we measure this in a manageable way?

How the brandED team builds a strategy

Teams may choose to set a goal or goals for each brand result—culture, performance, and resourcing—through a review of the initiatives in place that are connected to results, and identify one objective that leads to observable results. Some teams may decide to focus on one area, such as culture, and develop objectives that drill down into brand delivery. In either case, a team develops benchmarks for getting to the brandED goal. The team finds ways to engage with the community through the brand. Measureable objectives for these engagements may suit the targets for improvement: culture, performance, and resourcing. Again, team members can look for support from their networks in identifying reasonable, valuable ways to show evidence of brand success in academic and nonacademic results. Setting brand goals keeps the focus on results. Include these targets when creating your brandED strategy:

- What does evidence of our brandED goals look like in our culture, our performance, and our resourcing of the school? What tangible evidence can we expect to see from a community that is engaged?

- How will we creatively measure our progress toward the goals with manageable and tangible results? Will we want feedback in 3 months? Six months? One year?

- How will we communicate our progress to stakeholders? How will we share our work toward achieving our goals?

BRANDED DRIVER THREE: BRAND IDENTITY—TELLING THE STORY

When the promise of the school has been refreshed, a mission claimed, and goals for brandED strategy established, the storyteller-in-chief steps up. **Brand identity** for a school is established in the showcasing of the school's promise through stories in online and offline contexts.

William Arruda, a respected global brand consultant to business, believes that getting out the content and the message about a business brand is no longer relegated to a PR department. Brand communication belongs to the entire organization; it's everyone's mission. This can parallel the school organization's own need to tell its story as one united learning community. According to Arruda,

> School leaders need to give their permission—the mandate—to educators to be vehicles that tell the stories. This is a trend inside companies. In the past, all external communications went through the PR department. Today, innovative companies are relying on their leaders and employees to get the message out. This can seem scary because what you lose is control, but what you gain is more valuable: human connection. (W. Arruda, personal communication, April 28, 2016)

Arruda's example illustrates that this type of intrapreneurship in companies and edupreneurship in schools can support UBV.

Good content can highlight culture, demonstrate performance, and attract resources. To organize the delivery of stories in systematic ways, it's possible to develop Google spreadsheets on a monthly basis that track the posting of content that advances brand. The audience expects and welcomes consistency in the messages they engage with when they are in touch with the school's brand, so staying organized is key.

Identify where the brand identity can be advanced using text, audio, and visuals. New platforms like Instagram and Snapchat are now the darlings of visual storytellers. Big companies like Disney are already invested in these platforms and use them to connect and engage with their audiences every day, helping them deliver promise, set goals, and build brand identity. Schools also can engage with their stakeholders through the power of storytelling, on the very same platforms that legacy brands use. Who knows the school experience better than those creating it?

Part of building a brandED strategy is identifying the channels through which stories can be shared. For example, visual platforms have created new engaging and open passageways for images and videos where sharing with a variety of audiences can be achieved—where audiences are waiting for engagement with your brand. The legacy of a school brand can be shared on platforms from Facebook to Twitter to Pinterest, Snap, and beyond.

At New Milford High School, I (Eric) consistently utilized a variety of social media tools, such as Instagram and Flickr, to develop and enhance our brand identity and to promote and celebrate our story visually. My staff and I curated images to showcase innovative learning, events, student achievements, and social experiences. We then shared these images through the tools themselves or through a storytelling app, such as Storify. Video tools also served to strengthen our brand identity. YouTube channels were established to archive elements of our learning culture, and Ustream was used to share live video. With the image and video content in place, we were then able to amplify our work by sharing across such mainstream tools as Twitter, Facebook, and Google+.

How the brandED leader presents brand identity

In working with this third driver, brand identity, the brandED leader and team move the conversation to the value of storytelling. Developing content for promoting and sharing the school brand is the topic for the team. Remind your team of the phrase, "We are not *selling*, we are *telling*." Discussions are now focused on digital content and the value it holds in our world, the sort of content that will engage your audience. The team identifies the types of content for storytelling. Gallo's (2016) purposes for storytelling found in Conversation 1 can help categorize a range of possible forms of content that reflect the promise, mission, and goals of the school brand. His classification can help the team recognize school stories that inspire, motivate, educate, or build brand. Stories are the means of connection between the school and engaged stakeholders. If you have selected wisely, your team already has content experts on board. There are many sites like BuzzSumo (www.buzzsumo .com) that can help you and your team identify content from the macroenvironment that may be aligned with your brand. An additional way to curate content for brand identity is found in two storytelling frameworks: storytelling content and help content.

Build brand identity using storytelling content. Storytelling content captures the narratives (from both internal and external sources) that convey the awareness, values, beliefs, and emotions of the school brand. It showcases brand and validates the commitment of a range of stakeholders to the brand's promise. It inspires sharing and positive contagion in response. It should get people talking and remarking. Topics can form around the brand big ideas suggested by Carmine Gallo (2016), but simply thinking big as a brand leader can help you and your team develop topics for content. For instance, happiness is part of building a brandED brand, and it is a big idea that thousands of writers have approached in the online community. Find the match for your school and curate the idea of happiness from the range of stories of the internal culture of the school. Promote the stories of happiness and well-being. Use short content that might fit on a mobile device for a quick read or a longer piece for a school website. An array of educational content from educators like Tom Murray (@thomascmurray) and Dwight Carter (@Dwight_Carter) can be showcased for your community to enrich your own content. Video can also be part of a storytelling approach. Leaders have used short videos on Twitter and Snap; these can later be archived. This curating mirrors the digital content marketing that we see in our daily lives. When successful, educator content marketing yields positive responses and is a call to action for the community to engage. The power of interactive storytelling is also on the horizon as creative companies combine their software creation ability with engaging content that is presented with editorial and visual flair. A storytelling leader can grow professional relationships with creators in the tech space and with those creating editorial content, thus enabling a school's brand to be viewed even more engagingly by stakeholders. Watching for trends and signals in the tech world helps you build your storytelling power.

Build brand identity using help content. Help content is content that supports the overall brand in a utilitarian way. Surveying many school websites, one can see a showcase of features that are designed to inform and help stakeholders. This is valuable information, but not connected to brand. An effort to make this content more engaging and complementary of the storytelling content will elevate information to a connecting brand level. A balance of engaging help content and storytelling content is preferred on websites. Help content can become more in line with storytelling when it starts a conversation with stakeholders. Help content is seen in stories that serve to educate in a more functional way and may be tied to promoting other school initiatives. Content such as "How to Help your Child with Homework" or "Is AI Useful in Developing Your Child's Study Skills?" can evoke the caring feeling of the school brand. Understanding curriculum development or the transparent work of a school in developing a strategic plan can be part of the development of stakeholder help content. A Twitter feed on your school website may contain useful, engaging links to help content. These stories have less "evergreen feel" because help content is more immediate and needs refreshing on a regular basis. In some cases, it may be linked to timelines, so it has a briefer "shelf life." Topics for help content might be found on streaming sites like Periscope and Blab. Help content can be repurposed from across many platforms and supports the school brand as it is targeted to niches or subgroups of stakeholders (e.g., parents), a practice that further supports your brand transparency.

How the brandED team creates brand identity

In the spirit of distributed leadership, the team generates the content themes and topics that link to the brand. In developing and curating brand content, teams must keep in mind that an important part of choosing content comes from the first brandED Driver: knowing the audience and the promise. Know what your stakeholders are like and understand what they are looking for in messaging so that your content will engage them.

Segmenting different audiences gives the school opportunities to further develop a range of content. Part of the team's journey is finding and connecting to content providers in-house or in the community who have original content to share. Offering contests and enlisting challenges can also create interest for collecting content. The team will define processes for connecting to stakeholder curators of content valuable to the community. Keep content fresh and current. A team that invites the community in to help with sharing brand identity through curating and creating content will raise the brand profile in a sustaining, fresh way that keeps messaging current and relevant. This is content that people will want to like and share.

Testing content for brand identity awareness

As you create and curate content, look to four steps for collecting appropriate content that is original or repurposed from other sources to align with the essence of the school brand:

1. **Ask:** Why is this story or content important to share with the community?

2. **Match:** Does this content match our brand message?

3. **Sift:** What types of validating storytelling content and educating help content can we find in our school before going to outside sources? What external content can support our original content?

4. **Target:** Will this content resonate with our stakeholders? Will it fit their viewing time so that we can be assured that they will read it and even give feedback (e.g., short mobile content or longer Web-based content)?

Word of mouth, online content, face-to-face interaction, and traditional print all have value when it comes to establishing your school's brand identity. The genuine, unique, and remarkable voice found in the openness of school stories across many channels makes sharing the brand's narrative contagious.

BRANDED DRIVER FOUR: BUSINESS AS UNUSUAL—CLAIMING THE INNOVATION

The fourth driver, attending to **business as unusual**, unites your team through the celebration of innovation and new ways to message. Sharing the business-as-unusual message of brand is part of the creative work of brandED distributed leadership. Guide your group to share the positive experience of brand building with other stakeholders: staff, teachers, kids, parents, and community.

How the brandED leader presents business as unusual

Leaders think about this driver early in their efforts, long before they formally present it. It captures the spirit of edupreneurship. Adopting brandED sets your school apart from those leading the status quo.

BrandED schools survey the external environment where other schools exist and see the potential to partner, not to compete. In the transparent, digital world of a sharing economy, being unusual gets schools noticed in ways that go far beyond test scores. Focus with the team on how its power and understanding have grown. Encourage the team to take on the business-as-unusual role of school brand ambassador. Prepare the team to spread the word in new ways that get people talking, and claim the power of brand as a unifying, clarifying, and rewarding part of a responsive, modern school community.

How the brandED team sustains business as unusual

Working with this driver, the team identifies the possible channels—from word of mouth and print to digital and social outlets—through which to promote a school brand's promise. The business-as-unusual effort powers decisions as team members rely on each other to scour the digital landscape. Using Danny Meyer's brand behavior advice (discussed in Conversation 3), they "have each other's backs" as they look for ways to promote through new channels. They research and they reach to identify new places to promote storytelling content.

Many stakeholders embrace this innovative effort, especially Millennial teachers and parents in your community. These team members have networks, and they know about the constant arrival of platforms and apps and software on the scene. They are edge dwellers for the next big thing in content creation and sharing. Let them be the eyes and ears of the brand effort. Give your team the charge to be innovative in the business-as-unusual discovery of new ways to channel brand thinking and action.

In marketing plans, offline events as well as online connection work to sustain a brand culture. Challenge your team to create small, engaging touches with the community as well as bigger events with the wider stakeholder audience around the concept of the new brand, to convey the school's commitment to being brandED. BrandED events—fairs that celebrate edupreneurship, guest speaker series around the concept of brand, and alumni brand events—are all possible targets. Teams can develop creative content around panels that have brand-related messages. These can be no-cost community support activities featuring stakeholders who want to give back to the community by presenting topics related to brand development, such as digital transparency, online security, and building strong brand relationships. A business-as-unusual calendar of brand events built during brandED Driver activity and developed by your team will be a part of the strategic plan and ensure that brand will get attention from the community year round.

BrandED schools can be seen as curators of stories that engage their stakeholders in a way that spotlights up-to-the-moment connection to a range of meaningful cultural topics that are essential to learning. These stories can be shown across any of your school's visual channels, social channels, and platforms that feature school content. An inspiration for curating trends and topics that can instruct a brand on engaging with its stakeholders, the New York City advertising company sparks & honey (www.sparksandhoney.com), under the direction of media culture pioneer Terry Young, offers schools an adaptable thinking model that can quickly raise the awareness of trends that impact school content in the macroenvironment. The company curates storytelling in a way that can engage people in expansive and unique thinking. Curation of current trends informs a brand about the world outside the classroom. School brands feel the impact of trends in the macroenvironment, and conversations around these trends that impact a school community can engage stakeholders. Having a system for processing content that can engage a school community in discussions of aspects of culture—tech, art, music, fashion, literature, and sports—can help keep the community tuned in to school communication platforms in an exciting new way.

BrandED strategy improves culture, and an innovative way to show your brand's connection to building your school culture is to showcase stories—across all school platforms, the website, blogs, and Facebook or Twitter pages—of your own savvy and connected community as it responds to the macroculture that surrounds it. In short bursts of storytelling from students who are highlighting engaging stories from the microculture of the school and from the macroculture of the larger world, your school can behave as sparks & honey does. The company even has an app for this! Search with your collaborative team for "Now Next"/ N2N. It can inspire you as you plan your collection of content that can engage your community to watch, share, and comment on.

New opportunities for using digital content in this engaged spirit of a sharing economy keep the brand story fresh and innovative. Your "Digital Joneses," as they are referred to in Conversation 7, are facile at sharing content and can advance a continuous dialogue and storytelling among the tribe. These tribe members are already part of the innovative digital landscape. They welcome brand in their lives and have their own business-as-unusual stance that is different from previous generations of stakeholders. Promotion is in their comfort zone, thanks to digital and social sharing. They love the innovative sharing economy that allows them to leverage brand connection to further their reach in getting to needs and wants. (For instance, No car? Call Zipcar!) There is a bit of urgency in this generation. This group doesn't want to wait to achieve brand access. Make sure your plan includes targeted contact with this group. They are movers and shakers of brand on a budget. For these savvy stakeholders, tenets of brand that sustain the community are familiar in language and action.

It will take an "all-in" attitude to promote the story of the school brand, which has been carefully crafted and designed so that it can be claimed with pride and assimilated into the larger pond of the school community. Teams who focus on creating the sharing network and patterns of brandED messages introduce creative brand activity to the wider community. BrandED is promoted through the edupreneurial spirit of a team that has designed a brand that can bloom anywhere: at school events, social gatherings, and meetings; in classrooms and hallways; and, most important in our digital age, online. A brandED mindset keeps a community in the flow and empowered with feelings of well-being.

BRANDED DRIVER FIVE: ENGAGEMENT— SUSTAINING BRAND LOYALTY

The fifth and final brandED Driver is **engagement**.

Audience engagement builds the emotional connection to school brand loyalty. Leaders and team members determine ways to maintain the audience's attention to the school brand so as to sustain loyalty to that brand. Perception is key to your new brand messaging success. Unlike a "buyer" who can be hooked into loyalty with marketing plans, incentives, and deals, an audience for the school brand gets hooked on positive engagement and emotional connection that come from the connecting, consistent stories of the brand.

How the brandED leader presents engagement

Increasing support for the continuation of the brand will be important to a successful brandED Strategic Plan. In business branding, this eye on increasing awareness and engagement is known as *scale*. Scale in school branding means taking the temperature of an innovation. Is this innovation catching on? It is important for leaders to guide the team in ensuring engagement as a visible result of their plan. As a start, gauge support for the school by monitoring the quality of brand interactions that are found in online exchanges on Twitter, Instagram, Facebook, and school blogs. It is also possible to see scale—the growth of the brand presence—from email surveys, by monitoring of online responses, and in face-to-face meetings with stakeholders. The scale of the brand in the external world can be seen in the instances of students connecting in either online or offline exchanges that promote their school brand engagement. Leaders can use platforms such as Mentimeter (www.mentimeter.com) to get real-time feedback on the growth of the elements of the brand.

The feeling that schools care, that stakeholders are valued, is important in delivering service. A caring and supportive school mission will increase brand loyalty. Your stakeholders' positive engagement builds scale and creates that desired brand equity that shows goodwill. Help your team see that being open and transparent in the building of the brand will grow fans for the good work that the school offers every day and engages more supporters of the school brand, resulting in improved positive culture.

How the brandED team creates engagement

The elements of promise—the mission statement, positioning statements, website collateral, the school logo, and channels for sharing—all will be looped into your conversation around building engagement. Questions to start the team moving forward with thinking about engagement include those around the subject of affinity, which in marketing is defined as a repeated purchase based on consistent, positive feeling about the buy. The decision to purchase is truly automatic when affinity is present. The emotional juice just flows for the exchange. That's why some people can't start the day without Starbucks, and they don't really care about the coffee. It's about the positive grounding and good feeling from their routine. It's possible to bring affinity to school brand when a team keeps the following in mind:

- Affinity is built early on in the branding process. Brand loyalty is built on emotions. How can we create the emotional contact we need to keep school brand loyalty and keep the affinity for our work high?

- What can be shared from the earliest stages of brand development that will interest and motivate the community to build affinity? How will engagement fit into our strategic plan?

- What stories help us reinforce the value that the school is bringing to the audience daily? How can we inspire stakeholders to tell those stories so that affinity grows?

The team uses the results of these conversations to shape their school brand work on engagement. The collective's work on all the brandED Drivers is set on creating ways to keep audiences continually engaged.

Part Two: Your BrandED Strategic Plan

All brands need a strategy to make it in the 21st century. Your school brand is no exception.

The brandED Strategic Plan will serve as your map and touchstone. The process of using the brandED Drivers with your team is essential to creating your brandED plan. The goal is to embrace and implement innovative practices to better connect with stakeholders. These innovative practices are anchored in a unifying strategy for educators, not businesspeople, and these practices need their own road—one that a brandED Strategic Plan will capture. In your role of brandED steward, lead the creation and maintenance of a strategic plan inspired by the work of the team in delivering the brandED Drivers.

As you lead into the crafting of the brandED Strategic Plan with your team, set out to claim the unmistakable image, promise, and result of your school. Articulate brand for a very public showcase. Positive brandED culture, performance, and resourcing are supported in the creation of this model. A brandED Strategic Plan is your comprehensive map to adding brand thinking to your overall goal of school improvement.

BRANDED ADAPTATION OF AN ICONIC TOOL

The creation of the brandED Strategic Plan follows a respected foundational tool advanced by brand strategists Armstrong and Kotler (2015). The tool details the process of bringing a brand to market. A school plan adapts this tool using elements that purposefully outline a school brand journey to sustainability.

The Elements of the brandED Strategic Plan

The elements of the strategic plan combine the following into a powerful resource:

The leader's summary, stating the main goals of the effort

The rationale, outlining why the school is taking on a branding effort

The SWOT analysis, discussing strengths, weaknesses, opportunities, and threats that influence the delivery of brandED

The goals and objectives, targeting the implementation

The awareness channels for brandED, which detail the routes to messaging

BrandED actionables, describing the activities of the effort

Monitoring of progress toward goals, detailing the management of the strategy

After the collaborative team has completed work on the brandED Drivers, the skilled communicators on your team identify how to share the strategy with the community. The most skilled in "presentational literacy" can enthusiastically present the plan publicly. All brands have a visible launch. Don't skip that celebratory step! With the team, the leader shares the strategic plan offline in real-time settings and announces the brand and plan online, on websites, and through blogs. This plan is your road map, your brand guide to sustain the brandED effort. With a strategic plan in hand, you enhance the possibility of improving culture and performance and increase the chance for quickly engaging with resource partners.

Part Three: BrandED Stakeholder Relationship Management

With your plan ready, you as a brandED leader are secure in moving purposefully from brand promise to brand loyalty on the big stage of public sharing. Your plan identifies whom you serve. It guides you in how you will serve your stakeholders. It suggests how to engage the audiences you reach. How can you sustain relationships and maintain loyal audiences? Share the plan with pride. It is a call to action for the community.

The glue for keeping your strategic plan intact is your relational power. Relational power builds brand strength, loyalty, and partnerships. Brand managers in the business world employ customer relationship management (CRM) to help organize, understand, and satisfy customers. Once you own a clear brandED strategy, you can adapt this model of sustaining relationships to a more educator-friendly **stakeholder relationship management (SRM)** mindset. This adaptation focuses on strategic relationship building as a tenet of school improvement.

The educator's view of stakeholder relationship is based on keeping audiences on our leadership radar, knowing their shifting wants and how we can provide for them. Your brandED SRM is a modern-day Rolodex of connections for engaging every niche of audience with your school brand. The model of Elements of Stakeholder Relationship Management (Figure 4.2) identifies elements to develop in ensuring a connection to the community on many levels. An SRM model helps focus you on select avenues that sustain your brand. The model suggests the variety of elements available in brand development that create opportunities for building continued relationships that keep the brand connecting to its audience. Leaders choose where they want to place their efforts to gain the attention to the range of audiences that the school brand touches. The model offers possibilities of service and targets communication elements that sustain community connection for 21st-century schools.

Prior to the Internet and social media age, schools weren't comfortable with the idea of being providers of customer service. Times have shifted toward service to our audience, in part due to new trends in educational choice. Using a brandED plan, you can more easily adapt to this new environment of transparency and the necessity of engagement. By viewing yourself as a servant leader and educator, you see that the landscape is populated with stakeholders who desire engagement and experience. Managing this process is new for school leadership, so adopting an SRM frame can help you into a service-minded attitude.

Figure 4.2 The Elements of BrandED Stakeholder Relationship Management

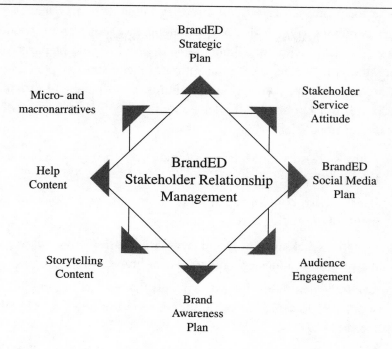

This attitude of service and gratitude for your stakeholders is a genuine part of leadership in today's world of communication. Having a brandED Strategic Plan is key to your management system. It helps you tune in to stakeholder service.

An articulated brandED social media plan can positively impact the scale of your audience engagement in the brand. You want to grow affinity. A stakeholder service attitude comes from continually promoting brand awareness to the community through elements of storytelling content and help content, which deliver the small stories and big-idea moments that keep brand messaging and stakeholder engagement flowing and positive.

Engaging with your stakeholders is about identifying who stakeholders are and what they want—not what you think they need. Participating in the brandED Drivers team experience helped you articulate the segments in the community awaiting school engagement. With new information, leaders exchange with their audiences of stakeholders and invite them into conversations, and they tailor their messages to the various publics. The SRM model promotes a range of brand-friendly messages that portray the school as you decide it should be portrayed. Your new processes for messaging outlined in your strategic plan lead to strong relationships across your communities in digital and real-time exchange. Touchpoints for thinking about building SRM for brandED action include the following:

- Actively identifying segments of audiences through the brandED Driver activity

- Purposefully building positive relationships, and targeting segments of the audience accordingly

- Mindfully making your brand story "stick" using powerful, engaging content and messaging that sustains brand

- Carefully identifying distinct segments that you serve and thinking about how to satisfy them through a service-minded attitude that creates loyalty

- Strategically developing trusted relationships internally with stakeholders under the school roof as well as with your community outside the school

- Thinking about how your team and the entire school community can be incentivized to recognize that branding is key to successful relationship building for the benefit of the school

Every relationship you develop can have a positive impact on students, staff, teachers, parents, and the community. Leveraging new relationships through your existing networks will benefit your school culture and achievement. As a result of your leadership in the creation of a brandED Strategic Plan through your team's work with the brandED Drivers, the goal of relationship building with stakeholders has never been as easy to address.

Conversation 4 Tips

- **Understand** the road map to brand through the brandED Drivers and reflect on creating a meaningful design prior to building a strategy with your team.
- **Lead** the discussions with your team from your understanding of *promise, strategy, identity, business as unusual,* and *engagement.*
- **Share** the leadership role through a distributed strategy as you collaboratively build the brandED Strategic Plan with your team to set the stage for brandED results of improved *culture, performance,* and *resourcing.*
- **Create** an understanding among members of the community about the value of a plan that builds stakeholder relationships.

Conversation 4 Reflections

Before holding public conversation around why business brand tenets inform educational leadership, think about these questions:

- Am I ready to lead strategy design sessions with the five brandED Drivers?
- How do I see myself facilitating the conversation on brandED strategy? Can I use the support of leadership information online and through my peer network to help lead the development of the strategic plan?
- Do I understand the necessity of using the brandED Drivers to lead to the creation a brandED Strategic Plan?
- Am I ready to communicate a public platform for the brand effort in a collaboratively built brandED Strategic Plan?
- How will I, as a stakeholder relationship manager, share the plan and provide service to my newly engaged community?

Conversation 5

Sustaining BrandED Innovation

In Conversation 5, a leader with a brandED Strategic Plan uses relational tools of traditional and new-age communication to implement and sustain the school's brand effort online and offline. Discussions build the leader's management of the narrative of a new school brand in sustaining ways, illustrating how this disruptive brand change brings three foundational, measurable outcomes: (a) improved school culture, (b) expanded school performance, and (c) increased school resources.

> Brand is a valuable asset . . . it should be treated like any other asset. This means it must be invested in, put to work to generate value and held accountable for results.
> —*Joanna Seddon, executive vice president,*
> *Millward Brown*

Focus on sustaining the results of your valuable, newly designed and built asset, your unique school brand.

Your brandED Strategic Plan includes many elements that create brand affinity, the necessary connection to good feeling with the stakeholder community. Use that goodwill to engage your 24/7 relational mindset that powers you to meet your school brand goals. Attention to human behavior, brand awareness, and communication access in your plan will improve culture, performance, and resourcing that sustain the long-term life of a school brand. Brand is about exchange at the deepest level. The life of a school brand depends on your conscious leadership investments every day in understanding brand and how people behave through exchange with the institutional brand you have crafted using channels that spread the word about your school.

Part One: Invest in BrandED Leadership

As part of your brandED Driver design journey, you claimed outside-the-box thinking as "business as unusual." The traditional school leadership role may originally have been one of distancing, but those days are done. Your officially claimed brand gives you access in daily exchange with your community and a lot to talk about as a lead communicator. Brand conversations that develop from your plan's implementation will open new doors. Leaders promote the school's brand using a model that integrates three tenets of brandED leadership behavior: the strategic recognition of the need to **associate, create,** and **engage** in a business-as-unusual effort to support the implementation of your institutional brand.

HOW BRANDED LEADERS ASSOCIATE FOR SUCCESS

The act of associating with others is a foundation of relationship building and is linked to the awareness of your own defined personal professional brand.

The act of associating is your daily exercise in the brandED leadership gym. Associating behavior is the essence of the classic model Management by Walking Around (MBWA). Sometimes referred to as Management by Wandering Around (Fisher, 2012), MBWA came to light in 1982 in Peters and Waterman's classic management book, *In Search of Excellence*. The authors profiled the innovative owners of Hewlett-Packard, who used MBWA as their signature way of communicating with their organization—not through emails, calls, or memos but by associating: They deliberately got to their people in repeated touchpoints, in regular face-to-face casual moments. It sounds commonsensical to do, but it was innovative at the time and still produces results. For those leaders needing practice in associating—in publically sharing their newly grown brand with others—this strategy can give you a chance to flex your relational muscle. MBWA isn't haphazard; it is achieved with strategic thought. Getting into a daily routine of associating with a wide range of stakeholders, internal and external, is of primary importance to leadership and to promotion of a school brand. Calling your original brandED buddy into the role of accountability partner can help you succeed in your goal to associate. Adding associating—the deliberate flexing of your communicative muscle as a part of your daily to-do list—builds brandED and forms a base for school leadership power.

Use any of the many free communication channels available online that support an associative online daily routine as you take MBWA onto the digital and social media stage. Check in with your brandED buddy and share on social media with those tools you are comfortable using—and challenge yourself with those you don't know. (See Appendix D for some suggested digital tools.)

Go on a hunt. Now that you have a brandED Strategic Plan, deliberately identify people you want to associate with in digital spaces and build relationships. There are opportunities for "walking around" in digital spaces today that weren't existent in 1982. The only reason you are reading this book is that one professional saw the chance to associate with another. It came from seeing that potential relationship source on TV. If you need structure, set your phone on a timer and give yourself 3 minutes for brand work at various points in your day. Push yourself to associate daily. Use the Google Calendar Speedy Meetings setting to keep your connecting to short (5–10 minute), meaningful, real-time or online meetings. Just the intention of reducing meeting length from 30 minutes on your calendar can help you be more efficient (M. Wong, personal communication, April 2015).

All stakeholders, including the kids, should be on your associating radar. Talk with them about your brandED effort. Ask for their impression of the school brand. Seek ideas and suggestions. Smile and say thanks, then follow up selectively with some of these new ambassadors.

Include aspirational associations. Associate through "reach" in real time or online. Look above you in a metaphorical sense. Whom do you want to build a relationship with who may have a higher stature? Start wandering around in digital spaces where your prospects are engaging. Twitter is a good resource for this, and once you have brand "collateral" to share that shows who you are, you can use it to associate for connection.

As you associate, "see" around your circle. See people whom you may have the tendency to overlook or to take for granted: Service providers of any sort, senior citizens, very young people, and diverse newcomers to your community can be part of your association plan. They are valuable contacts in their own right and may have additional associative power.

HOW BRANDED LEADERS CREATE ATTENTION

BrandED leaders go beyond business as usual as they create interest in education in new ways that elevate positive messaging to their communities. They are not humble when it comes to promotion of their school brand. Their aim is to capture attention and interest around the school's unique brand value (UBV). Leaders work to that end through their own consistent brand that becomes recognized and valued by the stakeholder community. The quest to get attention is part of sharing UBV. Call on your creativity to position yourself and own a strategy that leverages your school brand using your own leadership brand.

Diligence in building your network through associating will result in a new, collaborative peer community of fellow leaders, whom you can invite into your own efforts to raise the profile of education. This community can work to benefit one another's school brands, collaboratively generate interest, and create attention. Design new professional systems to tell stories of brandED school communities working together. Your own creative approaches to content development will build presence that can be shared with various publics locally and eventually even globally. BrandED leaders see themselves as being at the nexus of creative new projects that gather stakeholder attention online and in real time. A brandED leader can create new attention and be seen as a connector by facilitating sharing of information that provides value to different publics in education-minded communities.

Using strategies from the entrepreneurial community, leaders can create interest in growing a 21st-century brand style. Getting attention for your school as a committed brandED leader can begin in small ways. When working through the brandED Drivers, see yourself identifying channels that support interest. Step up with a few business-as-unusual strategies that show your ability to create community as a thought leader, boosting your own presence and giving value to others. This stance not only gets attention but also helps you partner.

Launch a brandED mastermind community, a group of four like-minded leaders. Include your brand buddy and ask him or her to bring another educator to the table. Meet regularly and support the creation of each other's brand efforts. Offer help to improve each member's school culture, performance, and resourcing using brand tenets. Thanks to the Internet, the masterminds can come from anywhere. Meetings can be held virtually. Use vehicles for sharing what the mastermind meetings bring. Follow up your sessions with blog posts, tweets, and content for school websites and even live streaming that can promote active creative brand leadership. Contact the local papers and pitch this new committed way for school leaders to work together on their institutional brand.

Marketing managers in companies are streaming their meetings online in an attempt to be seen as transparent to their loyal tech-savvy customers. School leaders can do the same. Be the steward of the effort and create accountability and a ritual around this mastermind gathering. Experiment with open, streamed meetings where you discuss education issues and trends. New platforms for sharing beyond Google Hangouts have developed on Instagram, which your youngest stakeholders can take responsibility for launching (with your guidance). Content about every aspect of educating students abounds online. Be an inclusive, transparent builder of relationships. Using the model of sparks & honey (noted in Conversation 4), be the leader who creates a place for interested educators to gather and discuss trends that are impacting education leaders and their schools.

Go bigger. Expand the mastermind group through lunchtime think tanks or morning coffees to focus on current topics that spark conversation around school brand. Find food and beverage partners who are interested in the topics to sponsor your group and add to the conversation with their own brand view. Invite members of the stakeholder community to these sessions. Survey the growing topics of interest to the stakeholder community, and develop small panels and invite your brandED buddy, your mastermind colleagues, and interested stakeholders to discuss and strategize. All participants are connected through brand. These communities are built informally, but can grow into powerful alliances. One historical case in point is Benjamin Franklin. He started a small club of interested community members, called a junto, that grew into an Ivy League brand we know today as the University of Pennsylvania. Creative efforts are part of that "You never know!" spirit (first mentioned in Conversation 2). In short, brandED leaders find good partners and become good partners, and the result gets attention. Don't forget that partnerships with the press, explored in Conversation 6, are also part of your brandED Strategic Plan to create attention. Imagine how inspiring a school leader is when partnerships, grown from creative attention getting and a new brandED focus, benefit the entire community.

You lead the positive attention-getting movement, but you will find your ambassadors who also can create connective attention. You need those supporters. A recent article in *Education World,* written by a team of principals, cites numerous ways for principals to gain resources for their schools without being the only ones who forge relationships and "knock on doors" (Anderson et al., 2016). Many agencies and companies have an interest in educational partnerships, enabling them to "do well by doing good." Social responsibility is of prime importance to potential resource partners. These entities will be inspired by your ability to get the word out in traditional and nontraditional ways. Teachers and staff in schools have created partnerships that include the services of the community; one such creative partnership resulted in a school-based service that actually reduced the tax burden of senior citizens who signed up to volunteer in the local schools. That effort created attention.

HOW BRANDED LEADERS ENGAGE USING BRAND PRESENCE

See yourself as the leader of a brandED education hub: an entity that attracts interest and partnering investment of all kinds—a school brand with a thoughtfully managed reputation that reflects the community's core. Engage your stakeholders in the process of building relationships. Your community will witness your engagement effort as you build your community of peer, aspirational, and foundational network partners. Your message spreads through word of mouth and through content on your school channels to attract the families of those who will be sending their children to your school.

Stay engaged with graduates who are resources with their own networks. Think like the Ford Motor Company. It engages the brand by hiring an army of high school students, many too young to drive, to mentor people purchasing smart cars in showrooms. Students work at the local Ford dealerships and serve as young consultants to seniors who may not understand the bells and whistles of their new cars and these cars' smart features. Right in the showroom, seniors receive help from these service-minded students and are more able to confidently manage their new vehicles.

A leader's ability to **associate, create,** and **engage** is captured in Figure 5.1, which is your map to brandED relational leadership. Use these behaviors.

Figure 5.1 Supportive Leadership Behaviors for BrandED

ASSOCIATE. . . BEHAVIORS TO SELF-ASSESS	CREATE. . . BEHAVIORS TO FUEL CREATIVITY	ENGAGE. . . BEHAVIORS TO POWER CONNECTIVITY
• Know your tech-savvy set • Evaluate personality type • Audit for communication skill set • Educate for broad goals across industries • Identify new communication channels to enhance current messaging • Launch something new that enhances your own brand identity	• Identify and reflect on leadership style • Consider educational philosophy • Self-monitor relational ability • Consider career vision • Forecast networking return on investment	• Forecast sustaining and scale—set your goals • Assess commitment to the community • Calculate risk • Evaluate your learning mode • Discover new partners daily • Form powerful relationships for the long haul

You now have a brand as worthy as any legacy business brand, one you have guided into existence. You must sustain it through your brand leadership as a steward.

An anchoring way to keep these deep commitments in mind is to ask yourself two questions daily, almost as a brandED leadership mantra to help you associate, create, and engage—and become a leadership **ACE.** Every morning, have a brief reflective meeting with yourself about your brandED plan and ask: "What will I do today to show that I am a brandED ACE as I associate, create, and engage my brand and my school's brand?"

As you close the door to your office each night, ask: "What have I done today to crush it as a brandED ACE? How did I associate, create, and engage my brand and my school's brand?"

Keep an online record as a journal in answer to that daily reflection. You can use it as your own guide for growth. You'll sleep better with the positive answers that come from your recorded effort, and wake refreshed in the morning to tackle those brandED goals that you will want to achieve.

Part Two: The Trend-Setting Stance of a BrandED leader

A positive brand presence is developed with consistent attention and is sustained by consistent communication. The leader of the brand has an eye on innovation and the trending possibilities that impact education in a fast-paced digital world. The business-as-unusual stance of a leader is clearly focused on innovation, which is linked to spotting trends. Working at the interface of education, psychology, economics, and marketing creates a 21st-century communicator whose Internet playbook of trends is enriched daily with new content. These cross-discipline and cross-industry stories fuel connection to school brand.

BrandED leaders identify important trends and link them to possibilities for school improvement across many avenues of information in the macroenvironment. These leaders inspire change informed by the digital and social community. Positioning the brand in response to trends further connects to the school's efforts to the look at the world beyond the schoolhouse door.

Validate initiatives that are part of the school brand by being a model for trend awareness of each school initiative that reflects the school brand. This is a forward-thinking, business-as-unusual way to keep an eye on the near future. Tracking trending issues of health, safety, justice, technology, and so on and connecting them through social channels to the work of the schools in those important areas expand the performance value that the initiatives currently offer. Long-term benefits from initiatives that are part of the brand can be extended with this trend-watcher view of leadership. Despite Alexander Pope's satirical statement, "Blessed is he who expects nothing, for he shall never be disappointed," brandED leaders are blessed because they expect the world to show up through digital content, and they are never disappointed in the wealth of information the content provides. Notable trends help them innovate for future success. BrandED leaders' openness to personal and professional learning using trends allows them to seek new and positive signals to guide them as they serve as steward of the brand.

This day-to-day eye on trends brings long-term result and is highly entrepreneurial. A leader switched on to the digital environment shows the attitude that welcomes the stimulating possibility for change. This is a leadership style that fits our fast-paced world of digital disruption, one that we will further explore in later conversations.

BE BRANDED WITH BALANCE

Use caution when trend spotting. BrandED leaders are on the lookout to innovate, but they do so with balance. Don't wear yourself thin chasing too many new platforms, apps, systems, programs, and even partnership connections. Have your brandED buddy, validators, or mastermind group keep you accountable for balance and focus. Use the same criteria for judging effectiveness that was used in the brandED Driver model for curating content. Ask yourself, "Is this trend, innovation, or connection in line with our school core brand?" Test it out. Revisit your brand promise and mission to check the value of a trend against the school brand before championing the signal to others.

A brandED innovation stance will lead you to many doors, but don't be tempted to throw too many open at a time. Don't feverishly try to keep options open on the chance that a particular direction may be the next big thing. Keep your image and promise in mind. By doing so, you will act as an innovative communicator bringing control over change in ways that create satisfying connections. What results is brand presence and a leadership innovation stance that is on trend and fresh and easily engaged with on many channels, but isn't seen as unfocused.

BrandED leaders don't look as though they are taking on things that might be important on the chance that something might pass them by. They model their ability to close doors to distraction; and thanks to the focus of a brandED Strategic Plan, they open only those doors that relate to the mission, vision, and values of the school. Discipline yourself to focus on innovative strategies for the development of culture, performance, and resources that positively impact students, teachers, parents, and the greater community and that can be successfully implemented out of the commitment to the brand. Your brand stance in a trending world honors the roles of continuous learner and edge-dwelling thinker. It will attract others to your work and allow you to promote and get attention comfortably.

As a result of this balance, you have the chance to create a new microenvironment where trends inform your leadership and bring new result: More qualified candidates applying for jobs, greater stakeholder support, and increased interest on the part of families to move to your district can come from this effort. A positive brand presence motivates and inspires your microenvironment of staff and coworkers. It can serve as an invitation to the macroenvironment as well, bringing colleagues near and far to your brand. Success is amplified when others see your models and replicate them. Your brand tells stakeholders about your school DNA. Beyond logos and mascots, tweets and hashtags, a shared positive brand presence throughout the microcommunity helps you tell the real story. A positive brandED presence clearly articulates to stakeholders what to expect from your district, your school, or you as a professional. This promise builds precious support and invaluable relationships.

EXTENDING THE BRANDED LEADERSHIP PROMISE

A balanced brandED strategy helps leaders stay focused on mission, vision, and values embodied in the brandED Strategic Plan, which supports the communication of the brand promise. By reaching people at an emotional level, you can build stronger relationships with key stakeholders. There is no better way to do this than by consistently sharing ways that you are making a positive difference in the life of kids each day.

A brandED mindset is a natural part of being a digital leader. You can communicate your innovative stance consistently, with social media as your public relations vehicle for storytelling. As the brand presence you build manifests itself, the brand promise is extended. You will develop familiarity and ease, posting your own work, ideas, and thoughts across a variety of platforms. Keep the following tips in mind to continually develop a mindset and the possibility of extending a successful brandED strategy:

- Be consistent. Develop a schedule for sharing content as well as creating content of your own. Regularly recognizing the work of educators and students in your school can be inspirational. The result can be greater levels of motivation and appreciation, which helps develop a positive school culture. Develop a template for curating on a monthly basis all the great work that's occurring. The report can then be shared in its entirety or broken up into numerous blog posts.

- Keep the message focused on work (school, district, your own) to provide value to stakeholders. Concentrate on elements that align with a thriving school culture, such as innovative learning, student achievement, staff accomplishments, college and career readiness, partnerships, unique traditions, and extracurricular activities.

- Engage in two-way communication to build and strengthen relationships.

- Maintain a presence across a variety of platforms. This allows you to amplify the great work that takes place by consistently sharing using a multifaceted approach that blends traditional (newsletters, email, phone, face-to-face) with digital-age tools (social media). With social media tools, make sure your account pages are up-to-date (in terms of website links, avatars, profile information, and the like). It is also wise to educate your stakeholders on social media tools and how you will be using them to increase engagement.

- Build consistency around logo, mascot, name, tagline, and so on.

- Review analytics and adapt when needed by embracing new tools to ensure the engagement of the community.

- Focus on transparency through honesty and sharing accurate information to build trust. The benefits here are numerous, including attracting families to move to your local district or, in the case of tuition-based schools (private, parochial, independent), to make a greater financial investment. It can also help when it comes to referendums, passing the school budget, and engaging alumni in the hopes of receiving donations of time, money, and resources.

- When it comes to sharing the story of your school, empower others to be active sharers, and avoid a gatekeeper mentality. Encourage different departments, student groups, parent organizations, and extracurricular activities to maintain social media accounts.

Developing a brandED mindset and strategy begins and ends with the amazing work you and your staff do with students that advances the profession of education. That's the hard part. The easy part consists of creating and then sharing content using a blend of traditional and new-age (i.e., social media) tools.

KEEP BRINGING BRANDED LEADERSHIP VALUE

> The role of a creative leader is not to have all the ideas; it's to create a culture where everyone can have ideas and feel that they're valued.
>
> —*Ken Robinson*

BrandED school reform conversations are led, not by executives, but by progressive school leaders harnessing and leveraging digital tools (Sheninger, 2014). A brand means value. With a brandED Strategic Plan, your delivery of value to your community is evident in the execution of the plan. The concept of brand provides value that can be articulated and threaded through every meeting, every class, every gathering. In the world of business, providing value is a key; similarly, in the business of schools, value is key to changing school culture, performance, and resourcing for the better. What further specific leadership behaviors can you advance to establish a brand presence that clearly articulates a promise of educational value?

The brandED leader ACE (associate, create, engage) framework can help you grow your value proposition as a relational leader in this new age, and it can foster a sense of trust, an integral component of a brand's ability to deliver promised value. Brand value is offered to us in the marketplace in many ways. Brands promise durability, health, style, safety, taste, convenience, or savings. There already are natural brandED leaders out there in the big world of education. School leaders are creating value in their business-as-unusual ways. Some may have never looked at their careers in an edupreneurial way, but now they can by using a brandED mindset: "I see my actions are directly connected to branding principles. What am I learning about branding? I'm discovering a school's brand promises value to residents of any district" (Sheninger, 2010). Using the overview of tools for being a brandED leader found in Figure 5.1, you can take a deeper dive into the continuous building of value for your school through focusing on your personal professional leadership brand.

As you become a student of brandED, you enhance your profile by learning in a variety of rich new areas—tech, management, and psychology, to name only a few—and you'll see new ways to incorporate current thinking into own professional growth to help you lead a school's brand development. School leaders who build a professional brand establish their own well-being based on philosophy, style, skill sets, vision, and innovative thinking that leads and inspires.

Part Three: The BrandED Competitive Advantage

The brandED steward's leadership role in showcasing a brand may bring out your competitive nature as you look to results. The companies behind all products and services measure themselves against the competition. Unfortunately, the only competitive measure we often see in education is the rank order of achievement in test scores published in the paper. We know that in the new world of school choice, there is a natural call to brandED leadership action. In these times, brandED leaders must raise themselves above the external definition of value placed on them from outside of the school, a value that considers only test scores; they do this by showcasing culture and performance in new ways, academic and nonacademic, that demonstrate value. Through a well-defined school brand, schools can show their authentic worth to parents and partners. Once schools start messaging strategically about their unique brand advantages, they become more competitive in attracting attention. It isn't the time to be humble. "Go for it!" as they say. Leaders have to look across this new landscape and see competition emerging in the world of education.

You have business-as-unusual thinking to do. You may have a diverse community of stakeholders who can leverage unique performance measures to show value beyond a standardized test score. Standardized test scores, curriculum, teacher and administrator quality, number of AP courses, college acceptances, and extracurricular activities are all part of the school brand's offering that is connected to positive brand result. But they are not the whole story. As you and your collaborative stakeholder team build your brandED Strategic Plan, you determine new evidence of the school's promise and mission and define new ways to value performance.

School leaders have a responsibility to create a competitive brand. By establishing a school's brand, leaders and other stakeholders are drawn to collaborate and can eventually partner. When you are thinking about school reform, your including branding conversations and strategies in long-term plans for a school helps develop a strategic path for continually improved pedagogical and management practices. Executing the strategies in a brandED Strategic Plan is one step to delivering a quality education to all students.

In business, a brand's competitive edge contributes to success. When you have identified the positive results of a brandED strategy, you will have the baseline for showing a school's tangible value. A brandED competitive edge is different from a business edge. This edge supports a culture that welcomes all demonstrations of students' unique abilities. It provides an attractive platform to showcase the community. Attention to a competitive edge builds a climate that offers an expansive view of performance that can attract resources for a school, which in turn further empower your students as learners.

BRANDED RESULTS THAT BUILD SCHOOL CULTURE

In a school adoption of brandED, the **image** and **promise** are showcased and communicated every day through the internal and external messaging of the school brand. It's easy to see that **results** are part of the expectations of a school that is brandED. The rich mix of stories of success provide the evidence of well-being that is important to sustaining a caring and productive culture.

Brand allows you to connect to a unified culture across the different initiatives already in place within the school community. Because of your brandED Driver work and brandED Strategic Plan, you can openly bring initiatives into your brandED big tent of messaging from across the curriculum: things like reading practices, tech initiatives, civics programs, cyberbullying initiatives, character development guides, sports, and the arts can all be connected to the school brand. A relational culture can take root that unifies the whole school organization.

Share the elements of culture you want to preserve, refresh, or launch. brandED strategies can improve culture and climate by showcasing how students are learning, achieving, and developing such qualities as leadership, perseverance, creativity, civic-mindedness, and big-picture thinking. Need more respect? More serious regard for each other? More attention to academics? More awareness of character development? More empathy among community members? Look to the brand. Through the building of a strategic plan, many initiatives will now become part of a singular unified voice with a clear and powerful school brand message. Lead the unifying process by showcasing the stories of the factors shared by your school's various initiatives and, to keep on message, positioning them through statements that relate to the school's mission. Aggregate the benefits of initiatives, such as why you are a STEM school, why you use DRAs or create a makerspace environment, or why you employ Habits of Mind as a district. Collect the combined power of programs under your school brand. Collect some initial data on a spreadsheet that tracks tweets and posts to blogs, Facebook, and Instagram to show the results of brand touch in relationship to your initiatives. Related brand events can be reported monthly to the community on a principal's blog or by students in student newspapers or student media productions. Result is found in new places with the business-as-unusual attitude. School culture comes from living the brand of the school, portraying the image, then tracking and celebrating the visible results that lead to emotional wins for the brand.

BRANDED RESULTS EXPAND SCHOOL PERFORMANCE

Academic performance is a traditional way to measure the success of a school brand, but the business-as-unusual brandED mindset is about nonconforming and innovative practices that also show results. Challenge yourself. How can evaluating school performance in broader terms be important to developing brand? Nonacademic performance is now gaining value, as a wider view of what describes a quality school is emerging. Leaders have met the challenge of valuing these performances. For example, Tony Sinanis and Joe Sanfelippo (2015) point to several ways to deliver results. As a principal and superintendent respectively, they have stretched their community to measure the social, emotional, and psychological development of their students. The combined energy and practice of these two leaders show a strategic commitment to developing a unique school leadership brand that focuses on result. They use the power of digital storytelling across numerous platforms, through podcasts and in blogs. They focus on their ability to facilitate the professional growth of their stakeholders. These forward-thinking leaders use their curating of stories and observations to begin the process of monitoring and reporting results. As early adopters of brand thinking, they are brandED leaders of the most natural kind.

As Sinanis and Sanfelippo are finding, leaders can think creatively about results and about measuring the growth of brandED initiatives.

What we decide to monitor, measure, and reward will grow a portfolio of new, expanded, and proven performance results. Monitoring the results of your PR outreach and your social media school presence, monitoring the number of quality partnerships you and your growing network of relationships build, and recording the transparent stakeholder efforts to show the core school brand across communication channels can create an initial baseline of data. Observation of the number of "touches," likes, comments, and exchanges that you use in your brand storytelling campaign can start the collection process. Having some form of data on the presence of the brand, even qualitatively reported, can be useful as you prepare to share your brand with potential resource partners. When a direction for monitoring the brand is determined during your work with the brandED Drivers, you can monitor the school brand's application using formal means. These are measures chosen by the design team—for example, surveys, online open-ended responses to prompts about the new brand, and monitoring of the school social and digital channels.

Traditional channels of communication in letters and emails can offer information and measure adoption of the brand. Focus groups can also be formed to test the effectiveness of the brand in the student, teacher, and parent communities. Informal measures taken from testimonials and observations during school events can be a measure of the integration of the brand. Evidence of visual presence of the brand online through student projects and postings, video, and written content can add to the picture. The partnering of brandED with other initiatives that connect to the school brand is explored internally. Look across school platforms for the common threads. With the introduction of new initiatives both social and academic, brand connection is part of determining the fit of the new direction. For example, testing the fit of an existing framework like an existing school character education initiative would certainly be easy. The promise of building more principled students is a match with the core principles of a school brand. Other programs might face a tougher test for inclusion in the school, depending on their fit with the core brand. Introducing performance into conversations is a part of the brandED strategy, and it can revitalize your brand results. Here are a few examples of how to gauge whether your strategy is working:

- Students' behavior can be an indicator. Fewer discipline referrals may suggest the power of brand in a new culture. Student attendance reports and volunteerism can be seen as connections to an effective brand message.

- Teachers' attitudes are indicative. How many have built and modeled building brand and its tenets of trust into classroom instruction? Consider using tools such as TodaysMeet or Mentimeter to collect anonymous perception data regarding the brand's presence in day-to-day classroom functions.

- Recruitment can indicate brand value. How many teachers who are hired understand the concept of brand and see its connection to their teaching role?

- Reach the larger community through associations and groups and their communication channels. Offer students in classrooms the opportunity to gauge the awareness, understanding, and support of the school brand.

- Students as brandED influencers for the larger community can be a resource for illustrating the expanded view of student performance, both academic and nonacademic.

- Strategies that focus on students' building relationships using digital tools can be measured, such as building high school LinkedIn pages for college or work or connecting to other classrooms around the globe for study. These can suggest an expanded view of brandED performance beyond getting good grades.

- Simple anecdotal feedback expressed as storytelling content can be a measure of growth of brand awareness in school performance.

BrandED leaders like principal Kevin Carroll track the comments made on various social platforms. Superintendent Robert Zywicki (personal communication, September 2016) posts the district-wide strategic plan on Twitter, which measures performance in a number of powerful and visible ways and links the ongoing conversation of performance to school brand.

What you, your staff, students, and parents do impacts how your school is perceived, trusted, and valued. The meaning of performance becomes more open for discussion. Your personal as well as school brand should reflect a commitment to the academic success and social and emotional well-being of the students. It is equally important that your brand shows the staff a determination to cultivate positive relationships in the name of school improvement. Your own performance can be measured against those tenets. Transparency can increase the possibility of attracting partnering resources for your school; partnerships from across many spectrums can only be initiated from a point of visibility and trust. Your school's consistent and continually fresh sources of brand collateral will compel others to connect with you as possible partners to advance the school community in myriad ways.

Performance is what you and every leader in your effort need to recognize as key to the "stickiness" of this effort. Expand the ideas of what meaningful performance is beyond the score on a standardized test. Another opportunity to impact the macroenvironment of education lies in the possibility of bringing students into the big tent for results through discovering their personal brand. The opportunities to track a student's performance over time are a strong match for building a learner's personal brand. This can be accomplished through the creation of standards-based portfolios that contain specific artifacts demonstrating conceptual mastery. As mentioned previously, whatever is posted online impacts your brand, no matter who you are. Students can now showcase their growth over time as well as unique skill sets that are attractive to colleges and employers alike. Educators who find new ways for students to compare their efforts to peers locally and globally through performance or collaboration help students share their brand and the brand of the school beyond the traditional structure of the ivory tower.

Social issues and issues of justice are often popular ways for students to interact through online engagement. Young stakeholders can engage in a mature manner regarding the real-world issues and problems of the day. During the Arab Spring, for example, youth took to social media to share and exchange a call for action with others across the world (Jacobs, 2014). Your school can share its culture—assignments, activities, and events—using student-led webcasts, broadcasts, and video presentations across school platforms and through social media. Technology has the potential to greatly magnify the opportunities to expand on performance that is captured digitally or socially. Students can transcend geographical boundaries and institutional limitations (Atkinson-Bonasio, 2016).

The developing field of massive open online communities (MOOCs) will fuel this phenomenon of connection for learners. BrandED Strategic Plans that set goals for expanding results linked to student performance in ways that are not connected to standardized tests can lead to a discussion of the types of performance that illustrate core brand values. Collaborative teams working with the brandED Drivers determine a range of new behaviors—new types of performance—that can be highlighted, valued, and monitored. Your team's collective work with the brandED Drivers features results as part of building the visible brandED strategy. In schools where a strong core brand is evident, results of increased collaboration, less bullying, or fewer referrals to the principal's office can be celebrated in stories that provide a view of new performance value that distinguishes the school beyond a number on a test. These stories can be told and measured for results in the response of the community. These are the attention-getting tales that grow word of mouth about the worth of the school. Stories of performance should resonate with such principles as support, modeling, listening, innovation, shared decision making, consensus, risk-taking, and lifelong learning. School leaders need to lead by example and sustain a personal professional brand connected to these principles.

BRANDED RESULTS THAT WIN SCHOOL RESOURCES

Communicating to build school resources in these tough economic times is essential. BrandED leaders develop strategies that distinguish them from the pack to help gain attention for resourcing.

Focus on being an ACE: Use your brandED leadership strategy of engaging, with an innovative eye on the range of partnerships available. Be active in seeing partnerships and sponsors for your brandED school message. Positioning yourself as a connected leader helps you engage partners in businesses that you want to attract for sponsorship. Before you can attract partners, your own brand identity and your institution's identity must be in order, along with stories to tell that connect potential partners to the school brand.

Get the word out about your competitive product: your school. Don't wait for stakeholder partners to find you; go after them. Operate in a strategic way through another ACE behavior: associating. Attract partnerships that can bring resources of material and service value. Use social media, which has become the power outlet for packaging and creating a brand identity. You can market for meaningful resource partnering. That kind of result happens fast, not at the pace of traditional grants. As the brand of the school is crafted and goals set, identifying and courting new partners becomes part of the brandED strategy. With a clear understanding of brand, it's easier to make an "ask" that opens the door for creating school partnerships. Dr. Melody Gunn, former principal of the Gibson Elementary School in St. Louis, saw that for some students, frequent absences were linked to their need to come to school in clean clothes. She chose a product partner in the good people of Whirlpool. Gunn asked for a donation of a laundry machine for her school. Whirlpool researched the need and saw a chance to "do well by doing good." Attendance improved by 90% for these students thanks to the presence of the machine. The partnership resulted in a growing campaign called Whirlpool Cares (Bland, 2016).

This is a striking example of business-as-unusual thought being put into action.

Before you ask, first attend to cultivating an authentic relationship. Identify your need and clearly articulate it before asking. Be ready with a great story to tell. If you speak in a genuine voice, connections can result even online, but in digital social spaces, take your time with building relationships. Approach any resource partners by first offering them value, not simply making an ask.

When you are armed with digital tools such as Hootsuite, Buffer, and IFTTT, you can present a brand that will live in messaging about your school success at any hour of the day or night. Partnerships can be made while you get some well-deserved sleep! Seeking resources in real time and on social platforms supports brand commitment and illustrates your dedication to professional growth, learning, innovation, and student success. Think expansively about possible resources:

- Have your antenna up. Be aware of possible connections anywhere you are during your day, personally and professionally. "You never know!" is the mantra of relational brandED leaders. The person sitting next to you while you're waiting to get your car repaired could be a great contact. You just need to say hello.

- Assess the networking circles you already have—family, friends, clubs, associations, social media—and then build on them using ACE strategies.

- Be consistent about asking one question of people when you have a conversation: "Who do you know that I should know?"

- Keep thinking about media. A relationship essential to the branding process is the one you build with the media. The world is driven by content, and your school is filled with great stories. There is probably nothing more powerful than storytelling that conveys and sustains a personal and institutional brand.

DIG IN ON THE RANGES OF BRANDED PARTNERING

Work proactively as you dig into partnering, either individually or with stakeholders, making relationships in the macroenvironment with external influencers and media through digital and real-time opportunities. Think with the mind of an educator marketer and aim to attract resources to your school around three communities of partners: emotional, service, and product:

BrandED *emotional* resource partners Find those who have positive feelings about your brand and are willing to act as ambassadors to spread the word. These are community members who can help share content. They may already be connected to the school community, but not in a systematic way. Offer them the chance to work toward the well-being of the school brand in ways that tangibly show their commitment to the stories of the school. Call them your brand scouts and have them use their networks to spread school content to others who would respond to positive stories of school. Retired teachers in all parts of the world make great emotional resource partners.

BrandED *service* resource partners Locate supporters who have skill sets to volunteer in the cause of promoting the brand. Push further into the world of service that connects to classrooms. David Eggers, author and TED Talk favorite, has built a national network of resourcing volunteers, service-minded partners who support the literacy development of needy kids. Under the title 896National, they provide a framework and system of support for over 32,000 students a year (Dylan, 2014). Again, retired educators may be waiting for an invitation to be relevant again, and they may simply want a connection to service rather than a substitute paycheck. Reach out to those who are nearby and develop them as a possible network of influencers who can be available to serve the school brand and its many initiatives.

BrandED *product* resource partners Identify those individuals, associations, small local businesses, and large companies who have products of value to the school's growth in culture or performance. Build relationships first before you make the "ask" for resources. Partners may have products that fit in the brand plan for your school. One such avenue is enlisting tech companies that want to support showcasing a school brand through partnering in developing products that are in their testing cycle. Think software, platforms, and apps. Think of a consistent school brand that is supported by using brand products, such as filters for videos or school-themed stickers that promote the visual connection to brand. In return, the school stories told through traditional and digital media channels will highlight how these products impact student learning or teachers' professional practice and add to the growth of the entire community. Partners can be small scale—small businesses that want to contribute to resourcing the needs of the school with products. In the end, both brands benefit.

Use the three communities of partners—emotional, service, and product—to start small grassroots efforts. It works. In 2012, a team of professionals created a small but powerful partnership that continues with schools today, called CORE 4, which the *Wall Street Journal* cited in an article about notable, giving partnerships (Grace, 2012). Michael Keating—a financial professional, husband of an educator, and father of school-age children—is the creator of this effort. He crafted a simple and targeted partnership to support kids, based on the power of four professionals who continually enlist the help of four other like-minded professionals. With an average contribution of $800, these professionals provide product support to schools with equipment or books, but they also bring service value to those school with which they partner, creating networks and relationships in the community that can bring results far beyond the small gifts of products and time. Educators who can communicate the narrative clearly can attract grassroots emotional partnerships such as this.

Conversation 5 Tips

- **Focus** on stakeholder relationship management to connect your strategic plan to relationships as a sustaining part of your school-wide brand, through the brandED leadership tools that build your relational power: *associate, create,* and *engage.*
- **Challenge** yourself to be a brandED ACE.
- **Reframe** the meaning of performance to include the stories generated around your school brand efforts. Measure their impact for tangible and intangible results.
- **Celebrate** results of your school's brand daily through showcasing around your brand's core tenets.
- **Identify** measurable culture, performance, and resource targets to show results.
- **Track** three types of resource partnerships: emotional, service, and product.

Conversation 5 Reflections

Before holding public conversation around why business brand tenets inform educational leadership, think about these questions:

- Who is the competition for my school's UBV? What does the competition have to do with my view of my school's brand? Do I see the need to have a competitive edge in light of school competition engendered by the implementation of "school choice"?
- How will I ensure my commitment to associating, creating, and engaging to build brandED relational success?
- Have I thought about how brandED impacts my school's culture, performance, and resourcing?
- Have I considered traditional and digital ways to show results that prove brandED ROI?

Conversation **6**

Communicating With BrandED Leadership Tools

The business-as-unusual journey continues in Conversation 6 for leaders who embrace new tools for leveraging their brandED plan, using offline traditional, social, and digital channels. BrandED leaders choose among many channels that engage the stakeholder community to implement their brandED Strategic Plan. Leaders expand their reach into the complex world of digital and social messaging with select tools that sustain the carefully crafted school brand, while they build necessary relationships online and offline through a brandED promotional brand-building process. This promotional process is an educator's adaptation of a campaign used by marketers. This brandED process fits a school leader's stance. Going beyond modeling your personal professional brand presence that spreads the good word, these tools are the engine for delivering your unique school brand to various publics.

What makes you unique, makes you successful.

—*William Arruda*

Get the word out with your brandED Strategic Plan. Give people something to talk about.

You've identified the Drivers of your brandED work with staff, teachers, students, parents, and the community. You own a brandED Strategic Plan. Your business-as-unusual stance is ready to be displayed daily through developing new, strategic relationships. Promotional channels for your new brand messages await. Sustain your role as a brandED steward as you strategically spread the word about your institutional brand.

Part One: The BrandED Payoff of Distributed Leadership

Brand development has traditionally been either product or service driven, but today it seems that the line between service and product has blurred. What distinguished a service was once found in its marketing characteristics. Service was classified as *intangible* because unlike products, services aren't seen, tasted, felt, or smelled before "purchase." Also, services are *variable,* meaning that the quality of service depends on who is providing the service. Service is *inseparable* from a provider. Services are delivered in the moment; they are *perishable.* You can't store service for later use (Armstrong & Kotler, 2015). Because of the rate of change and the digital delivery of value, services are now viewed as products. It is a view that is evolving daily.

BRANDED LEADER OF SERVICE OR PRODUCT?

Schools don't need to get caught up in the debate about products and services. There is no right or wrong way to view what we provide to our stakeholders. BrandED leaders can use their judgment. Both product- and service-oriented delivery are about keeping stakeholders happy. Educators who are in a brandED mindset, those who see the worth of delivering stakeholder relationship value, may favor the view of being service providers rather than product deliverers. After all, most educators are service-minded individuals who have social skill and the desire to impact well-being. Other educators may feel that although we are not packaging in the ways merchandisers do, we do work to enhance our students' lives with tangible features, and these products, their skill sets, carry them successfully into the future. Skills that they possess will distinguish them in a "packaged" sense when they apply to college or for jobs. Because of the blurring of the brand lines in business today, viewing education as a combined delivery of product and service may serve your thinking about your brand effort. Either way of thinking promotes the engagement of a school with its stakeholders.

It is in the channels of content that a combined product- and service-minded orientation may become part of the education brand. The results of your communication and public relations efforts are tangible products. Just as in a PR agency campaign, these touchstones of earned content are tangible products that hold valuable places across media channels. The stories of your school or district that stakeholders see, celebrate, share, and appreciate may show your attention to service. They have value as collateral. Lines are blurred in the world of marketing, and content that is produced in text and video constitutes valuable products that engage stakeholders. Content that captures innovative practices demonstrates the learning of students, provides evidence of gains in student achievement, and presents progress in unique ways that are products for schools to point to with pride. The products prove that standards are being addressed. They celebrate staff accomplishments, and collaborations that have provided enhanced learning opportunities for students.

Brand is about perception, and if there's no "there" in your school brand, if there is only a static website and one-way messaging, there's little to see. These brand products, communicated to stakeholders using various digital channels, guarantee eyeballs. People will look, and will like and share your brand. This engagement is the result of your service-minded efforts to develop learning.

Keep in mind that the product and service attitudes you display depend on the premier channel of an engaging website. You may have a website that gives a laundry list full of the wonderful features your school offers, but be aware that features are not themselves communicating a cohesive brand. Brand communicates benefit, and storytelling products communicate benefit that connects to emotions. No benefit means no reason to care, no reason to engage. Make the perception of your brand immediately authentic, clear, and connected so that your stakeholders see benefits. In developing a product stance to share the narrative of your school, give your stakeholders a daily dose of the unique benefits that your school brand provides.

SHARING RESPONSIBILITY TO PROMOTE THE BRAND

A powerful step in spreading the word about brand is to recognize that brandED's connection to distributed leadership is a valuable element of the school brand effort. A useful tool as the brand was designed, distributed leadership can continue to set the expectation of shared responsibility in promotion of the brand, internally and externally. The affiliative model of brandED leadership shown in Figure 6.1 illustrates how collaborative leadership powers your promotion. Your purpose is to create collaborative support and frameworks for telling the story of the brand and promoting it locally and globally. The **awareness** of the brand, its designed **value,** the **beliefs** the brand embodies, and the **emotions** that have been part of creating and sustaining the school brand provide connectivity. Using the affinity of distributed leadership, the brand is shared with the internal microenvironment and the external macroenvironment for increased reach and power. Spreading the word through any powerful tool of sharing online and offline becomes more powerful because of the collaboration, energy, and reach of distributed leadership. It's an "all hands on deck" for brand attitude. Moving beyond early brand adopters, new ambassadors are continually identified in the stakeholder pool of students, parents, staff, and the greater community. The energy of brand is contagious, and a distributed leadership model speeds the process of spreading awareness. The acceptance of an affiliative attitude makes the team a network of brandED storytellers and stewards who grow the brand in service to the school's mission using digital and traditional channels of communication, working as effectively as a Madison Avenue marketing team to deliver the brand message.

Figure 6.1   The Affiliative Model of BrandED Leadership

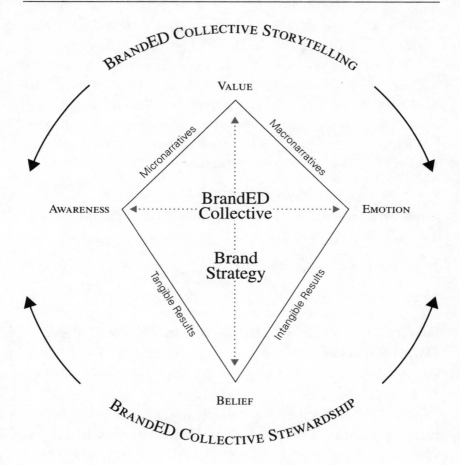

Part Two: Press, Networking, Digital Presence, and Thought Leadership

Two words capture brand marketing at its basic core: *identify* and *satisfy*. The terms are foundational to the definition of marketing offered by Philip Kotler, world-renowned marketing educator and consultant to global corporations (Armstrong & Kotler, 2015). Throughout history, merchants and traders identified a "need" and "satisfied" it. The world of disruptive innovation in business today is proof of people's continuing desire to identify and satisfy.

As you build brandED, you are looking for ways to identify and satisfy, a task that becomes even easier in this new-age media world where stakeholders want to engage with you around their needs. Your school audience wants to be satisfied. This audience includes parents, kids, teachers, staff, and the community at large, as well as resource partners. Communication can enhance your team's effectiveness in getting the word out about brand image or identity. A 21st-century communication toolbox for school leaders includes the following:

- Public relations: connectivity to press and through new media
- Networking: relational connecting and influencer partnering
- Digital presence: knowing your audiences and engaging them online
- Thought leadership: achieving a respected expert stance that educates internally and externally in your organization

BRANDED PUBLIC RELATIONS IN THE NEW DIGITAL AGE

What's your purpose in developing brandED public relations (PR)? Why do educational leaders need to know PR?

According to PR professional Renee Blodgett, "Public Relations in its true sense is about human connections and the art of mastering human connections at a deep level" (Cohen, 2011b). In the early days of PR, it was about relationships with not just the press but communities; the difference was that these audiences were not online. When delivered from a place of passion and purpose, PR in the new world will not only take social media, branding and marketing to the next level but also elevate the people and products that are changing the world (Cohen, 2011b). Proactive school leaders see the value of this newly defined world of PR. Educators come from a place of passion for learning and can use the accessible tools of PR to fuel a positive brandED culture. They own products and services that can be promoted to show the value of the school. Good PR recognizes positive school performance beyond test scores in the expanded Brand ED mindset. It highlights the positive social norms that define performance in an educational setting through narratives that are authentic human interest tales capable of attracting worthwhile resources.

PR is part of a free "earned" channel of advertising that schools can use. Leaders with a brandED mindset function as the guides of their own PR machine for school brand. Luckily, the walls have crumbled in the PR world. These days, people don't fax a press release or mail a press kit to get attention. The digital world moves too quickly for that. Once upon a time, a "second day" story was still seen as relevant to print and TV media. Today, the "second hour" story is old news. Don't let the idea of content moving at the speed of a click concern you. Your brand story, if it is solidly defined and placed continually for sharing, will attract eyeballs online. The resources of a collaborative team and growing brand ambassador network will provide many brand stories that can capture local press or even beyond.

In brandED Driver discussions, your team selects channels to promote brand messaging that includes PR. Building your strategic plan evokes commitment to find the best ways to showcase a new school brand identity.

A strategy built on relational behavior gets attention. There are thousands of new digital partners in the macroenvironment of education who want engaging content and unique story angles to share with their audiences. There are countless outlets for telling your story. A leader doesn't have to be the sole source of content for the effort. Empowering staff, teachers, students, and parents to tell stories through your brandED Strategic Plan distributes the showcasing effort. I (Eric) found great success with the New York City media with our innovative practices. Through either social media sharing or direct phone calls, news outlets were extremely interested in how education was changing to prepare students better for the real world. National media outlets such as *USA Today, Education Week,* and *Scholastic Administrator* also were interested in innovative ideas and strategies that aligned to more rigorous standards in relevant ways. All media outlets were intrigued by how school leaders were adapting to a digital world in order to better engage stakeholders.

Unfortunately, bad press is a fact of life. The best way to counter it is to be proactive with consistently sharing all of the positives that happen in schools every day. In 2009, I (Eric) began my brandED journey, and from that point forward used social media and traditional means to tell our real story about how we were meeting the needs of our kids. After 5 years, our transparency became our greatest asset in the battle against negative press. In the spring of 2014, some of our students were caught after successfully counterfeiting money for over a month using an inkjet printer and resume paper from a local office store. When the news broke, every major NYC news station was at my school. Guess how many phone calls and emails I received from parents about this? Zero! The best defense against negative press is a brandED offense.

Defining and discussing the term *content* with your team is part of your strategy. In your development of brandED Drivers, defining the content and positioning of brandED will help people confidently identify what's PR worthy about your school. Check out the platforms and sites of other schools—the competition—that are actively sharing their brand. PR delivery continues in the distributed leadership model. In starting a PR movement, enlist brandED collective members who are naturals at promotion.

A START-UP PR PLAN

PR is partly about building strong relationships with media professionals. In our digital world, it now also means taking control of the story of yourself, your school, and your district. New media have ushered in a whole new way to characterize professionals who want your content. Today's PR family has expanded to include influencers, bloggers, webinar leaders, and podcast and radio show hosts who are creating or curating the kind of content you want your brand to be part of. You want these communities to appreciate your school brand and support your culture in a relational exchange.

Print journalism

First of all, recognize that print media aren't dead. The industry is changing, but still valued and still part of a brand awareness plan if thoughtfully executed. There are several ways to get connected to assignment desk editors and reporters, ranging from quick fixes to long-term friendships. BrandED leaders also set goals for engaging press and media as part of their eye on result. Leaders can set the bar for media attention to the brand. For instance, one PR placement a month in some schools is seen as a goal. Here are a few tips to start:

- Buying a media list of reporters through a service such as Media Contacts Pro (www.mediacontactspro.com) is a quick way to launch. It's a small investment that gets you focused on assignment editors in your region whom you can call to introduce yourself and your ideas. You can also find reporters' names and sometimes online addresses in the opening pages of print magazines.

- Develop a small media kit that can live on your website or that is part of your personal professional blog. It acts as a promotional PR tool that makes it easy for journalists, bloggers, and influencers to highlight your brand. They were once traditional text-based collateral. Today, they are a mix of promotional content about your school. There is no set formula. Build it as a PDF and include the stories, the visuals, and links to your school brand.

- To approach editors about events and press-worthy accomplishments, use a short media advisory template. You can find models for this online (also see Appendix E). Media advisories can be standardized by your team and used again and again with each new form of content you offer to an editor or news desk. The advisory should have a catchy title and contain the basic facts of the story you are presenting, including the traditional who, what, where, when, and why. Using the advisory helps you develop a "pitch" conversation about your school's brand and the content you have to share. Write out a few lines for the pitch that you can use and that the members of your team can make to editors.

- Editors have little time, so be friendly and direct with your media contacts. Get their names, keep them on your list of contacts, and follow them on social media even if they don't take the pitch. Use your brandED mission statement and ask them if they would accept a media advisory. Avoid overused words like "amazing," "interesting," or "cool" when you pitch. Let them know why this is important news for their audience.

- Practice your pitch in real time. When you meet reporters in the course of school events, such as sports reporters at your school games, or reporters covering school meetings, let them know some of the things you want to showcase. If you have made a relational connection, they may refer you to another reporter or another outlet, such as an online website.

It may take a while to get your first story in print, but keep calling editors with stories of your brand. Invest in building relationships with every pitch you or your team members make. You will become "known," and a relationship forms with the press based on trust. It takes time to develop these efforts, but they are well worth the work.

Reporters online

Today print outlets have online platforms. You can often get reporters' email addresses directly from their online articles. You can advance PR efforts directly to reporters' online addresses, although keep in mind that they are also getting assignments from the desk assignment editor, so make friends there too. If you are new to this business-as-unusual media approach, check out these tips:

- Begin your relationship by reading and commenting on a writer's articles first, before pitching your content.

- Check out Twitter or other social media spaces to find the reporter's profile and content. "Listen" online and collect data about the reporters with whom you want to begin an online relationship.

- When appropriate, retweet (RT) or share their work and comment. Do it regularly and respectfully, and they will notice you. Start a Twitter list of reporters on whom you are focusing your relational efforts. If you include a quote RT, you may get a follow from a reporter, and then you can directly speak to him or her in a Twitter direct message, but avoid being "stalky."

- Use an open mind when searching out reporter relationships. Anyone from sports to financial reporters could be a connection.

Influencers

Use Twitter, LinkedIn, and other social media and news feeds as well as search engines to search for keywords and see who "owns" the space for whatever piece of content you are trying to promote . . . STEM? STEAM? professional capital? tech? literacy? assessment? Use the Twittersphere to show these influencers "social love" by retweeting and quoting them. Like and comment on their other platforms. Look at these influencers on Twitter. Do a search through their followers and learn more about them to see if they might also be good connections. Investigate keywords as hashtags and see who is writing great engaging content that has made an impression. Follow, RT, and repeat! The same can be said of YouTube, where a world of influencers are creating content that you can connect with and create relationships around. A great comment goes a long way in establishing digital connection to online influencers.

Twitter chats

If you want to build your presence through Twitter chat engagement, you can venture out into the realm around a topic of interest to you or to your school. Popular Twitter chats include #edchat and #satchat. To support the global community, #edchat takes place every Tuesday at 11:00 a.m. and 7:00 p.m. EST. Through an open poll, two different questions are selected as topics of discussion. At 7:30 a.m. EST on Saturdays, administrators and teachers can engage in leadership topics during #satchat. For more information on Twitter chats, visit cybraryman.com/chats.html.

Identify something that connects to your brand that can be shared with other educators. Find out which teachers and administrators you have on staff who are engaged in this way and make an effort to provide them with value for being part of the connected community of educators. This could come in the form of allowing them to lead professional development opportunities with colleagues on what they have learned in online spaces (and being compensated for it if there is money in the budget). You could also develop means to provide professional development hours through the use of digital badges to acknowledge their learning in these spaces.

Blogging

Today, blogging is a big business. Ask your team, staff, and community to identify K–12 guest bloggers for your school. Set a goal to connect with 10 educational bloggers who have high presence. Leaders like Derek McCoy, Todd Nesloney, and Amber Teamann are superstars in the educational digital space. Target the best voices in education who are blogging, and build relationships that can lead to shared content and presence. Comment on and support bloggers' thinking. Follow them on Twitter and develop the relationship. You can offer bloggers the chance to have their content featured on your district website. Offer up guest post ideas and content.

Leaders who create their own blogs as a means of building a personal professional brand see a relational value beyond storytelling. A blog address is a way to connect with other writers. These colleagues will help you get your voice out to their readers and followers. Sharing engaging content from your school blog on your own blog as well as others' builds your presence.

Another brand value is found in the creation of your own principal or superintendent blog where you can build your personal professional presence as you promote and inform the institution. Leaders who have blogs have used them successfully as they have pivoted from using traditional print and email channels of communication with stakeholders to using blogs to message their community on topics related to curriculum, policy, or organizational change. A blog isn't an add-on for these leaders; they have left the email chains and newsletters behind for a brand-driven experience that shows continued presence online. The transparency available with a commitment to blogging is powerful and viewed with genuine appreciation by all community stakeholders.

Webinars

Content abounds and conversation is king using the vehicle of webinars. Start by participating, and encouraging your team to participate, in webinars given by members of the educational community. As in connecting to bloggers, set a goal of participation. The brandED leader can model this and promote appearances. Your connected, innovative teachers can also be spokespersons for the brand on webinars. Once you've shown up on webinars, follow up with positive feedback and maintain your relationships with webinar influencers. Developing a relationship with the webinar community can get you positioned to be a guest, enabling you to share your school brand story. You skill at telling your story will grow. As much as you can, model your own transparent behavior and show up anywhere to showcase the school or your work. The ultimate goal is to begin facilitating webinars of your own on platforms such as edWeb (www.edweb.net) to share the amazing work taking place in your school or district. Many districts see this as an aspirational channel for getting the word out about their school.

Video

Visual presence that can be shared and liked and commented on is another sure way to engage to communicate your brand. Many leaders have embraced this means of digital storytelling in thoughtful, targeted ways. A Snap or a quick Instagram video post can be a quick shared media promotion across numerous social media sites; something longer and more story-like can appear on the school's website as well as on partner websites and on YouTube. For those drawn to Instagram, efficiency can be found with the Schedulegram app that manages more than one Instagram account. Schedulegram is great for those who want to build brand presence on the Instagram platform through multiple views of the school that are serviced by the school itself, which keeps the brand visual story consistent. Instagram's newest version of Instagram Stories makes sharing visual content even easier. The latest model of note with which brandED leaders and their teams can establish their video footprint is a new platform called Knowsy (knowsy.co). This new outlet is a model for your search to develop help content for your school brand. The site can give you plenty of ideas about how to engage your community in sharing and curating 1-minute videos that create engagement, answer questions, teach, or entertain. Video content, easily produced on mobile phones, can be submitted, curated, and shared on the district channels. It can take only a minute to engage your community and make your brand contagious.

Live streaming

Mid-2015 saw the birth and rapid development of two new live streaming platforms: Periscope and Blab. Periscope has proven over the last year to be of particular interest to educators, many of whom have experienced Google Hangouts as a professional learning tool. Periscope brings something new to the experience. It's a free app linked to Twitter. These sites are terrific for capturing and broadcasting real-time content. No press kit needed, just an account and a mobile phone. Many educators are becoming creative in their initial application of this tool. Teachers like Sarah Thomas have been identified in professional journals as pioneers. Sarah uses the Periscope app in connection with her innovative makerspace (Madda, 2015).

Through live video, Sarah has been able to show stakeholders all over the world how her students are learning with their hands by creating, tinkering, inventing, and making. Her use of Periscope video provides a more detailed view into the practical nature of how a makerspace supports high-level learning and engagement, and inspires others to pursue this innovative practice. Periscope and other live video tools can also be used take virtual field trips, connect with experts, give homework help, reach students who are out ill for extended periods of time, showcase live performances, or even let people attend an art show without their physically being there. Educators are interested in the value of this tool as a means of promoting the good work of their school in a free and far-reaching way.

One of the leaders in the Periscope community is Sheila Jane Chako, whose website Sheila Jane Teaching is a textbook for developing brand presence. Sheila Jane's brand tagline on her colorful, engaging website is "Teach Happy. Live Happy. Be Happy." She sees herself as a teacher who is also a teacher advocate. Her homepage refers to itself as the "staffroom" that teachers wish they had! Her understanding of building brand is driven by her need to serve and support her fellow educator colleagues; she does this energetically through her YouTube channel, where she broadcasts, honors, and interviews the "Teachers we Love." A blog post recently highlighted her fellow movers and shakers in the Periscope universe for teachers (Chako, 2016). Follow them and research others in this growing community to understand its pros and cons. The pros seem to outweigh the cons, but know them both. Privacy can be a concern when streaming younger students. Adjust features such as location, posting to Twitter, and chat to protect your kids. Also make sure that all appropriate media waivers have been signed when posting any video online. Another con is that the communication is only one-way, which takes a bit away from the authentic engagement factor. Take a deep breath and dive into streaming. To get started, check out the account of elementary principal Todd Nesloney (@TechNinjaTodd) to see how he uses Periscope as part of his brandED strategy.

THOUGHT LEADERSHIP: DRIVING THE CONVERSATION

As the leader of your brandED Strategic Plan, you will have a chance to take on a new role, one of a strategic thought leader. There is a growing audience for content related to teaching and learning and leading. Educators are scouring *Huffington Post Educator* articles and the *Edutopia* platform. The role of lead learner comes with a responsibility to share in the dialogue about school-related topics. In the mix of PR, the role of thought leadership becomes a genuine and compelling part of a school brand story. The emergence of an informed, connected educator armed with digital tools and a passion for learning is an integral part of promoting school brand. As you build your personal professional brand, don't wait to identify the audiences for sharing. Do your homework, research Google, and search for topics you are interested in. Find your voice for expressing your school passion. Building the brand without a strategy for sharing can short-circuit your impact as a thought leader. Seeing yourself as an expert thought leader helps you build trust in your community. Don't be shy—report on your brand. Build your professional identity to share with your school community and then with the bigger world.

What is a thought leader in education? Someone whose voice can power the value that your school brand captures. There are many channels through which you can share or market your messages. For a complete list of platforms that you can approach with content, or simply monitor for possible relational use, refer to Appendix G.

TRACKING JOURNALISTS: HARO AND MUCK RACK

Another way to search outlets that may be new for educators is the website HARO (Help a Reporter Out, www.helpareporter.com), a free publicity tool. With HARO, you can be connected to reporters who are looking for sources and for content. You can also set yourself and community up to be found as resources for educational stories on a grand scale. HARO allows you to pitch thousands of influential reporters who work with them daily in their search for good content and notable experts. With HARO, you can use your expertise in education to speak as a thought leader to the postings sent by journalists each day for experts in the field. HARO presents an opportunity to connect to a high level of PR with a stroke of a few keys and a media advisory or an attractive, interesting few lines about your topic. Another outlet for connection to journalists is Muck Rack (www.muckrack.com). Log in as a blogger (with or without a blog) and input *education* or other related words to see the latest content in articles from journalists who are writing about education or trends that impact learning. You see their contact info immediately. Follow them on Twitter first and use your listening and retweeting before reaching out for a pitch or an ask.

CORPORATE NEWSLETTERS/VOLUNTEERISM

Another little-known outlet for your content is corporate PR and newsletters. These outlets generally have high-quality presentational value. Corporate or in-house magazines, which number in the thousands, are written for the company's customers. Apple, Dell, and IBM are among the biggest outlets. Don't forget associations like law journals or health journals that have professional audiences. They welcome content that can give their readers a break from the typical articles. Companies also are looking for ways to show their social responsibility to their readers. Coming up with creative hooks using the work of students can get you close to publication quickly.

Use your network to approach people in companies with the topics that you think are a match, topics that you can cleverly spin. Do some research on the sites that you want to connect to for publication. A quick look at the Dell main website can take you to their social responsibility goals and topics that align with educators. Head to the online blog and see what is featured there. Get the names of those who write for and produce the magazine and use your best pitch.

Identify your favorite brands and query their marketing departments about their use of guest writers who are brand fans or have complementary content. Organizations with intranets also have need for content. Volunteer to help them communicate their messages using the skills of your savvy students in the school community who can capably update agency intranets and make their content fresh, and who receive resume-building experience and credit. Have your students also connect and publish on a voluntary basis for a corporate newsletter. Through connecting to potential partners on Twitter, teachers have been able to make connections to HR department specialists who can offer topics for students to provide editorial support and visuals that go along with the brand of the company. Students' views of health topics that are important to them or their families can be features in hospital and pharmaceutical newsletters. Real estate newsletters can be enriched by students' views of what makes a residential neighborhood desirable for kids or teens; tech companies can welcome the entrepreneurial students of tech and their range of ideas and potential suggestions for tech tools for Gen Z. These are only the beginning. The key to connection to corporations is relationship development. Go out on Twitter with students and search the companies to which you want to provide interesting content from students. You can use these opportunities to bring value and begin a relationship that may eventually lead to emotional, service, or product resourcing.

These tools hold communication power for school leaders. In business, growing a connected, targeted brand that is constantly in touch with audiences is fueled by two different marketing camps: "big data" and "creative." The tension between these two camps has persisted in business for years. Researchers and creatives have a different view of telling the story of brand. In education today, there are movements toward collecting and analyzing big data. This isn't the direction for brandED storytellers; we don't aggregate big data, yet information, both anecdotal and formative, serves as important feedback regarding the implementation of brand principles and the results. The lesson for educators is to serve both camps within your brand approach. Creativity inspires strong brand development, while data collection verifies its results. A balance of creativity and data collection can also sustain brand relevance through interest and positive attention to the brand.

Part Three: The Law of BrandED Attraction

Armed with the school narrative, tools for promotion, a collaborative network to tell the story, and content about school performance, you have credibility to approach supportive partners.

The Law of BrandED Attraction comes down to honing your image, promise, and result into a clear and compelling pitch that makes it easy to ask those with whom you have developed genuine connection for an opportunity to partner. Test the power of your brand using the Law of BrandED Attraction that has garnered you attention through use of online and offline communication tools. For example, use social media to connect with "big fish" corporate brands. Find those who share the parallels between their organization's brand and stories with your school's content. Build a digital relationship. They may not be the unlikely candidates for attention that you first imagine. Develop a trusting exchange of common narratives. Build awareness with them online through content. See them as part of your aspirational targets for relationships. Forward-thinking schools today have experimented with partnerships with colleges and universities; some have captured the attention of nonprofits. Historically, schools have hesitated to get too close to business partnerships, but the world of technology and the vast number of tech businesses on the scene provide opportunities to change the view of exchange with business.

A BrandED Short Story of Attraction: Eric Sheninger

Adobe is a major player in the corporate and educational technology market. Many of Eric's teachers wanted access to Adobe tools, but in a small school, budgets are tight. However, we were able to secure access in one of our computer labs where teachers and students alike flocked to unleash their creativity. Eric would routinely use his blog to share all of the amazing ways his students were demonstrating conceptual mastery and attainment of standards. These blog posts were then shared across Twitter, Facebook, and other social media tools. Eric also began to use some of the tools to support his professional practice.

(continued)

Then one day, Adobe Education contacted Eric, as company employees had read about how his teachers were effectively utilizing Adobe tools. He was invited to join the company's prestigious Adobe Education Leader program. (The Law of BrandED Attraction in action!) Admittance to the program provided him and his teachers access to any Adobe tool for free. This access then led to the embracement of even more innovative strategies in his school. For example, one of his math teachers began using Adobe Captivate to flip her class. She created elaborate lessons with embedded formative assessments that provided her with real-time feedback. Students watched these short lessons at home, which then freed up more time in class for the teacher to work with students. After a while, more teachers were using Adobe and other tools to flip their classes. Naturally, Eric made the time to blog about the pedagogy behind the approach, which caught the eye of both CBS and NBC in New York City. In no time, both television stations were at his school covering the story. This partnership benefited Adobe in many ways, from the major media coverage to the gathering of practical examples of how their tools were being used to improve learning. From the school's standpoint, they got access to awesome tools and were able to be innovative in their practice.

SEEK AN ARRAY OF PARTNERSHIPS

The creation of partnerships using brandED tenets can be a grassroots effort, rather than a full-out campaign to become involved in a structured public-private partnership that formalizes relationships on a grand scale (Claypool & McLaughlin, 2015). As the brandED short story shows, because of the transparent world, it's easier and easier to make an ask, which opens the door for creating school-corporation partnerships. But before you ask, first attend to developing an authentic relationship. Approach any resource partners offering value. When you do, go back to the building of relationships through human behavior.

Use the "giving behavior" suggested by Adam Grant (discussed in Conversation 2) to introduce the possibility of creating a lasting bond. The most important way to approach is through the lens of resource partners suggested in Conversation 5. After a search of the brands, notice if you see promise in potential partners as emotional, service, or product resource sponsors. See relationships through those categories. Don't just focus on "stuff"—materials or product—look carefully at the story of the brand online. Begin by social listening on all the brand sites until you understand their interests. Then begin to connect with the brand on all of its platforms, and like and share them. Retweet and show up as a fan. Depending on the size of the company, you may be surprised at how quickly you can connect and get into a short online exchange.

Look for connectivity between your crafted school brand and mission and the social responsibility stance of any company you want to partner with, and use that as a common feature as you develop awareness online. This stance is part of a trend identified as "Moral Imperative" in the database built by the cultural trend strategists at the innovative New York City sparks & honey agency. See those who match the moral imperative of your brand, what it genuinely stands for in society. Often leaders can make online connections through community outreach, human relations, and even social media departments. When you make the connections, make them on the basis of what you have in common and come up with a creative hook for giving value to a potential partner. The content of your brand, your online stories, are marketing collateral that builds understanding. Content is seen as a value to a partner. Although doing so takes patience, building an ask from nothing using social media is worth it. Don't forget that face-to-face may work even more quickly, so keep in mind the partners you want to meet, and start looking for connections in your network or on LinkedIn for introductions. Also look for and plan to attend any public marketing events that are hosted by your potential partners to make face-to-face connections.

ENGAGE YOUR COMMUNITY

Use the "1,000 people who know you" rule from mass marketing as a guide for resourcing your campaign. As you begin, focus your efforts on serving a small part of the market and keeping them happy. Your most loyal fans are already with you. Tell them your brand story through social media and digital contacts. These people will be your biggest supporters, and they will enlist more fans to the cause.

In your brandED initiative, regular digital marketing and communicating with wider audiences about your school are imperative. In the digital world, supporters could be sitting down the street or 8,000 miles away, so engage them with messages that keep them supportive of your school. Your brandED strategies can attract and retain people who care about education, not just those in your school or district or even community. Just think how many more budgets would be approved if school brand was consistently shared and marketed more personally every day.

A BrandED Short Story: Mike Wong

BrandED leaders don't have to focus on big corporate connections. You can find people like Mike Wong in your local community. You have local supporters who aren't directly connected to the school, but who could benefit from connecting with you. Seniors, stay-at-home moms with small children, merchants, professionals, and small businesses are all in your community of stakeholders. Think about how they can benefit from the value of your school brand.

Mike Wong, an engineer and alum from Park City, Utah, went back to his school to mentor students and wound up launching four students in a business called IKOS, which went on to create a toy that was awarded "2015 Best Product of the Year" by *Creative Child* magazine (M. Wong, personal communication, April 2016). Mike came to the project to give back to his school, but connected with several students who became excited about a real-world application of their interests. His short visit turned into a commitment that changed the lives of the students who helped engineer this toy.

As the story of Mike Wong shows, the alumni community can be of strong brand power for your efforts in all ways: emotional, service, or product relationships. If a true brand bond is forged with your students before they become your alums, you will have a more connected brand community after graduation. With the digital connections that your grads value in their daily life, you can keep them close as fans. Think about the storytelling value that can connect your alumni beyond a homecoming game or a high school reunion. You have a tribe already who could resource through mentoring, connecting, and donations. Even developing simple ways to connect through surveys or short contests around your school brand online can get your young alums engaged.

Other local relationships come in the form of connecting to business. The business world can touch the school community at any scale—small, midsize, and large. Using associating, creating, and engaging (ACE) tools (see Conversation 5) will create a mix of partners in your leadership professional network. The possibility that you are only one link away from a valuable partnership for resource is always there if you attend to growing your network.

Conversation 6 Tips

- **Explore** the full range of traditional and new-age communication tools available to tell your story to local and global audiences, and use the distributed model of leadership to promote the school's message through selected channels.
- **Address** the community and teach the value of brandED as a relational tool for school improvement.
- **Understand** the opportunities that exist for partnering and build avenues to relationships.
- **Identify** and describe the needs in your community for emotional, service, and product partners.
- **Imagine** what a school calendar for a brandED year may look like following the development of your strategic plan.

Conversation 6 Reflections

Before communicating your brand with the public through a variety of your identified channels, think about these questions:

- Which tools of traditional and new media communication are a fit for the brandED strategy we have developed that will be shared using our affiliative model of brandED distributed leadership?
- How can the selected communication tools help us expand the idea of performance by our students and staff beyond test scores?
- Knowing that brandED leadership builds resources, how can we target the right partners?
- How can we maintain the messaging of our brandED Strategic Plan as brand stewards?

Keeping Up With the Digital Joneses

Conversation 7 supports a leader's effort to align with today's connected digital and social media stakeholders: the active online community of students, teachers, parents, and the greater community. This effort sustains the school brand mission with an eye on continual innovation for the future. Using the inspiring world of disruptive innovation that has made its way to education, brandED leaders further their new media efforts in partnership with the digital tribes they lead and learn to engage their most connected digital communities in support of the school brand.

> The Millennial Generation . . . the "Me" Generation. Well, it's true. We do have a sense of entitlement, a sense of ownership, because, after all, this is the world we were born into, and we are responsible for it.
>
> —*Evan Speigel, CEO, Snapchat*

Part One: Disruptive Digital Behavior That Innovates Schools

In its definition, the word *disruptive* seems extreme.

Disruption is described as *troublesome* and *unruly,* but the word also has other meanings that fit a brandED effort, like *innovative* and *groundbreaking.*

Disruptive change can result in better value in the eye of a consumer. Embracing innovative and bold ideas involving technology has led to some amazing advancements for end users of products and services in the last few decades. Education is ripe for disruptive change leading to innovative practices that improve learning outcomes for our students. What might have worked in the past will not necessarily have the same impact today, as the world has changed dramatically in a short period of time. It's safe to say that the seismic shifts we are witnessing as a result of technological advances will continue to reshape our world in ways that we could never have imagined. Disruption is really the "new normal" in the view of Scott Kerr, Time Inc. executive director for Strategy+Insight (personal communication, December 13, 2016). Kerr credits the growth of innovation in our new media age to great disrupters who are tuned in to the culture. These innovators see gaps in current "best practice" conventions that others miss. These spirited leaders smartly execute and change entire industries. In his work growing the next generation as a sought-after speaker in colleges, Kerr presents the value of disruption across industries and sees disruptive practices like brand adaptation as a fit for educators who now have the ability to engage their community in transparent, open ways. Disruption has become commonplace in the new world, and organizations have moved from adaptation to evolution in order not only to survive but also, more importantly, to thrive.

The past offers us many lessons about change and disruptive leadership, as certain organizations have embraced innovative ideas while changing the ways they learn. Let's take a walk down memory lane to see firsthand some powerful examples of disruptive innovation in action.

Remember the days when many of us had a Blockbuster video card? If you didn't have one, you couldn't rent a VHS tape of your favorite movie. If you did, your joyful anticipation of watching the latest new release was often squashed upon your arrival at the store, when you discovered that all the copies were already rented out. This didn't change much with the shift from VHS to DVD. So where is Blockbuster today?

You know the answer: Netflix caused the demise of Blockbuster. Netflix was willing to innovate and changed the way we got our video: no brick-and-mortar stores, DVDs by mail, and eventually streaming. The Blockbuster leadership never really knew what hit them until it was too late. The innovative ideas embraced and employed by Netflix were much more consumer friendly. They also aligned nicely with the technological changes that were occurring. The stubbornness and shortsightedness of Blockbuster along with its unwillingness to move away from business as usual resulted in its ultimate demise.

Let's look at another example. How many of us had a Blackberry as our first smartphone? Many members of Eric's personal learning network still make fun of those who held on a bit longer than most. Well, the story of Blackberry ended just about the same way as Blockbuster's. Apple and Steve Jobs disrupted the smartphone business with the iPhone. Not only did the iPhone annihilate Blackberry and forever knock it off the pedestal as the gold-standard device, but it also sparked the smartphone wars. Virtually every touchscreen smartphone device today has come to us thanks to the iPhone. This is another example of how a willingness to innovate resulted in a fundamental change in how we work and learn.

Here is one final example that is unfolding right before our eyes. The taxicab industry has been steadfast in its opposition to change. Any attempts to innovate now are futile, as Uber seized on an industry that was not very consumer friendly. Uber owns no physical cars, yet is now valued at around $68 billion (Chen, 2015). Anyone can use the Uber app to hail a ride for a fraction of the cost of a cab. In some cities you can even order food, helicopters, and jets. Don't think for a minute that Uber is waiting around for the next disrupter to come along and eradicate its business model. The company truly understands the nature of disruptive leadership and change and is committed to being ahead of the curve. It is doing so now by investing in driverless cars. Uber's commitment to embracing innovative ideas will keep the company relevant for a long time.

There are powerful lessons that schools can learn from the stories of disruptive leadership and change. In many ways, there are similarities between Blockbuster, Blackberry, the taxicab industry, and our education system. Even though there has been incremental change resulting in some isolated pockets of excellence in schools across the world, system change has been hard to come by. By employing disruptive strategies, we can begin the process of creating a more relevant learning culture for our students. If we don't, history has already provided a glimpse as to what might happen.

With those salient examples in mind, think about your brandED leadership. Disruptive leadership compels educators to go against the flow, challenge the status quo, take on the resistance, and shift their thinking in a more growth-oriented way. Disruptive leadership will lead to disruptive innovation. If we hang on to the same old type of thinking, we will continue to get the same old results . . . or worse. This is why digital leadership is so important in a time of rapid change. There is time to go down the path less traveled and create systems of excellence that will be embraced by our learners and in turn better prepare them for their future. Think differently. Learn differently. As I (Eric) noted in a recent blog post, "Innovation, in an educational context, is creating, implementing, and sustaining transformative ideas that instill awe to improve learning."

BrandED leaders understand and embrace disruptive change. They understand that a century-old education model will prepare students for a world that no longer exists. This is unacceptable. BrandED leaders look to actively disrupt the system by embracing evolving technologies to improve student learning outcomes and their own professional practice, transform learning spaces to make them more reflective of the real world, and implement bold ideas that challenge the status quo and have yet to be implemented at scale in the education system. Just the use of social media as a consistent means of communicating and taking control of public relations is an agent of disruption, as our stakeholders are not used to a transparent school. BrandED leaders are undeterred when it comes to tackling issues in education that are broken, such as grading, homework, observation and evaluation, and lack of accountability when it comes to professional development.

Possibly the most crucial area in education that needs disruption is in how schools meet the needs of today's changing learners. It's not that learners today are learning differently per se, but more that the environment in which they learn has changed dramatically. How can school meet the needs of learners who are immersed in highly engaging and fun games such as Pokémon Go and Minecraft outside of school? Traditionally, schools have worked better for the adults than they have for the kids. Disruptive change flips the script in order to create schools that work for kids.

A school brand must embrace and align with the digital transformation of teaching, learning, and leadership that is occurring or about to occur in order to meet the diverse needs of changing learners. The idea of "keeping up with the Digital Joneses" reflects a spirit of meeting all stakeholders where they are in digital spaces, a spirit fueled by the culture of disruption that brings us new professional value. The Digital Joneses welcome disruption, and they create it.

The young Millennials who are working on augmented reality and virtual reality will change the way we present content in schools. Wearable technology will soon help teachers connect with students. Thanks to this crew of innovators, creative thinkers, researchers, edupreneurs, streamers, geeks, policy wonks, Millennials, mommy bloggers, and pundits, change will gallop even faster than it is today. Why? Because simply put, they are people of ideas. One idea leads to another and another in this generation, and these ideas take shape quickly and come to market fast. The abundance of good ideas makes for a world of possibility for those who are lucky enough to be digitally savvy, and their numbers are growing. Giving up control, trusting kids, and creating the conditions where they can select the right tool for the right task to demonstrate conceptual mastery and empower ownership of learning are a prime example of a type of disruption needed now. BrandED leaders are not only catalysts for this change, but they also utilize the tools at their disposal to educate key stakeholders as to the need and value of these changes. The new digital world requires a proactive approach.

Our schools have characteristically changed in a slower fashion. It's tough to keep up personally and professionally with the sea of information we deal with in our busy lives. Yet we want to be continuous learners in these digital times. We want to model that for kids, teachers, staff, parents, and the community. Technology allows us to be in the race and keep the pace. It's the new normal for educational leaders to be part of the bigger world beyond the schoolhouse door. The saying that content is king no longer applies, yet it still applies to a brandED mindset where culture is just as, if not more, important. Content is *what we learn about,* and culture is *what we are learning to be.* Building and sustaining a district or school brand in an environment of disruption thus becomes even more important. It is creating and sharing content that not only accurately describes culture but also helps continually push its evolution. As learning now takes place at an intense rate, our Digital Joneses are setting the pace. Leaders and their respective organizations not only have to keep up but also must try to set the pace.

BrandED is not about change simply for the sake of change. Disruption creates a new order. BrandED leaders exhibit habits of truly disruptive leaders. They know that they must be purposefully authentic, they must be decision makers, and they must be ready to guide their community to well-being. Finally, while they are rewriting the rules, they are always explaining *why* (Hoque, 2015).

THE LEADERSHIP BENEFITS OF DISRUPTIVENESS

Taking on a brandED leadership mindset makes a school leader disruptive in the best possible way, as an innovator creating value and change around the question of "Why?" Answering "Why?" drives a leader's decisiveness, authenticity, and responsiveness, and the transparency behind the question benefits the community. The brandED leader who likes to ask "Why?" is the edupreneur who is questioning business as usual. These edupreneurial leaders are taking a risk, but know that the answers to questions like "Why do we do it this way?" "Why isn't there a better way to reach the goal?" "Why can't we think like this?" can yield new thinking that inspires innovative, disruptive practice.

A BrandED Short Story: The Power of "Why?"

As the principal of New Milford High School, Eric strategically approached the question of "Why?" as a disruptive school leader. He utilized an array of social media tools to explain why and how technology initiatives were being implemented for the betterment of their learners. Going beyond why, this was also an opportunity to explain how the school was still meeting the demands of higher standards. When the school dramatically increased the Advanced Placement (AP) scores, Eric blogged about the action plan that was put into place and how hard his teachers worked to help their students succeed. Social media was also used in another case to explain changes to how they were going to grade their students.

In the end, all stakeholders should know the power of a leader using the question "Why?" Communities appreciate knowing how a leader arrives at a particular decision and how that decision impacts the system. The end result of efforts to be transparent, authentic, decisive, and responsive with New Milford's strategy resulted in unprecedented mainstream media coverage of the school's work. For example, CBS Channel 2 New York City visited 14 times in 5 years to cover New Milford's innovative practices. Examples like this helped solidify the school's positive standing with the local community and provided evidence of success. This type of innovation is linked to the question of "Why?" at every step of change.

SHARE THE DISRUPTIVE STAGE

Bringing new and disruptive changes to education requires a risk-taking attitude, but it is the need to see a better way that not only shifts result but is powerful enough to create a new world built on new practices and beliefs. When Henry Ford was asked about his disruptive invention of the automobile, he said he knew that his job wasn't going to be engineering a faster horse. Then he set about showing the world how an engine would revolutionize lives through mobility.

This type of leadership is a unifying force that promotes the connection of your school in ways that strengthen its culture, performance, and resourcing. A disruptive stance yields far-reaching benefits that can benefit the community at large.

The seeds of positive disruptive behavior take root in strong communication that the digital world provides. Disruptive leaders use those channels, always explaining why, always promoting change. Being a successful disruptive leader is based, in part, on radically candid communication, attending to honest and open messaging, clearly identifying what's working, and then challenging what's not working for the good of the school brand identity.

Transparent brandED disruptive leaders do not micromanage. They give credit to others when initiatives succeed, and take the blame if things fail. As a brandED leader, you can tackle the constant perception battle by providing more frequent and accurate updates about the daily work occurring in schools. This requires sharing challenges as well as successes and opening yourself to feedback from anyone. In the end, transparency helps build positive relationships with key stakeholders in your community, including the media.

BrandED leaders work toward disruption by leading with authenticity, an element of any successful leadership brand. They are the *protectors* of the brand, stewards who are the champions of innovation and are prepared to promote and defend the reputation of their carefully crafted school brand. The thinking that has given way to disruptions and innovations like flipped classrooms, makerspaces, and global exchanges are part of the early "adoptership" spirit of a brandED mindset. This shift is one that begins the process of upending the entrenched "factory-based" model of school structure and moving toward models of learning that will continue to become increasingly disruptive in our changing connected world of learning. It is only the beginning.

Part Two: BrandED Partners in a Digital World

BrandED leaders place technology at the core of their strategic plan. Reach out to the Digital Joneses, our stakeholders: the staff, teachers, parents, and community members who look at tech as lifestyle, not as an "add-on" to their lives. They are your brandED stakeholders, a key audience with which to engage and to build powerful relationships. Engage the Millennials, born between 1982 and 2000, who are on staff. Connect with the Millennial parents who are sending their young children— Gen Z, or Plurals—to the door of your school. Observe the entrepreneurs, most of whom are Millennials, who are part of your external community. They are the largest cohort that your school brand serves, regardless of demographics.

Millennial stakeholders can contribute in many important ways because of their ease with digital and social media communication and their forward-thinking view of the world of technology. Recognize that there are differences in the patterns of tech use between early and late Millennials. This differing behavior segments them into two different tribes, and your brand messaging must match their beat, so when messaging these audiences, consider their varying styles.

Much continues to be written about Millennials, and Gen Z will now be grabbing more of the attention and headlines as they age into their young adulthood. Big data yields information on these very digitally transparent cohorts. We see how different they are from previous generations. Some consider these groups to be narcissistic to the point of distraction. But you can capture the attention of these groups of your school community. They want to be connected. Greg Petro, writing about Millennials in *Forbes,* goes so far as to say that "they are *reliant* on being connected" (Petro, 2013, emphasis the author's). Use that desire for connection to bring these generations to your brandED plan as informed and active stakeholders in cocreating and delivering the school brand.

Millennials grew up with tech. They tell stories online at the drop of a hat thanks to their attraction to social media. They collaborate, question, and are of necessity entrepreneurial in a challenged economy. As part of the brandED campaign, they can be a priceless resource for creating, curating, and systematically sharing content. Their flexibility allows them to meet different situations without balking. They know what they don't want as they learn. They are passionate about what they do want to know, and find answers quickly. Millennials want engagement, like to think out of the box, and welcome sharing. Provide opportunities for these distributive leadership cocreators, and you will earn their loyalty to the brandED mission.

THE MILLENNIAL TEACHER AND BRANDED

There's tension between the benefit that proactive parents bring to the school and their pressing need to be connected to the education of their children in ultraresponsive ways. According to Lauren Benjamin (personal conversation, June 6, 2016), the founding member of Benjamin Staff Development in Briarcliff Manor, New York, and parent of a Gen Z child, the quickly shifting pace of change in instruction weighs heavily on parents who want to know, "What can I do to support my child when I see her education in 2017 looks nothing like my own education in the 20th century?" Factor in research which shows that Generation X and Y parents are not as accepting of the ivory tower distancing that Baby Boomer parents accepted prior to the social and digital age. Today's parents want to be included. Lauren looks across her desk as a Millennial educator and asks herself another question: "How do I educate my students' parents about the changes in curriculum so that they can support their children? In a world of debating about teaching and learning, is digital reading considered 'screen time,' 'reading time,' or both?" As a Millennial, Lauren feels a tug between her parental self and teacher persona in this digital age.

Despite the "rookie" status that veteran teachers may assign to them, Millennial teachers, as a rule, take risks for the purpose of disruption that can lead to innovations like flipped classrooms and learner-centered models. They embrace the entrepreneurial promotion of their own lessons on connecting platforms like www.teacherspayteachers.com. Immersed in tech, young Millennial teachers and the Gen Z students in front of them experience a far less daunting communication gap than the one their older teaching colleagues face. Their team-oriented behavior makes them perfect as ambassadors for brandED. Their comfort with the concept of brand in their personal lives makes them a fit. As engaged end users and customers of the top brands of the world, they can advance the rationale for use of brandED thinking and help with building authentic relationships.

A Brand ED Short Story: Amelia Tran

Amelia Tran is a Millennial working in both the digital world of business and in education. Her career path, like many in her generation, is focused yet fluid and distinctly upwardly mobile. A senior digital strategist at the Firebrand Group for the past 4 years, she is now project manager for The Marketing Arm. In the world of education, Amelia serves as a continuing education teacher, specializing in digital marketing strategy, at New York University and Baruch College. Tran epitomizes the educational Digital Joneses. Her world is one of live-streaming apps, Periscope, and Facebook, to name a few of the many digital tools she accesses. These same platforms offer stakeholders a glimpse into a school's programs, activities, and initiatives in real time. Parents can be engaged with streaming video, and can

(continued)

engage with faculty through discussions on specific topics, which can be broadcast for other parents to view. This getting the word out and creating a climate for "getting ideas to spread" is the essence of what Seth Godin believes to be brand awareness magic.

Amelia sees the power of schools attracting stakeholders by using live-streaming apps as a way to share knowledge outside classroom walls. Her school provides streaming lessons that establish it as a content resource provider internally and to the external community that helps increase awareness of the school's brand. She believes that other real-time streaming apps, such as Snapchat, though only able to showcase a "story" for up to 10 seconds, can also be used to enhance virtual experience between brand and stakeholders. (A. Tran, personal communication, April 30, 2016).

With Amelia in mind, brandED leaders are advised of a necessary call to action in building the ranks of teaching professionals. We must find talented, innovative Gen Y teachers and keep them close. Our charge in reaching Gen Z lies in focusing on hiring Millennial teachers who show the connected digital skill set, a passion for inquiry, and the ability to be relational. On the fringe of educational professionalism are tremendously skilled young people who need to be nurtured into our profession. Case in point is Janine Perry, who tested her love of learning, passion for culture, and interest in the digital world by taking on an education minor in college. Janine went as far as a practicum experience in a school situation that was as void of the connection of brand as could be experienced. If Janine had been part of a brandED community as a young prospective teaching professional, she would have stayed. She would have impacted the lives of children in a long career, yet the lack of a powerful school brand, the lack of a compelling image, promise, and result changed her direction. She is currently a cultural strategist at the innovative New York advertising agency sparks & honey. Janine still dreams of a possible route back to teaching. Let's call her "the one that got away" and use her experience as a lesson. BrandED leaders must increase the number of professionals like Janine. Be on the lookout for Millennials to teach your Z generation. Invest in them. Partner more actively with colleges and universities. Find prospects in informed schools of education. Search for them online as they develop their skills in the academy. Hire them. Give them the professional learning experience that can mature them into lead teachers who are 21st-century digital-savvy and lifelong learners. Surround them with coteaching partners and mentoring that gives them the basics for managing classrooms filled with Gen Z students. Millennials have a confidence that creates belief, and the collaborative work ethic that can fuel the story of the brand using their own unique perspective, which they gladly share in their open and transparent way.

GENERATION Z

Get ready. Brand Z is here.

You can also call them Plurals or Generation Next. MTV, whose own brand has changed, calls them "the Founders." Call them what you will, they are formidable. They are a smaller demographic group than Gen Y. These are our current students, those under 17 years of age. Yet their economic potential—the money to be made from this demographic in marketing and branding—will far overshadow the value of Gen Y. They will rule as consumers. Is there any way to keep up with them as learners? It will be a challenge. These are people who eschew anything that isn't engaging them. Leave a voice message? No thanks. Email? No way. Cable TV? No chance. They are wary of the world, having grown up with almost daily instances of terror threats, school violence, gun violence, social unrest, and economic uncertainty during their formative years. Their future is in question. They've experienced a long economic downturn, and question the relevance and high price tag of college. They live their young 24/7 connected lives in a quickly changing, complex world. They attend schools where teaches try to prepare them for a future in the workplace that may or may not be there for them. They wonder about jobs and tools to do jobs that have yet to be created. They are as much survivors as their heroine Katniss from the Hunger Games.

These minds figure into developing a school brand. Winning them as brand supporters in our classrooms is key today and important for loyalty to the school brand in the future. Their ability to multitask makes them important contributors to many of the avenues of messaging for sharing the brand. Their problem-solving skills make them open-minded about figuring out strategy. They don't fear new technological lanes for sharing their savvy selves, and they enlist their peers in local and global endeavors in a digital heartbeat. As you approach brandED, keep Gen Z close to the development process. The fast-food brand Taco Bell, a favorite of Gen Z, learned this faster than anyone. It started to invite Gen Z into corporate marketing and branding meetings through an app. The company incentivizes these contributors to engage with the brand by giving discounts. As educational leaders, see their worth in what they can contribute to brandED development in the moment. Leaders need to harness legacy brand power through this generation that can be a direct pipeline to emotional, volunteer, and product partnering. These students in our classrooms can be the "founders" of a more connected alumni brandED strategy that you launch by focusing on this demographic as potential alumni digital and social media legacy partners from the day they enter your school. Bond through their understanding of brand to create active resource partners for the school's future brand success. By doing so, you will have active brand ambassadors and partners following their graduation and into their meaningful, giving adult years.

Part Three: Connecting With Parents on the Digital Playground

BrandED strategy seeks the engagement of Gen X and Gen Y parents. These two demographic segments represent the bulk of the parents of the Gen Z students in our classrooms today. Millennial parents are expecting a lot from their child's school experience, and it includes engagement. Listening to the Millennial parent is essential as you develop and share your school brand. Including the voice of Millennial stakeholders in your collaborative team strategy is necessary in a digital brand effort.

This stakeholder group comes to the digital table wanting to "like" and "share" with partners; they bond easily and look for tribes to join, to influence, and to interact with daily. They also expect the exchange with a provider of a service or product to be transparent, authentic, and responsive. Even in the face of helicopter parents, "hoverboard" parents, tiger moms, and panda dads, we can engage with our parents for positive result. We can build genuine trust with our parental stakeholders by being transparent about how schools work, how we make our decisions, and how we can partner with them in the education of students.

Give today's parents their due: 72% of Gen Z students entering our schools have a history with tech and digital devices thanks to their tech-savvy parents (Sales, 2016). Millennial parents and the education of their Gen Z kids pose a complex challenge. Gone are the distancing days of the ivory tower and the attitude that Baby Boomer parents carried, a traditional mantra of "the teacher is always right." We have a new order where that message is challenged. That's why attending to a unifying, communicative innovation like brandED is essential to your digital leadership style. Meeting stakeholders where they are in digital spaces and engaging them in two-way communication through a multifaceted approach is vital (Sheninger, 2014). Using a variety of digital tools allows families to choose the best way to interact with you, thus forming another great way to build relationships. This is not a substitute for face-to-face communication but a needed complement.

The newest crop of learners possesses digital savvy, but we must also offer a school brand that is rich in digital tools for their future. We must prepare them, not only in language literacy expression, but in their tech literacy. We must ready them for their future—even without knowing what that future may be. Build a brand that supports students who are learning in this uncertain time. One that is rich with tech, literary, and even presentational literacy. Gen Z will surpass Gen Y and Gen X as end users of technology, and their time in public school must offer them relevant learning experiences that will help them grow into the opportunities of a rapidly changing world. The brandED mission for schools lives in the stories of engaging learning environments that look different from traditional school settings.

Bringing the cross section of demographics into the development of a brandED school strategy not only makes the work of brandED relevant in the moment but also evokes a trust in the combined vision of stakeholders who build and sustain a school brand. As school choice options expand, developing an identity that is relevant in a digital world is more important than ever. In the context of education, the identity of your school (or even yourself) is determined not only by the work but also by how the work is shared and consumed. It stands for who you are and what your school and district are. Being cognizant of this fact allows you to be proactive in creating an identity that resonates with all stakeholders. Think about the identity that you, your students, and staff want, and harness the tenets of brandED to make it a reality.

Conversation 7 Tips

- **Prepare** yourself for brandED leadership by understanding the disruptive nature of innovation.
- **Find** every opportunity to understand the range of demographics of your stakeholders—Baby Boomer, Gen X, Gen Y/Millennial, and Gen Z/Plural—and the tools they use to communicate and consume content.
- **Segment and position** messages in ways that appeal to each demographic of your stakeholders.
- **Focus** on the Gen Y and Gen X parental demographics as they are becoming your brandED allies.
- **Enlist** participation on your team collective for members of all demographic groups. Form a brandED team that blends their stakeholder strengths.

Conversation 7 Reflections

Before holding public conversation around how innovation, disruption, and the range of demography for supporting brandED, think about these questions:

- Can I develop my brandED Strategic Plan and include parents—Gen X and Millennials—and bring Gen Z into the brandED conversation to ensure success?
- Am I ready to take on new challenges in my digital professional life with the support of my digital natives?
- How will I welcome a world of disruption and connectivity and celebrate the openness that's evolved post ivory tower?
- How will I bring value and safety to the disruption of communication that brandED offers?
- Am I confident enough to use distributed leadership to move responsively onto an ever-changing digital and social playground?

Return on Investment in the BrandED School Community

The closing discussion, Conversation 8, addresses the leadership stance of *steward* of the school brand in a deeper relational commitment to brandED sustainability. The continued attention to preserving the brand, monitoring the promise, maintaining relationships, and celebrating results with an eye toward the future is modeled as a shared responsibility among the community. The stewardship role suggests the possibilities of the local and global return on investment (ROI) for brandED leaders and their communities. Brand behaviors demonstrate a mindful approach to building relationships that can benefit the entire community, including teachers, students, parents, and other stakeholders. You will recognize that being part of a brandED community can give a school a competitive edge as it showcases itself and its unique value.

> Relationships are like muscle tissue . . . the more they are engaged, the stronger and more valuable they become.
> —*Ted Rubin, marketing consultant and author*

In business, ROI is measured in dollars: if the business is to be sustainable, a dollar spent must result in at least a dollar earned. ROI is richer in education.

BrandED educators see evidence of their ROI in many ways. The public commitment to brandED goal setting results in markers of school improvement that can be evidenced by data (achievement and perception), innovative practices, staff accomplishments, and student achievements (academic and nonacademic). This evidence of results then makes the case daily for sustaining a relevant brand. There's added value in the intangible ROI in a school brand: building and sustaining relationships.

Relationship building should be top priority when innovating. Leaders must understand how innovation can bring forth powerful ideas to displace established norms (Bass, 2016). In a world of digital disruption, attending to relationships figures into a brand's survival. In business, brands that are displaced by new ideas often realize too late the need for a continual relational presence. Brands that prevail are muscling their way to success because of the returns, tangible and intangible, that their targeted relationships bring.

Part One: Be the BrandED Relationship Steward

In the course of gaining a competitive leadership edge, especially in these times of school choice, brandED tenets help educators adapt their management of schools to a style of marketing that has existed since the mid-20th century. The stance for educators isn't found as a chief brand officer (CBO), but as a storyteller-in-chief. In Figure 8.1, Brand Business Model vs. BrandED Leadership Model, the continuum of presence that advances a brandED mindset is contrasted to the sales function of a CBO. The ROI is markedly different.

The brandED school story will always be different from the story of business. In schools, stories are key to creating emotional well-being in

Figure 8.1 Brand Business Model vs. BrandED Leadership Model

IMAGE PROMISE RESULT	SELLING	CHIEF BRAND OFFICER	IMPROVED • Sales • Scale	SALES SKILL SET • Persuade • Negotiate • Generate leads	CHIEF EXECUTIVE OFFICER
IMAGE PROMISE RESULT	TELLING	BRANDED STORYTELLER-IN-CHIEF	IMPROVED • Culture • Performance • Resources	BRANDED LEADERSHIP SKILL SET • Associate • Create • Engage	BRANDED STEWARD

the organization, rather than a tool for scaling the market and building sales. The school brand storyteller introduces stories and their value with the goal of engagement and to promote stakeholder bonding. As the branding effort matures, stories help sustain the innovation. Leaders who practice and grow their professional storytelling skill will experience a ROI. They become brandED stewards who are able to use a new communication skill, one that is recognized and valued, as a powerful model for others in the microcommunity.

The distributed leadership model again offers leaders a team approach for supporting relational activity that can sustain a brandED initiative. The growing brandED collective of ambassadors and supporters can play a integral part in the stewardship of the brand. In a shared model of leadership, fellow brand storytellers and stewards evolve from every corner of the community to support the brand and transform the school culture, create new performance indicators, and build partnerships that lead to resources. Every member of your collective has an extended network in the macroenvironment that can bring value to the school. Leaders can rally their teams and charge them with actively networking for brand awareness and relationship development, even designing processes that can bring more "eyeballs" to the school brand online, which in turn lead to resources for the school. The ROI increases with the collaboration of a community. The model supports the brandED leadership stance that honors image, promise, and result through a leader's commitment to associating, creating, and engaging for brand strength and relevance. The model of leadership represented in Figure 8.1 is a snapshot of the new thinking and new possibilities that your brandED mindset will bring. It is adapted from business, but powered by education.

Stewardship sustains the school brand. BrandED stewards are watchful about relationships and nurture them. If stewards lack a keen understanding of how to sustain a relational base through the digital and traditional tools of brandED leadership, results will fall short, producing a low ROI.

SHARE THE ROLE OF BRANDED STEWARD

As previous conversations illustrate, brandED leaders do not micromanage the brand. They allow it to grow through the desire of teachers and learners to make connections and to be relational. The school microenvironment will show the adaptation of the edupreneurial brand spirit among teachers who can serve as storytellers and stewards of their disruptive brand innovations. For instance, teachers who teach the writing process using the digital tools of Evernote, Kazenia, and G Suite bring new levels of effective learning, including relational experience. Using these tools and more that are developing young writers increases teachers' digital comfort, which leads them to expand teaching and sharing opportunities beyond their classrooms. Platforms like these have opened the doors for building relationships in a way that enhances experiences for students and teacher. These relationships create content and stories that spread the positive word about the school.

Another case is seen in the concept of Genius Hour, now being adapted by communities of teachers whose writing and sharing about innovation are making the concept a bit of a contagious, disruptive idea. Educators see their relational power in new concepts like Genius Hour, which provides a new view of instructional time for students that looks just like a Google work model for independent thinking (Juliani, 2015). During the Genius Hour, time is put aside during the school day for students to explore their own passions. It gives them a choice in what they learn during a set period of time. Teachers use the Genius Hour to advance to the highest level of synthesis for learners. They give students permission to be inquisitive and curious, to question, to research, and ultimately to problem-solve on topics of their own choice.

Teachers who create and connect to these innovations immediately benefit from widening their relational networks for themselves and their students. Teachers using engaging, innovative curriculum are enhancing ROI for learning, but also for the community. Learning from the feedback received from engaging in this way, teachers have continued to refine their use of these tools in the classroom to meet the needs of their own connected students.

Our teachers also become brandED stewards, modeling a fearless spirit and living a call to action for building and maintaining relationships through real-time and digital and social experiences. Teachers also are able to monitor brand messages from their classrooms, making them more engaged as stewards of the school brand. Brand ownership is evident when people see themselves as stewards. BrandED school leaders value teachers' stewardship efforts, encouraging and valuing the building of authentic relationships internally and externally that enrich the school no matter where they are initiated. Every teacher is an important part of a brandED school.

As you lead the stewardship effort, be inspired by a model of success. Your brandED stewardship can be informed by the 70/30 formula of leadership that worked for Steven B. Sample (2002), president of the University of Southern California. He spent 30% of his time on substantive matters and the remaining 70% on the routines that helped others and connected the community. It is a model to bring to staff and to teachers that shows your commitment to building relationships that sustain the brand effort. Innovative teachers can be inspired by this thinking in your school community. Sample was a legendary leader, a true steward who was revered by the USC Trojan family for the relational leadership he lived.

Part Two: Local to Global BrandED Investment

When built with a brandED strategy, a school brand unifies.

At a local level, it streamlines many school initiatives that were previously fragmented. It "de-silos" the community, taking people from an isolated view of their place in the school (the silo) and moving them into a shared mindset for the school mission. BrandED isn't a top-down mandate. It creates a web of complex relationships that sustains and creates a return on the effort.

A school brand in this rapidly changing world of technology must be responsive, open to growing beyond the local stage. The key here is supporting a connected educator's worldview using the digital and social tools that build relationships.

As you develop your own brand and the school's brand, keep an eye on the global community. Some of your teacher leaders are already connecting to other educators around the world, building an informal networked model of education that cracks those limiting silos to benefit students. Focusing on global thinking may not be part of your earliest stages of brandED development, but keep the big world of connection in your sights. Awareness of a few basic possibilities of a global relational plan, no matter where you are in your school's journey of digital connectivity, will set the stage for global sharing of your built brand.

LEVERAGING BRANDED REACH TO GLOBAL BRAND CONNECTION

Never before have the communities of education and business shared as much as they do today in their connectivity to the world outside their respective backyards. Connected relationships can be leveraged and continually modeled by a brandED leader's using the vision of return on relationship.

Because your school storytelling and content creations don't come from a marketing department but from the connected communities of educators, they can resonate with real truth. They speak of the truths that excellent education offers anywhere around the globe. Many educators use the acronym TIME, which means *totally investing myself in education,* as they engage in worldwide connected communities. When schools turn their brandED view to a global stage, giving and goodwill are truly at work (Grant, 2013).

As teachers share their stories in connected educator communities, PLNs, and PLCs, as they reach out to blog and share on powerful platforms like *Edutopia* and connect through social platforms online, they forge professional relationships that benefit their students, create new ideas and vocabularies, and help them think deeply about communication. This is visionary partnering on a global level through discussion of innovation, leadership, and discovery of new platforms. Educators share tools for storytelling on the global stage of digital platforms. They promote sharing and professional learning through SchoolTube and TeacherTube to build their skill set and connections to the tribe of educators interested in globalization. They share PR tools (e.g., press releases and notices) that help them position their storytelling. School leaders need to welcome, search for, and hire connected teaching professionals, making them part of the distributed leadership model for brandED. Leaders come from everywhere in the ranks of educators and possess unique tools to spread the word.

Linda Darling Hammond spoke of taking 10 hours per week to collaborate to build teachers' professional skills. This can now be maximized through the sharing of global practice in connected online communities (Hammond, Chung Wei, & Andree, 2010). Investigating programs and innovations from as far away as Finland, where the best of educational practice is creating results, and taking professionalism to a new level, are two powerful lessons that can be learned through a global lens.

CONNECTED GLOBAL PRESENCE CAN ADVANCE RELATIONAL RESOURCING

Educators in connected communities are marketers. They build brand value. Connected educational leaders know the power of advancing their personal professional brand. Their efforts bring tangible results for their students. Educators build brand out of empathy for others. It is something that connected global educators share in online chats and discussions about resource partnering. They dream big and talk about building connections to big media brands like *USA Today* and television networks. They brainstorm in their communities online about the ways to network to all sorts of industries, from hospitality to tech companies, to form relationships and partnerships to benefit schools.

One such example is seen in a relationship built between New Milford High School (NMHS) and a company called Proton Media; Proton provided an enterprise solution called Protosphere, intended for corporations, to explore the possibilities of 3-D virtual learning and collaboration in the cloud. The school's brand presence as an innovative school was well developed, and because of that, the amplified social media led this company to the school's doorstep. The partnership resulted in the creation a 3-D virtual learning environment for the school.

Using the Protosphere platform, the school explored unique pedagogy in a virtual environment, and technology *as* the learning environment. In the virtual NMHS campus, they explored the possibilities of 3-D virtual learning, collaboration, and technology to personalize learning for students. Teachers and students saw how communicating and collaborating are different in a virtual environment, due to the integration of avatars. The relationship brought NMHS students (represented by their avatars) and data together in an engaging and stimulating virtual world.

The school used Protosphere as a tool for face-to-face interaction in the virtual space in order to raise student achievement and to improve student performance overall, while enabling teachers to deliver classes more efficiently and effectively. Learners were able to talk, view, and interact with presentation and media content; record notes; and access the Web, all at the same time, from anywhere. Teachers were able to embed learning into collaborative processes to improve performance, extend the learning outside the school day, and prepare students for a 21st-century workforce in which many of them will have to communicate and collaborate virtually.

A brandED mindset and strategy allowed the school to partner and receive this $200,000 tool for free. Once we were able to integrate this amazing program, they were able to put into play the media relationships they had previously formed as a result of having shared we work consistently using social media. This resulted in news coverage, which further validated the innovative practices that were positively impacting kids. Social media allowed them to then share this news with local stakeholders as well as those across the globe. Culture, performance, and resourcing were all improved thanks to brandED thinking.

The school brand effort must include a plan for being relational at all levels of the organization. The popular American film *Field of Dreams* included the memorable phrase, "If you build it, they will come." Successful partnerships like the one NMHS formed with Proton Media illustrate the power of brandED leadership. Once a collective team, using a shared leadership model, builds the brand and launches a strategic plan for connecting, "they"—the relationships—will come. And opportunities will grow. If your potential partners don't know you are out there looking to collaborate on the global stage for the good of your kids and community, they can't work with you. You must be as clear as you can be about what your brand is and connect with those who want to be part of it. Your kids deserve every effort as you do this. It is an investment in their future.

THE BRANDED RELATIONAL COMMITMENT

As you imagine the possibilities of bringing the business principle of branding to grow your leadership development skill set and to improve your school's culture, performance and resourcing, think about the positive impact branding will ultimately have on improving stakeholder relations. As an early adopter of brand thinking, as a leader of brand relational behavior, you will take your school or district to new heights by celebrating and amplifying success like never before.

A BrandED Short Story: Tony Sinanis's Relational Key . . . Storytelling

Tony Sinanis, principal of Cantiague Elementary School in Jericho, New York, has been modeling a brandED mindset for years.

For Tony, the journey began with an iPad in 2013. He was fortunate in that his whole school had WiFi access, so he made a conscious decision to spend as little time as possible in his office and as much time as possible walking around the building visiting classrooms, talking to children, taking pictures, posting on social media about the school's daily adventures, emailing parents with the highlights of the school's work, and blogging about successes in a weekly staff newsletter.

"Well, I am thrilled to say that almost three years in, our school's brand story is really solid and consistent throughout the entire building! The best part of the journey has been that I am not the only one telling the story; it is a collective story being told throughout the building featuring all teachers, students, and family members" (T. Sinanis, personal communication, May 16, 2016). Every classroom has an active Twitter account; some classrooms have "social media interns," kids who are taking the pictures and posting the content with teacher approval on social media. Students and families are using the #Cantiague hashtag in their own social media posts in order to tell their collective community story.

Tony says, "I don't share this information as a way to toot our own horn, but instead to share that when a conscious decision is made to brand your school and tell your story, the possibilities are endless." (Tony has seen conversations at PTA meetings go from talking about the logistics of fundraisers to discussing the concerns over high-stakes testing or the power of book clubs as a way to differentiate instruction. The community is informed, and there is a commitment to transparency. It means that the school leaders have to be confident in choices that are made, that they have to be open to feedback—good and bad—that the school has to show that with every success there are at least three failures, and that there is a level of comfort in flattening the walls of the school and proudly telling their story to shape perceptions and build realities. This is the epitome of brandED, and there is no doubt that it has been worth it for Tony and his stakeholders.

Part Three: Sustain a BrandED Community Through Return on Relationship

Sustainability of any initiative is imperative to transformational change. The beauty of a brandED mindset is that it seamlessly aligns with the work that educators are already doing. The key shift is in building communities and relationships with a clear message of a school brand, one that empowers sharing of the great work taking place every day in schools. As the world becomes even more digital, it is important to develop strategies that harness digital tools to meet stakeholders where they are living. By embracing the strategies outlined in this book in a consistent fashion, you will experience what Ted Rubin, a leading social marketing strategist, dubbed a *return on relationship.*

Return on relationship (ROR), simply put, is the value that is accrued by a person or brand due to nurturing a relationship (Rubin & Rose, 2013). "ROI is simple dollars and cents. ROR is the value (both perceived and real) that will accrue over time through loyalty, recommendations, and sharing" (Ted Rubin, personal communication, May 13, 2016).

In Ted Rubin's view, Facebook fans, Instagram followers, retweets, site visits, video views, positive ratings, and vibrant communities are not measurable financial assets—they aren't reflected on the balance sheet and can't be counted on an income statement—but that doesn't mean they are without value. Instead, these are leading indicators that a brand is doing something to create value that can lead to financial results in the future. In addition, these relationships can be leveraged through initiatives, campaigns, and events to create real dollar value for a brand.

Like many, Ted realizes that social media has enabled us to connect with an infinite number of individuals; it has given us the tools to extend relationships that years ago would have been impossible. Yet make no mistake: As Ted says, "Social media is a facilitator of relationships, but it is not the relationship itself." You have to give to get; it's so simple in concept, yet not always easy to wrap your arms around when online, as giving and getting are not as simple as favors, hugs, or handshakes.

Ted believes that everything we do in our personal lives and business revolves around relationships—now more than ever. With effort, an online relationship may begin from a Facebook friend request or by following someone on Twitter; but don't kid yourself: That initial request or follow will never create the relationship. Trust is built on interaction, when you're true to your word, authentic, and genuine. To build relationships online, you (as a brand or individual) have to offer value in return. Whatever form this value takes, be it information or personal introductions, engagement and interaction will remain key. Ted says, "By asking questions and proposing ideas, you can engage your followers in such a way as to give them the ability and *reason* to respond. Then, when they do respond, interact with them to solidify your relationship, lest it fade away." Directly acknowledge their response, ask follow-up questions, and share their insights with others. Connect on Twitter with Ted (@tedrubin) and you'll see what he means. The more responsive you are to your audience, the more responsive they'll be to you. That's where relationships are born. As Ted states, "A network gives you reach, but a community gives you power! Networks connect . . . communities care."

A Closing BrandED Short Story: Changing the Narrative

For Dr. Joe Sanfelippo, the superintendent of Fall Creek School District in Wisconsin, brandED matters in schools for a number of reasons. He believes that changing the narrative of what schools are and helping leaders define their role in schools are two main components to brandED. Both have a profound impact on how you and your school district are perceived by the community. Schools serve communities. In rural America, the school serves as the hub of the community. People utilize school buildings from sun up to sun down, and the relationship that is built throughout that time is key to the success of your district (J. Sanfelippo, personal communication, April 29, 2016).

Joe understands that the narrative of public education needs a fix. The work done in schools all across the globe is spectacular. Kids gather, learn, and leave with the hope that they will make the world a better place. The issue with our educational system is that the stories about schools are being told by people who have no affiliation with those schools. Joe says, "The idea of branding schools isn't about selling kids or making false promises . . . it's about promoting the amazing things happening for those not experiencing them on a daily basis." Telling the story of schools helps create a narrative that builds culture and gives everyone in your community an identity. Utilizing social media and being the storyteller-in-chief in your district is a great way to celebrate the success of students with parents and the community. Kids who tell stories to their parents about school turn into adults who tell stories to colleagues, neighbors, and friends. Oftentimes those stories don't reflect the work that is happening in our schools today. Joe states, "As a school leader, it is imperative that we honor the work being done in our schools by giving

(continued)

the public an accurate assessment of what is happening in those spaces."

Branding our particular spaces allows students, staff, and community members to share in an identity. Joe reports that "in Fall Creek, Wisconsin, we put Go Crickets on everything. T-shirts, hats, license plates, umbrellas, towels—everything. We give all of these things away at games and events. We also bring our gear everywhere we go. If staff present at a conference, they take gear to give away." The cost for Joe? Very little in a monetary sense. As part of his district budget, there is a line item for community outreach, which is where the money is allocated for Go Crickets gear each year. The other cost factor is the time put forth to research and design the items.

For Joe it is less about cost and more about the reward gleaned from his brandED mindset. One picture emailed or tweeted to the district is added to their "Where in the world is Fall Creek Pride?" board that hangs outside the elementary office. They currently have pictures from people in Go Crickets gear from 40 states and five countries. The district asks families and community members to take Go Crickets gear on their vacations and send a picture from their destination. They want everyone in their village to share in the identity of the school. "We use Twitter, Facebook, Instagram, and Snapchat to celebrate the work of our kids. Our teachers tell the story of their classroom through these mediums, and the #gocrickets hashtag has allowed all of them to contribute to a shared story that helps create the true narrative of our building." The #gocrickets stream is live on the school's webpage and can be viewed on eight big-screen televisions that line the school hallways.

Their learning is transparent, and everyone can come along for the ride. This approach also completely changes the discussion at home for parents and kids. As Joe points out, "It is our job to help create a bridge between school and home. For years, kids have been going home at the end of the day, and when they are asked about what happened in school by their parents, the response is almost always "I don't know." In Fall Creek, parents can change the question to "I saw on Twitter that you were launching rockets today in 7th hour. Tell me more about that." The connection is real and specific and allows families to have conversations about the great things that are happening in their spaces.

In the absence of knowledge, people tend to make up their own. As superintendent, Joe is the highest paid staff member in the building. Whether he likes it or not, that comes with a stigma. "I have no idea who the superintendent in my school district was when I was a kid." The job of a school leader is difficult. However, Joe doesn't think school leaders do themselves any favors by not leading the charge in branding their space. Being active in helping develop that brand experience is useful in many ways, the most relevant of which is that people now know what you do. "Visiting a second-grade classroom is fantastic. Sitting down with kids shows them you are invested in what they are doing and helps develop a relationship that lasts for years. Taking an extra 30 seconds to tweet a picture of what you are doing not only shows the student that you are proud to display their work; it shows the public that you are not sitting behind your desk moving papers from one side of the desk to the other." The social capital that is gained through this process can certainly help leaders offset any issues that arise during their tenure in the building. The community is much less likely to disparage you for a mistake if they know what you do on a regular basis. Joe notes, "If you make a mistake, and you will, the social capital you have developed over time will clearly help you get through the misstep in your leadership role."

One thread that runs through all the brandED short stories we've shared in this book is that the brandED effort is well worth it. It's time for you to define yourself and your school through an authentic brand. Create your own brandED short story with an eye on growing it to long-term brand legacy success. Your brandED professional development journey can distinguish your leadership in this digital age. As storyteller and steward, share the brandED journey to new results that build your own unique ROR. Tell your story, empower learning, and create ROR that matters to you and to your school in this changing and engaging digital world.

It's time to be brandED. Are you in?

Conversation 8 Tips

- **Understand** that distributed leadership holds the key to brandED awareness, value, belief, and emotions as you implement this change. Your school brand is sustained by the community of stakeholders invested in creating and maintaining the unique brand value of the school story.
- **Recognize** that relationships are key to the roles that brandED leaders play as storytellers who create the school narrative and stewards who sustain the school brand.
- **Remember** that social media facilitates relationship, but it is not the relationship itself. Leaders use tools of brandED leadership to build authentic partnerships and relationships.
- **Think and act** locally and globally. "Go big or go home" can be the mantra for connecting the school brand in a transparent, digitally connected world.
- **Support** the sharing of brand by education professionals who are acting out of the leadership ethic of giving and empathy.

Conversation 8 Reflections

Before holding public conversation around how brandED brings worth to the entire community, think about these questions:

- Can I articulate what ROR is, and its value to nurturing a brandED relationship?

- Am I building my social capital through brandED leadership and inspiring my stakeholders to do the same?
- Am I energized by the possibility of innovating as a brandED leader?
- Do I see the connection of my role as storyteller-in-chief to my role as a brandED steward?
- Can I compellingly communicate that brandED is worthwhile as a tool for professional leadership development?
- After learning about this innovative way to create professional and institutional improvement, can I positively respond to the final brandED leadership question: *Am I in?*

Appendix A: Developing a Mission Statement

As you craft a new mission statement, or refresh an older one, lead your collective team in a market-focused direction that defines a school. Create a short statement that captures the core belief of the entity: the school. This isn't a simple task, but it is well worth the effort.

BrandED is about building relationships. Make certain your mission statement includes language that makes the commitment the way any market-focused mission statement would. The statement identifies the community and the relationship that is being forged through the core belief of the brand.

Elements of a BrandED Mission Statement

Short

Evocative

Clear

Inspiring

The image, promise, and result should be unique and evident in your school mission statement. As Seth Godin would suggest, it must be **remarkable.**

To begin the process of creating the mission statement, use these five simple prompts:

1. WHO are we?
2. WHAT do we promise?
3. HOW do we deliver?
4. For WHOM?
5. WHY are we relevant?

Appendix B: Crafting Positioning Statements

Created by the collective team to support the market-focused mission statement, positioning statements can be a series of multiple messages for target populations of stakeholders, intended to more deeply connect them to the school's brand and mission. They can be a part of websites, blogs, and other brand messaging collateral that is directed to a segment of stakeholders.

Sample school brand positioning statement directed to parents:

> For caring parents of K–2 students who want to partner in their child's educational experience, [name of school] is an informed, connected, and giving community that creates a supportive, developmental school experience that we demonstrate every day as a dedicated faculty and staff.

Sample school brand positioning statement directed to students:

> For students in grades 9–12 who need the best preparation to meet their career goals, [name of high school] is a place of authentic, connected, caring learning that will prepare each student for the world awaiting them tomorrow.

Positioning statements serve as additional messages that can be repurposed as need arises in exchange with the targeted groups of stakeholders. The examples above illustrate targeted positioning statements that support a school mission statement. Use this pattern to achieve yours: To/For [target segment] who [identify need], our [school name] is [brand concept] that [point of difference]. (Adapted from Armstrong & Kotler, 2015).

Appendix C: Stewardship Model of BrandED Development

Early Implementation of BrandED Professional Development	Middle Stage of Implementation of BrandED Professional Development
Leader creates a personal professional brand that is the basis for the institutional brand journey. Leader assumes the brandED "storyteller-in-chief" position, identifies stakeholder fans, and holds initial discussions to build a collaborative team based on distributive leadership. Leader gathers the collective team and leads a professional brand building and personal SWOT experience before launching development of the strategic plan. Leader meets with collective to discuss vision, purpose, and big ideas for creating and articulating the school brand. Initial discussions focus on brand collateral with deeper and consistent messages that unify the diverse community and engage the segments of audiences.	Meet with the collective to create brandED through the series of brandED Drivers from promise to engagement. Introduce brandED Drivers to the community as the foundation for the planning initiative. Develop positioning statements and create or refresh the school mission statement with a deeper message that unifies the diverse community and is focused on engaging audiences. Establish measurable goals for brandED improvement in culture, performance, and resourcing. Develop processes for highlighting stories that link to the brand goals. Provide staff development for teachers to help them develop a personal professional brand and understand how to support the school brand. Look for ways to include students in valuing school initiatives as part of their personal brand.

Mature Stage of Implementation of Professional Development	
With the collaboration of the brandED team, craft the brandED Strategic Plan, which is then presented to the public.	Find ways to meet with segments of the resourcing population, informally or formally.
Conduct an assessment of each identified goal for the sustaining of brand and showing growth.	Invite media, bloggers, and influencers to school events and activities, large and small, that promote the school brand.
Promote the development of students as emotional brand partners in academic and nonacademic settings.	Target social media for celebrations of a year of brandED.
	Focus on relationships for the emotional, service, and value they potentially hold for partnerships.

Appendix D:
Suggested BrandED Digital Tools

Tool	Link	Description	Use
ASCD Edge	edge.ascd.org	If you are a member of ASCD, join this community to share blog posts on its site about successful strategies and ideas that have been implemented in your school/district.	PR
Blab	blab.im	Share live conversations where stakeholders can watch, join, and interact with you.	Communications, PR
Blogs	www.blogger.com wordpress.com medium.com www.tumblr.com	Share news, achievements, opinions, and reflections on various topics in detail using a variety of media. There are multiple platforms to choose from.	Communications, PR
Buffer	buffer.com	Work smarter by sharing social media messages at preset times to save time and extend influence.	Brand management
edWeb	home.edweb.net	Conduct webinars to share successful strategies and ideas that have been implemented in your school/district.	PR
Facebook	www.facebook.com	Facebook is the world's largest social networking service. Create a professional page for your district or school. When you develop your personal professional brand, establish a page for yourself.	Communications, PR
Flickr	www.flickr.com	Create picture galleries and share across other social networks.	PR

Tool	Link	Description	Use
Google Alerts	www.google.com/alerts	Track your digital footprint and brand. Use keywords to get email notifications about your district, school, or yourself.	Brand management
Google photos	photos.google.com	Back up, save, and share, photos quickly.	PR
Google+	plus.google.com	Google+ integrates both Twitter and Facebook features.	PR
Hashtags	tinyurl.com/brandEDU	A hashtag is a keyword or phrase preceded by the hash (#) symbol to include in social media posts. Hashtags make the content of your post accessible to all people with similar interests, even if they're not followers or fans. Create one for your district/school. Use pre-existing ones to amplify your message.	Communications, PR, brand management
Hootsuite	hootsuite.com	This is a social media management system that integrates with 80+ applications	Communications, PR, brand management
IFTTT	ifttt.com	Create "recipes"—chains of simple conditional statements—among the social media tools you use to save time and maximize messaging impact. Sample recipe: If I post to Twitter, then the same message will go to Facebook and Google+.	Communications, PR, brand management
Instagram	www.instagram.com	Instagram is a photo and video sharing site that integrates with both Twitter and Facebook. Use hashtags to maximize exposure.	PR
LinkedIn	www.linkedin.com	Manage your professional identity.	PR, brand management

Tool	Link	Description	Use
Mention	mention.com/en	Track your digital footprint and brand. Use keywords to get email and/or mobile app notifications about your district, school, or yourself.	Brand management
Periscope	www.periscope.tv	Periscope is a free, live video streaming app for iOS and Android devices. Stream directly to Periscope and Twitter followers.	PR
Podcasting	vocaroo.com soundcloud.com www.audacityteam.org	Create audio recordings that can be shared using digital tools or by embedding them on a website.	Communications, PR
QR codes	www.qrstuff.com	Create a code to a website that can be scanned using a mobile device. Download and place QR codes on announcements and paper flyers. When users scan the code, they will be taken to the website.	Communications
School apps	crescerance.com www.schoolmessenger.com	These apps enable you to send push notifications to stakeholders.	Communications, PR
Smore	www.smore.com	Easily create instant newsletters that can be shared across existing social networks.	Communications
Snapchat	www.snapchat.com	Share live stories in the moment through video, text, and images. Stories disappear after 24 hours.	Communications, PR
Storify	storify.com	Create engaging stories using social media and traditional elements.	PR
TodaysMeet	todaysmeet.com	Engage stakeholders in the process of sharing information.	Communications
Tweetdeck	tweetdeck.twitter.com	This is a dashboard specific to Twitter. Set up columns to track conversations about your school/district, hashtags, and yourself.	Brand management

Tool	Link	Description	Use
Twitter	twitter.com	Twitter is a microblogging platform that allows users to send 140-character messages called tweets. Tweets can be text, images, video, and websites.	Communications, PR
Ustream	www.ustream.tv	Stream live video and then archive on a district/school channel	Communications, PR
Voxer	www.voxer.com	Voxer is a push-to-talk, walkie-talkie app for communication with stakeholders and other educators.	Communications
WhatsApp	www.whatsapp.com	This is a messenger app and provides calling for free.	Communications
YouTube	www.youtube.com	YouTube is the world's largest video creation and sharing site. Create a channel to share announcements, news, and events.	Communications, PR

Appendix E:
Media Advisory Template

A school's promotional efforts to attract traditional press are served by understanding the power of a *media advisory*. This is a message targeted to specific journalists and editors. It isn't a mass mailing of a press release. Use the advisory to further develop relationships with editors, producers, journalists. Send a short and attention-grabbing announcement about an event, a special project, or notable recognition received by the school that illustrates pride in the school brand. The advisory email is sent to your best contacts. It is followed up with a phone call directly to the media outlet editorial desk or city desk, or to a reporter. It's a warm touch that can open a quick, personal follow-up phone conversation. You can use the following template for planning purposes.

[YOUR SCHOOL LETTERHEAD/LOGO HERE]
MEDIA ADVISORY

Write a Short Headline

Write the date of the event/occasion/project

CITY/TOWN—Write a short description of the event/occasion/project

<u>Rewrite the Title of the Event/Occasion/Project</u>

WHAT: Brief description (one line)

WHEN: Time for media to report

WHERE: Where media will report

WHO: List names of important participants who will attend

CONTACT: Phone(s) and email of point person to contact

About: Briefly add important details of the school mission and brand, including website. Add any other partnering entities in the event to show connection and value.

Add three hashtags to signal the end of the Media Advisory to look professional!

###

Appendix F: A BrandED Leadership Timeline

A suggested timeline can guide you in leading the development of school brand. Use the benchmarks of **informing, visioning, launching** and **assessing** to focus your workflow and test your role as a steward of brand development.

INITIATE BrandED Leadership: Monitor Personal Leadership Development

1. **Informing:** Develop a personal professional brand through reading, discussion, creation, and sharing in real time and online.

2. **Visioning:** Craft your first personal professional brand in reflective activity.

3. **Launching:** Determine channels through which to share your brand in public using real-time and online channels.

4. **Assessing:** Meet with many stakeholders using the MBWA (Management by Walking Around) style and practice the communication of your brand. As you informally share your own new brand presence, identify early adopters who may become part of your collective team in developing a schoolwide brand.

SHARE BrandED Leadership: Develop Support for Your BrandED Schoolwide Story

1. **Informing:** Select team members to join your distributed leadership collective for your brandED strategic campaign; refer to Assets of the BrandED Collaborative Team (Fig 3.2).

2. **Visioning:** Invite stakeholders to informally meet. Convey the need, purpose, and goal of brandED as a unifying strategy to improve culture, performance, and resourcing. Use the assets of the collective team to enlist help in creating a brandED Strategic Plan. Gather stakeholders from all segments of the community: teachers, staff, students, parents, community, and businesses.

3. **Launching:** Plan an initial session with select point people from your team who are strategic and comfortable in sharing the lead. Discuss how the assets of the collective will be focused. Introduce the elements of brand history and personal brand connection, and use structured frameworks, such as the PERMA dashboard and SWOT analysis, to enlist their supportive engagement.

4. **Assessing:** Evaluate the assets of the collective to ensure that a range of assets is represented for the workflow of developing the brandED Strategic Plan, the strategy for schoolwide brand delivery.

ACTIVATE BrandED Leadership: Own Your BrandED Stewardship Role

1. **Informing:** Meet with your team: Guide the team to design with the tenets of branding and brandED. Discuss the digital and print collateral and messages that are currently characterizing the school. Introduce the foundations of **image, promise,** and **result** that the school will convey. Explore the vision, purpose, and core idea of the school.

2. **Visioning:** Activate thinking using the brandED Drivers. Begin to develop the new brand messages and systems for communication. Define the promise, mission statement, and optional positioning statements. Identify brand goals and objectives that can be benchmarked through the Drivers. Identify the existing and new systems for sharing the brand. Develop a calendar of brandED activities that invites all stakeholders to create business-as-unusual brand events.

3. **Launching:** Capture your brandED Strategic Plan and share it with the community through public channels. Begin the visible connection of the brand online and offline with the support of the collaborative team.

4. **Assessing:** Assess the community's engagement with the brand: seek digital or real-time feedback using creative ways to observe the brand in action through digital content and offline brand events.

Appendix G: Online Marketing and Brand Resources for Educator BrandED Adaptation

Any of these online resources can expand the marketing and brand adaptations of leaders who wish to follow and curate trends. This is a deeper dive into brand thinking for leaders who want to be seen as future oriented "edge dwellers" who curate trends that connect to education through the industry of marketing and communication.These sites and others can provide brand content for stakeholder engagement in as current a time frame as possible. Content from these sites can easily be promoted on social media and in digital forms. In addition, leaders can use this curated content to develop relationships with possible resource partners for promotion or for emotional, service, or product resourcing partnerships. This is a list of suggested resources that can be adapted by any leader using a search engine.

www.adage.com: *Advertising Age*

www.adweek.com: *Adweek*

www.aef.com: Advertising Educational Foundation

www.ama.com: American Marketing Association

www.brandingmagazine.com: Independent daily brand journal

www.brandingstrategyinsider.com: Information about brand building www.clickz.com: *Click Z* marketing news

www.dmanews.com Direct marketing news stories

www.heidicohen.com: Actionable marketing guide

https://muckrack.com/daily/: Muck Rack newsfeed for PR and marketing

www.marketingprofs.com: Practical advice through text and podcasts

www.marketingtechnews.net: Collected current technology marketing topics

Affinity   The state of connected good feeling between a brand and its audience that is evident in the long-term engagement and loyalty shown by the audience. It is up to the brand to deliver its genuine promise in order to keep the affinity of its fan base.

Affiliative brandED model   An adaptation of Daniel Goleman's thinking about shared responsibility, an affiliative brandED model for promoting brandED messaging illustrates how distributed leadership among a collaborative team spreads the word about the good work of schools to the microenvironment and macroenvironment of education.

Brand   A name, term, sign, symbol, design, or a combination of these that identifies the products or services of one seller or a group of sellers and differentiates them from those of competitors (Armstrong & Kotler, 2015).

BrandED   An adaptation of the business brand function found in marketing that differentiates a product or service from the competition, brandED is an educator's professional learning strategy for defining 21st-century schools through their unique story of core value and for engaging the community in digital and real-time exchange that results in improved school culture, performance, and resources.

BrandED contagion   How things catch on in the marketing sense in a school environment, especially in the social media and digital space; the concept of going viral.

BrandED culture   The components of basic values, perceptions, wants, needs, and behaviors that are shared by an audience of stakeholders in a school community and are communicated consistently through the messaging of a school brand.

BrandED Drivers   The identified elements of a model-building process, adapted from marketing, that results in a clear brandED strategy to articulate the school's goal and brand message.

BrandED image   The components of the visual and visceral representations that are perceived by an audience of school stakeholders and are communicated consistently through the school brand.

BrandED mission statement   A mission statement defined in terms of satisfying stakeholder needs, highlighting commitment to the long-term welfare of the community.

BrandED parent brand   The overarching brand of a school that gives rise to extensions that relate to the core school brand. Usually found in cases of large school districts that create a core brand that is supported through connected positioning statements of schools within the district.

BrandED performance   The extended ways that student learning and achievement can be measured to show capacity in thought and expression beyond the limits of standardized tests and that reflect the school values that are communicated consistently through the school brand.

BrandED promise   What a school promises to deliver to its audience of stakeholders; this reflects the core value of the school's brand in an authentic and trusted delivery of service.

BrandED resourcing   The result of dedicated attention to building relationships that showcase the school's strategically crafted brand; resources come from partnerships with like-minded individuals or companies that improve the school community through emotional, service, or product resourcing.

BrandED result   Select, measurable, and attainable goals to show progress of the school brand to improve culture, performance and resources.

BrandED stewardship   An ethic adopted by a brandED leader that demonstrates the responsibility of managing and guiding the elements of a brandED Strategic Plan.

Brand equity   The differential effect that knowing the brand name has on customer response to the product or its marketing (Armstrong & Kotler, 2015).

Chief brand officer   In business, a recent addition to an organizational chart that places an individual in the lead for all aspects related to brand development and management.

Competitive advantage   An advantage gained over competitors by offering greater customer value, either by having lower prices or providing more benefit to justify higher prices (Armstrong & Kotler, 2015).

Customer relations management   The overall process of building and maintaining profitable customer relationships by delivering superior value and satisfaction (Armstrong & Kotler, 2015).

Emotional partnership   One of three directions for a brandED leader's building of relationships and resources for schools. Emotional partners may lend ideas through content and activity that help support promotion of the brand, which creates the good feeling that continues connectedness to the brand.

Event marketing   Holding or sponsoring events that highlight the development and use of a brand. Using the school brand as an anchor, events can serve as promotions across the district to build relationships and celebrate the school brand.

Evergreen content   A form of content that can be used for the long-term communication of your school brand. The school mission and content connected to the mission are evergreen. The mission remains in the public eye and is changed only over time.

First Moment of Truth   A traditional way, prior to the advent of the Internet, that consumers made purchasing decisions face-to-face with products on store shelves.

Generation X   The 49 million people born between 1965 and 1976 in the "birth dearth" following the Baby Boomer demographic (Armstrong & Kotler, 2015).

Generation Y/Millennials   The 83 million children of the Baby Boomers born between 1977 and 2000 (Armstrong & Kotler, 2015).

Generation Z/Plurals   Those born after 2000 (although some analysts include people born after 1995), who make up the teens and tweens markets that are the most ethnically diverse of any US generation to date.

Ivory Tower   An idiom suggesting an educationally remote place or situation lacking in engagement with the stakeholder world outside of the internal school structure.

Macroenvironment   The larger societal forces—demographic, economic, natural, technological, political and cultural—that affect the microenvironment (Armstrong & Kotler, 2015).

Macronarrative   The big-picture story of the school brand advanced by the storyteller-in-chief to engage the audience of stakeholders.

Madison Avenue   Originally, the New York City street location of the first top 20th Century advertising agencies. The term today refers to advertising business as a whole in the 21st century.

Marketing   The process by which companies create value for customers and build strong relationships in order to capture value from customers in return (Armstrong & Kotler, 2015).

Marketing return on investment/ROI   The return on effort in the investment divided by the cost of making it happen.

Media kit   A collection of stories, links, and visuals that can promote the school brand. Built as a PDF, it can be located as a button on the school website. In efforts to share the school brand, a media kit saves a leader from reinventing the wheel when approaching journalists, bloggers, influencers, and potential partners.

Microenvironment   Those factors close to the school brand that impact its service to the audience.

Micronarrative   Those small stories that support the big ideas of value, belief, awareness, and purpose that the school brand embodies, which are collaboratively gathered by the stakeholder community for sharing across many communication channels.

Mission statement   A statement by the organization regarding its purpose and what it wants to accomplish in the larger environment (Armstrong & Kotler, 2015).

PERMA Model   Positive psychologist, Dr. Martin Seligman's theoretical model of well-being employed by brandED leaders in support of their collaborative team approaching brand innovation.

Perception   How people target, organize, interpret, and judge what they see and hear so as to make a meaningful picture of their world (Armstrong & Kotler, 2015).

Positioning   Arranging for an offering of a product or service to occupy a clear and desirable place relative to other similar products in the minds of an audience (Armstrong & Kotler, 2015).

Positioning statement   Statement created by the collective brandED team to support the mission statement; it can comprise multiple messages for different target populations of stakeholders to more deeply connect them to the school's brand and mission.

Public relations   Building good relationships with various publics by obtaining favorable publicity; building up a good image; and mitigating unfavorable rumors, stories, and events (Armstrong & Kotler, 2015).

Product partnership   The result of developing authentic relationships with economic partners in the macroenvironment who share affinity with the school brand and can supply their products in service to the school through donation.

Reputation management for brandED   Collective resources in digital and real time that help leaders form positive, connected, and authentic brandED personalities.

Return on relationship (ROR)   Value that is accrued by a person or brand due to nurturing a relationship. ROI is simple dollars and cents. ROR is the value (both perceived and real) that will accrue over time through loyalty, recommendations, and sharing.

Social marketing   A principal of sustainable marketing, which holds that a company should make decisions by considering customers' wants and society's long-term interests ("Do well by doing good").

Stakeholder relationship management (SRM) An adaptation for education leaders that differs from the business tool of customer relationship management, but has the same intention for schools: the understanding of who are the end users of a brand and how to keep them satisfied and engaged.

SWOT analysis An overall evaluation of an organization's strengths (S), weaknesses (W), opportunities (O), and threats (T). The analysis can also be applied to an individual profile (Armstrong & Kotler, 2015).

Unique brand value (UBV) The ability of a school, organization, or professional brand to distinguish itself from others and to form authentic positive relationships based on its brand personality.

Unique sales proposition Identified by leading television advertising executive Rosser Reeves (1961) in the mid-20th century, the concept used to highlight the differentiator that a brand brings that leads to a buy.

Word-of-mouth influence The impact of the personal words and recommendations of friends, associates, and other consumers on buying behavior (Armstrong & Kotler, 2015).

Zero Moment of Truth (ZMOT) Term coined by Google that refers to the powerful role that the Internet plays in influencing the behaviors of consumers making buying decisions online.

References

Agbor, E. (2008). Creativity and innovation: leadership dynamics. *Journal of Strategic Leadership*, *1*(1): 139–145.

Anderson, L., Corcorran, J., Davis, L., Elliot, E., Greene, P., Henderson, B., . . . Weiner, A. (2016). School-business partnerships that work: Success stories from schools of all sizes. Retrieved from http://www.educationworld.com/a_admin/admin/admin323.shtml

Armstrong, G., & Kotler, P. (2015). *Marketing: An introduction* (12th ed.). Boston, MA: Pearson.

Arruda, W. (2013). Seven questions to ask when uncovering your personal brand. *Forbes*. Retrieved from http://www.forbes.com/sites/williamarruda/2013/11/12/7-questions-to-ask-when-uncovering-your-personal-brand/#709c3c577400

Atkinson-Bonasio, A. (2016). Getting an early start. *Research Information*. Retrieved from http://www.researchinformation.info/news/news_story.php?news_id=2117

Balmaekers, H. (2014). The one word answer to why innovation fails. *Innovation Management*. Retrieved from http://www.innovationmanagement.se/2014/09/22/the-one-word-answer-to-why-innovation-fails/

Bass, R. (2016). Disrupting ourselves: The problem of learning in higher education. *Educause Review*. Retrieved from http://er.educause.edu/articles/2012/3/disrupting-ourselves-the-problem-of-learning-in-higher-education

Bierly, C., Doyle, B., & Smith, A. (2016). Transforming schools: How distributed leadership can create more high-performing schools. *Bain & Company Insights*. Retrieved from http://www.bain.com/publications/articles/transforming-schools.aspx

Bland, M. (2016). Whirlpool put laundry machines in some schools and increased attendance by 90%. *Scary Mommy*. Retrieved from http://www.scarymommy.com/whirlpool-care-counts-improves-attendance-in-schools/

Chako, S. J. (2016). 5 teachers to watch on Periscope [Web log post]. Sheila Jane Teaching. Retrieved from https://sheilajaneteaching.com/5-teachers-to-watch-on-periscope-a-periscope-linky/

Chen, L. (2015). At $68 billion valuation, Uber will be bigger than GM, Ford, and Honda. *Forbes*. Retrieved from http://www.forbes.com/sites/liyanchen/2015/12/04/at-68-billion-valuation-uber-will-be-bigger-than-gm-ford-and-honda/#6c2413ea5858

Claypool, M. K., & McClaughlin, J. M. (2015). *We're in this together: Public-private partnerships in special and at-risk education*. Lantham, MD: Roman & Littlefield.

Cohen, H. (2011a). Thirty branding definitions. Retrieved from http://heidicohen.com/30-branding-definitions/

Cohen, H. (2011b). Thirty-one public relations definitions. Retrieved from http://heidicohen.com/public-relations-definition/

Connick, W. (2012). The seven stages of the sales cycle. *National Association of Sales Professionals*. Retrieved from https://www.nasp.com/article/AE1B7061-3F39/the-seven-stages-of-the-sales-cycle.html

Csikszentmihalyi, M. (1990). *Flow: The psychology of optimal experience*. New York, NY: Harper and Row.

Csikszentmihalyi, M. (2004.). Flow: The secret to happiness. TED. Retrieved from https://www.ted.com/talks/mihaly_csikszentmihalyi_on_flow

Dahlstrom, E., with Brooks, D. C., Grajek, S., & Reeves, J. (2015, December). ECAR study of undergraduate students and information technology, 2015. Research report. EDUCAUSE Center for Analysis and Research. Retrieved from https://library.educause.edu/~/media/files/library/2015/8/ers1510ss.pdf?la=en&channel=Eloqua&elq_mid=15944&elq_cid=7691272

Darling-Hammond, L., Chung Wei, R., & Andree, A. (2010). How high achieving countries develop great teachers. Retrieved from edpolicy.stanford.edu/sites/default/files/publications/how-high-achieving-countries-develop-great-teachers.pdf

De Swaan Arons, M. (2011, October 3). How brands were born: A brief history. *Atlantic*. Retrieved from http://www.theatlantic.com/business/archive/2011/10/how-brands-were-born-a-brief-history-of-modern-marketing/246012/

Dua, T. (2015). How brands can remain relevant today. *Digiday*. Retrieved from http://digiday.com/brands/advertisingweek2015-advertising-week-2015-what-brands-need-to-do-to-remain-relevant/2015

Dweck, C. (2007). *Mindset: The new psychology of success*. New York, NY: Ballantine Books.

Dylan, J. (2014). 826 and the future of education [Web log post]. *Huffington Post*. Retrieved from http://www.huffingtonpost.com/jesse-dylan/826-and-the-future-of-education_b_4848387.html?utm_hp_ref=fb&src=sp

Eisenberg, B. (2016). The value of a unique value proposition. *ClickZ*. Retrieved from www.clickz.com/clickz/column/1698681/the-value-unique-value-proposition

Ferrel, O. C., & Hartline, M. (2014). *Marketing strategy*. Mason, OH: South-West Cengage Learning.

Ferriter, W., Ramsden, J., & Sheninger, E. (2011). *Communicating and connecting with social media*. Bloomington, IN: Solution Tree.

Fisher, A. (2012). Management by walking around: 6 tips to make it work. *Fortune*. Retrieved from http://fortune.com/2012/08/23/management-by-walking-around-6-tips-to-make-it-work/

Friedman, T. L. (2015). *The world is flat: A brief history of the twenty-first century*. New York, NY: Farrar, Straus & Giroux.

Gallo, C. (2016). *The storyteller's secret*. New York, NY: St. Martin's Press.

Giang, V. (2012). 9 tips on creating a remarkable product. *Business Insider*. Retrieved from http://www.businessinsider.com/seth-godin-9-tips-on-creating-a-remarkable-product-2012-2

Gill, C. (2016). Snapchat for business: How to reach millennials through storytelling. *LinkedIn*. Retrieved from https://www.linkedin.com/pulse/snapchat-business-how-reach-millennials-through-storytelling-gil

Godin, S. (2008). *Tribes: We need you to lead us*. New York, NY: Penguin Group.

Goodwin, T. (2016). Marketers should stop ignoring instant messages. *Guardian*. Retrieved from www.theguardian.com/media-network/2016/jan/22/marketing-instant-messenger-whatsapp-facebook?CMP=share_btn_link

Grace, M. (2012). Helping non-profits with hula hoops and kickballs. *Wall Street Journal*. Retrieved from http://www.wsj.com/articles/SB10001424052970203806504577183263558500868

Grant, A. (2013). Action happiness: Give and take with Adam Grant. YouTube. Retrieved from www.youtube.com/watch?v=7ogXvSwwFns

Grant, A. (2014). *Give and take: Why helping others drives our success*. New York, NY: Penguin Press.

Grant, A. (2016). *Originals: How non-conformists move the world*. New York, NY: Viking.

Grant-Halvorson, H. (2015). *No one understands you and what to do about it*. Boston, MA: Harvard Business Review Press.

Gunelius, S. (2008). Six hats of a chief brand officer. *Corporate Eye*. Retrieved from http://www.corporate-eye.com/main/the-6-hats-of-a-chief-brand-officer/

Gunelius, S. (2014). The psychology and philosophy of branding marketing needs and actions. *Forbes*. Retrieved from http://www.forbes.com/sites/work-in-progress/2014/03/05/the-psychology-and-philosophy-of-branding-marketing-needs-and-actions/

Hahn, N. (2014). Rosetta Consulting's customer engagement survey part I: The marketer's perspective. Retrieved from http://www.rosetta.com//assets/pdf/Customer-Engagement-Survey-2014.pdf

Hais, M., & Winograd, M. (2012, July 7). A new generation debuts: Plurals [Web log post]. *Huffington Post*. Retrieved from http://www.huffingtonpost.com/michael-hais-and-morley-winograd/plurals-generation_b_1492384.html

Hammond, L., Chung Wei, R., & Andree, A. (2010). How high achieving countries develop great teachers. Retrieved from edpolicy.stanford.edu/sites/default/files/publications/how-high-achieving-countries-develop-great-teachers.pdf

He, L. (2013). Google's secrets of innovation: Empowering employees. *Creativity Post*. Retrieved from www.creativitypost.com/business/10_practices_from_the_most_innovative_organizations

Hiler, T., & Erickson Hatalsky, L. (2014). Teaching: The next generation. Third Way. Retrieved from http://www.thirdway.org/report/teaching-the-next-generation

History: 1960s. (2003). *Advertising Age encyclopedia*. Retrieved from http://adage.com/article/adage-encyclopedia/history-1960s/98702/

Hoque, F. (2015). 5 habits of truly disruptive leaders. *Fast Company*. Retrieved from http://www.fastcompany.com/3052725/hit-the-ground-running/5-habits-of-truly-disruptive-leaders

Horn, M., & Staker, H. (2015). *Blended*. San Francisco, CA: Jossey-Bass.

Interbrand. (2016). Best global brands 2016: Rankings. Retrieved from http://interbrand.com/best-brands/best-global-brands/2016/ranking/

Jacobs, H. (2014). *The new literacies*. Bloomington, IN: Solution Tree.

Jobs, S. (2013, April 21). Think differently. The crazy ones speech of 1999. YouTube. Retrieved from https://www.youtube.com/watch?v=keCw RdbwNQY (Speech given in 1999)

Juliani, A. J. (2015). *Innovation and inquiry in the classroom.* New York, NY: Rutledge.

Kapferer, J. N. (2012). *The new brand management.* London, England: Kogan Page.

King, G., Rose, C., & O'Donnell, N. (Interviewers). (2016). Janah Hayes chosen national teacher of the year 2016. *CBS Morning News.* Retrieved from http://www.cbsnews.com/videos/connecticut-jahana-hayes-named-2016-national-teacher-of-the-year/

Kline, D., Duprey, R., & Noonan, K. (2016, January 11). 3 ways Chipotle Mexican Grill can win back consumers' trust. *Motley Fool.* Retrieved from http://www.fool.com/investing/general/2016/01/11/3-ways-chipotle-mexican-grill-can-win-back-consume.aspx

Kosoff, M. (2015). Sheryl Sandberg once told an employee she sounded stupid and why this is a great management lesson for everyone. *Business Insider.* Retrieved from www.businessinsider.com/the-reason-sheryl-sandberg-told-kim-scott-an-uncomfortable-truth-is-a-great-management-lesson-2015-12

Kotler, P., & Armstrong, G. (1996). *Principles of marketing.* Upper Saddle River, NJ: Prentice Hall.

Laird, P. (2006). *Pull: Networking and success since Benjamin Franklin.* Boston, MA: Harvard University Press.

Madda, M. J. (2015). A peek at Periscope's potential and privacy concerns in the classroom. *Edsurge.* Retrieved from www.edsurge.com/news/2015-06-11-a-peek-at-periscope-s-potential-and-privacy-concerns-in-the-classroom

Maslow, A. (1998). *Maslow on management.* Hoboken, NJ: Wiley.

McCulloch, L. (2000). Learn what a branding campaign is. *Inc.* Retrieved from http://www.inc.com/articles/2000/03/18889.html

Meyer, D. (2008). *Setting the table: The transforming power of hospitality in business*. New York, NY: Harper.

Miletsky, J., & Smith, G. (2009). *Perspectives on branding*. Boston, MA: Cengage Learning.

Mineo, L. D. (2014). The importance of trust in leadership. *Research Management Review*, *20*(1), 1–6.

Monroe, D. (2014). Confessions of an edge dweller. *Transition Voice*. Retrieved from http://transitionvoice.com/2014/01/confessions-of-an-edge-dweller/

Murphy, M. (2016). Facebook hints at how it could become a big player in the ride sharing business. Quartz. Retrieved from http://qz.com/605156/facebook-hints-at-how-it-could-become-a-big-player-in-the-ride-sharing-business/

National Association of Secondary School Principals and the National Association of Elementary School Principals. (2013). Leadership matters: What the research says about the importance of principal leadership. Retrieved from http://www.naesp.org/sites/default/files/LeadershipMatters.pdf

National Policy Board for Educational Administration. (2015). *Professional standards for educational leaders 2015*. Reston, VA: Author.

Ogilvy, D. (1987). *Confessions of an advertising man*. London, England: Southbank.

Penhollow, S. (2014, February 25). Chalk it up to experience. *Britton*. Retrieved from http://www.brittonmdg.com/the-britton-blog/chalk-it-up-to-experience

Peters, T. (1997). The brand you. *Fast Company*. Retrieved from https://www.fastcompany.com/28905/brand-called-you

Peters, T. (1999). *The brand you 50: Fifty ways to transform yourself from an "employee" into a brand that shouts distinction, commitment, and passion!* New York, NY: Knopf.

Peters, T., & Waterman, R. (1982). *In search of excellence: Lessons from America's best-run companies*. New York, NY: Warner Books.

Petit, Z. (2014). Legends in advertising: Bill Bernbach, the original Don Draper. *Print*. Retrieved from www.printmag.com/featured/legends-in-advertising-bill-bernbach/

Petro, G. (2013). Millennial engagement and loyalty—Make them part of the process. *Forbes*. Retrieved from http://www.forbes.com/sites/gregpetro/2013/03/21/millennial-engagement-and-loyalty-make-them-part-of-the-process/#62cbbc5d44c7

Pink, D. (2012). *To sell is human: The surprising truth about moving others*. New York, NY: Riverhead Books.

Rao, J., & Weintraub, J. (2013, March 19). How innovative is your company culture? *MIT Sloan Management Review*. Retrieved from http://sloanreview.mit.edu/article/how-innovative-is-your-companys-culture/

Reeves, R. (1961). *Reality in advertising*. New York, NY: Knopf.

Riviere, A. (2009, December 21). 10 tips for a better account-ability partnership. *GIGAOM*. Retrieved from https://gigaom.com/2009/12/21/10-tips-for-a-better-accountability-partnership

Robinson, Sir K. (2006, February). Do schools kill creativity? TED. Retrieved from https://www.ted.com/talks/ken_robinson_says_schools_kill_creativity?language=en

Rose, J. (2012). How to break free of our 19th-century factory-model education system. *Atlantic*. Retrieved from http://www.theatlantic.com/business/archive/2012/05/how-to-break-free-of-our-19th-century-factory-model-education-system/256881/

Rubin, T. [Ted], & Rose, K. (2013). *Return on relationship*. Mustang, OK: Tate.

Rubin, T. [Trish]. (2009). Branding lessons: Meet a MADman princi-pal [Web log post]. Trish Rubin's EdVentures in a New York Minute.

Retrieved from http://theedventuresgroup.blogspot.com/2009/11/someone-give-me-seatbelt-because-ride.html

Rubin, T. [Trish]. (2016, December 11). The storyteller and steward of brand leadership[Web log post]. All Roads Lead to Relationships: Trish Rubin's Blog. Retrieved from https://trishrubinnyc .squarespace.com/blog/2016/4/11/the-storyteller-and-steward-of-branded-leadership

Sadeghi, T., & Tabrizi, K. G. (2011). The correlation between feelings and brand perception on purchase intention. *World Applied Sciences Journal, 12*, 697–705.

Sales, N. J. (2016). How social media is disrupting the lives of American girls. *Time, 187*(6/7), 26.

Sample, S. (2002). *The contrarian's guide to leadership*. San Francisco, CA: Jossey-Bass.

Scott, K. (2016). Radical candor. Retrieved from http://www .kimmalonescott.com/

Seligman, M.E.P. (2012). *Flourish: A visionary new understanding of happiness and well-being*. New York, NY: Free Press.

Shaffhauser, D. (2014). Schools could do better teaching tech. *The Journal*. Retrieved from thejournal.com/articles/2014/07/29/millennial-parents-schools-could-do-better-teaching-tech.aspx

Sheninger, E. (2010, January 19). Guest blogger: Eric Sheninger, The value of BRAND in education [Web log post]. Trish Rubin's EdVentures in a New York Minute. Retrieved from http://theedventuresgroup.blogspot.com/2010/01/guest-blogger-eric-shininger-value-of.html

Sheninger, E. (2014). *Digital leadership: Changing paradigms for changing times*. Thousand Oaks, CA: Corwin Press.

Sinanis, T., & Sanfelippo, J. (2015). *The power of branding: Telling your school's story*. Thousand Oaks, CA. Corwin Press.

Sipe, J. W., & Frick, D. M. (2009). *Seven pillars of servant leadership: Practicing the wisdom of leading by serving.* New York, NY: Paulist Press.

Smith, A. (2015). US smartphone use in 2015. Pew Research. Retrieved from https://www.pewinternet.org

Solis, B. (2011a). *The end of business as usual.* Hoboken, NJ: Wiley.

Solis, B. (2011b). *Engage! The complete guide for brands and businesses to build, cultivate, and measure success in the new web.* Hoboken, NJ: Wiley.

Srinivasan, T. S. (2015). *The five founding fathers of American psychology.* Positive Psychology Program. Retrieved from https://positivepsychologyprogram.com/founding-fathers/

Vanauken, B. (2015). *Brand aid.* New York, NY: American Management Association.

VW chairman says parts of company "tolerated breaches of rules." (2015, December 10). *Automotive News.* Retrieved from http://www.autonews.com/article/20151210/COPY01/312109975/vw-chairman-says-parts-of-company-tolerated-breaches-of-rules

Walkin, L. (2013). Brand reputation management: Your 7 point game plan. *MarketingProfs.* Retrieved from http://www.marketingprofs.com/articles/2013/11004/brand-reputation-management-your-seven-point-game-plan

Whitehurst, G. J. (2009). Don't forget curriculum. Washington, DC: Brookings. Retrieved from www.brookings.edu/papers/2009/1014_curriculum_whitehurst.aspx

Zenger, J., & Folkman, J. (2015, November). We like leaders who underrate themselves. *Harvard Business Review.* Retrieved from https://hbr.org/2015/11/we-like-leaders-who-underrate-themselves

Acknowledgments

ERIC'S

First and foremost, I offer my sincere thanks and gratitude to my wife, Melissa, and my kids. Their unwavering support allows me not only to follow my passions but also to dedicate time to share my thoughts on education and leadership. This book would have never become a reality had it not been for Trish Rubin, who introduced me to the concept of branding in education back in 2009. Her wisdom and guidance influenced my leadership, which ultimately played a part in the transformation of my former high school. I am indebted to the practitioner voices of Joe Sanfelippo, Tony Sinanis, Brad Currie, Ryan Imbriale, and Ted Rubin. The work of these leaders helped us illustrate the impact of a brandED mindset. Finally, a special thanks goes out to Jossey-Bass, specifically Kate Bradford and Connor O'Brien. Their watchful eye and honest feedback helped keep us on track while creating a valuable resource for school leaders.

TRISH'S

In the development of brandED, I am grateful for the support of many dear people in my worldwide personal and business/educational network. With a professional tagline that reads "All Roads lead to Trish," I have been exceptionally fortunate to have been taught, inspired, mentored, and cared for on the road—especially now as I proudly stand at the energizing intersection of education and business. Thank you to all for your love and your laughter shared online and offline during the development of this work. I appreciate the brandED storytellers Alexis Bonavitacola, Kevin Carroll, Rob Zywicki, Amelia Tran, and Mike Wong for their stories. I especially thank my daughter, Alexandra Rubin, for her steady support and tough love as I drafted. Thank you to my team of marketing students from Baruch College for their energy and unique Gen Y ideas. A heartfelt thank you goes to Ms. Yoonjung (Jennifer) Lee for interpreting our thinking into all of the original figures in this text, and to Jessica Stuart for her early work on illustrations. Thank you to the Wiley/Jossey-Bass editorial team of Kate Bradford and Connor O'Brien, whose straightforward thinking and targeted inquiry were a priceless editorial gift. A special thank you to Mr. Walter Vail, my first educational mentor in Glassboro, New Jersey, who gave me the chance to be his disruptive partner in school reform many years ago and offered me my unique brand value in an educational worldwide experience that influenced the lives of thousands of teachers and their students years before the birth of the World Wide Web. Finally, my sincere thanks to my coauthor and friend, Eric Sheninger, for inviting me on this journey. Our brand is serendipity. I'm proud to be your disruptive partner in a 21st-century idea that you embodied and inspired into the creation of our book. Thank you for believing and for genuinely living as the first brandED school leader.

Index

111; reputation management and, 108; sharing, 102–104; of storyteller-in-chief, 98, 105; SWOT analysis and, 99, 107; transparency and, 103, 105, 111; Twitter and, 111; UBV and, 59, 98, 100, 135; visual communication of, 105; well-being and, 107; Zywicki and, 119. *See also* One-word brand

Persuasion, 56

Peters, Tom, 76; on "Brand You," 99; *In Search of Excellence* by, 168–169

Petro, Greg, 225–226

Pink, Daniel, 72; on persuasion, 56

Pinterest, 51

Plurals, 32

Pokémon Go, 221

Pope, Alexander, 175

Positioning, 16; collaborative team and, 118; of edupreneurs, 134; statement, 112, 147–148; Zywicki and, 119

PR. *See* Public relations

Presentational literacy, 161, 231

Press, 172; negative, 200

Primacy effect, 109

Print journalism: media advisory template for, 201; Media Contacts Pro for, 201

Proctor & Gamble, 14

Product personalities, 16–17

Product resource partners, 191

Products: services as, 194; skill sets as, 195

Promise, 2, 12–13, 32, 144; brandED mindset and, 177–179; community connectors and, 145; engagement and, 159; as evergreen, 145, 146; James and, 143;

messaging and, 176; mission statement and, 146–147; process of articulating, 146; promoting, 29; UBV and, 146

Promotion: as advertising, 25; affinity and, 26, 27; Currie on, 45–46

Promotional brand-building process, 193

Proton Media, 242

Protosphere, 242

Psychology, 62, 94, 136; Apple and, 63; artificial intelligence and, 64; of a brandED leader, 74–75; business-as-unusual model and, 69; change impacting, 85; demography and, 65; digital decision-making behavior and, 71; Dweck on fixed and growth mindsets, 69–70; Facebook and, 63; giving nature and, 93; Hierarchy of Needs and, 73–74; positive, 73; promise, image and result and, 71–72; relational behavior and, 76–77; tenets of brandED and, 71–72

Public relations (PR), 198; blogging and, 204–205; content for, 200; corporate newsletters and, 209–210; HARO and, 208; influencers and, 203; live streaming and, 206–207; Muck Rack, 208–209; performance and, 199; print journalism and, 201–202; reporters online and, 202–203; thought leadership in, 207–208; Twitter chats, 203–204; video and, 205–206; webinars and, 205

Pull: Networking and Success Since Benjamin Franklin (Laird), 78